W9-ACX-103

419 Eastwood Drive
Salisbury, NC 28144

Vocal Solos
for
Christian Churches

A Descriptive Reference of Solo Music for the Church Year
Including a Bibliographical Supplement of Choral Works

by

Noni Espina

Third Edition

The Scarecrow Press, Inc.
Metuchen, N.J., and London   1984

The title of the second edition was <u>Vocal Solos for Protestant Services</u> (1974).

Library of Congress Cataloging in Publication Data

Espina, Noni.
    Vocal solos for Christian churches.

    Rev. ed. of: Vocal solos for Protestant services.
2nd ed., rev. and enl. 1974.
    Includes index.
    1. Sacred songs--Bibliography. 2. Choruses, Sacred--
Bibliography. I. Espina, Noni. Vocal solos for
Protestant services. II. Title. III. Title: Vocal solos
for Protestant services.
ML128.V7E8 1984   016.7836'751   84-51398
ISBN 0-8108-1730-6

This Third Edition Is Dedicated To

The Memory Of

DR. HUGH PORTER
1897-1960
Director, The School of Sacred Music
Union Theological Seminary, New York

and to

SERGIUS KAGEN
1909-1964
Juilliard Voice Pedagogue
the writer's mentor who suggested
the compilation of this work

Acknowledgements

Sincere thanks to the publishers and composers
for supplying the needed information and material

CONTENTS

P R E F A C E

The first two editions of this reference work, under the title
VOCAL SOLOS FOR PROTESTANT SERVICES, have been used by church musicians,
recitalists, teachers of singing, and music students. Interest for a tool
of this nature exceeded expectations. A third edition, therefore, is being issued, this time under a new title, VOCAL SOLOS FOR CHRISTIAN
CHURCHES. The change was made in response to suggestions that this book
should have wider use.

Both the old and new editions follow the same organization, format,
and approach to basic information. The expected changes are in the introduction of new and current material and the elimination of those that are
out-of-print. With the third edition, the owner of the first two (1965
and 1974) would now have a set of three references that are partially
different from each other.

The titles in this new edition have been thoroughly checked with
publishers. No one has control over the availability of any piece of music because no one controls the behavior of the market. A piece may be
available one day and be out-of-print the next. Even if publishers ex-
haust their holdings, some music dealers may still have some copies. Fur-
thermore, after a few years some out-of-print sheet music reappear in new
collections or are reprinted in the original sheet form. Also, for a fee,
many publishers are willing to make copies of any music in their files,
if requested.

There is no claim that this book is a "complete" reference of sacred
solos. In an ongoing research, the word "complete" does not exist. The
search for materials of quality is time-consuming and often a frustrat-
ing and complex job. If there are worthwhile solos that do not appear here
it is because their scores have not been made available. Library sources
are unreliable because their holdings are not always current.

The songs and arias reviewed here were examined with quality in mind
in regard to the music and text. Oftentimes an otherwise fine text is
made weak through the insensitive handling of musical prosody. Translations of foreign languages also create some difficulties. Besides music
and texts, practical use and professional acceptance are considered.

The practice of adapting sacred texts to music based on secular as-
sociations and inspirations does not always work favorably. Although ex-
pertly handled, most of the resultant material distract the worshipper
from his desire for complete spiritual upliftment. The practice is not
altogether bad - that is, if one can get away with it. Great musicians
of the past, to mention Bach and Handel, for example, "borrowed" secular melodies for some of their sacred works. The point is not that they
did it, but that the finished product, clothed differently, surpassed
the original. In most cases, the original was no longer remembered. Man-
y arrangers unsuccessfully ape this method.

In this reference the user will find a few originally non-sacred
melodies published with new texts which would fit the needs of certain
occasions in the church. These new English versions seem to be adequate
and useful and their general character not outside the original. They
are also better than the greater bulk of original sacred solo material
in the market. Among the songs included are "Wedding Song" by Schutz,

the music of Schutz with text from Ruth 1:16-17, and "Be Thou with me",
the music of Bach with text by the late Metropolitan Opera baritone,
Mack Harrell. After all, when considering the music of the masters,
does one really find a distinction as to what is sacred and what is
secular? Great music defies classification of this sort. The music of
Bach, for example, transcends the classifications of sacred and secular.
In saying thus, this writer does not encourage any further adaptations,
for this method has already been overused. In our contemporary world,
intelligent musicianship also means knowing when to leave things alone.

This book is not intended to be a musicological dissertation, but
a useful and practical guide for musicians in search for materials to
perform. Only the basic facts about each song are given. Critical anal-
ysis of composers' styles do not belong here. This reference should also serve the needs of people who do not have the schooled knowledge
of music.

Most of the songs reviewed here are based on the voice-keyboard
combination. There are piano reductions of solos with orchestral accompaniment, such as arias in large choral works. One will also find a few
other combinations such as Gustav Holst's "Four Songs for Voice and
Violin" and Vaughan Williams' "Four Hymns for Tenor Voice and Viola Obbligato".

A few explanations are necessary so that the user may fully under-
stand the principles that guided the organization of this reference.

1.   The dates of composers known to be still living are not included. Many do not wish their dates used.

2.   When the work is not originally in English, the English version of the title is given first. English titles are not word-for-word
translations.

3.   Excerpts from choral works are alphabetized by aria.

4.   The title of a cycle or group of related songs may appear as
the main heading. Most songs within the group may be performed separately.

5.   Designations of range (lowest note to highest) and tessitura
(where most of the notes lie) are determined by the code of pitches.

6.   Comment on the type of voice refers to that type the song in
the key published would sound best. When indicated that a song may be
performed by "All Voices" although published only in one key, it means
that the song may be transposed for use by all voices. There are also
songs which composers indicated to be used only for the type of voice
specified.

7.   "Remarks" refer to the basic structure of the piece, with a
few other information thrown in.

8.   The Code that appears after Accompaniment (Acc) indicates
the material or edition on which the Remarks and other information are
based. Codes following the first one refer to other available editions.

9.   The suggested Occasions at which a song may be performed
comprise one of the most important features of this work. Exlanations
follow.

(a) "General Use" means that a song may be performed on any Sunday or occasion that is not a special holiday or feast day, such as
Christmas or Easter.

(b) "Special Use with Sermon Theme" means that the song may be
performed in conjunction with the theme of the sermon. Under this

designation are listed those songs which, because of the worth of the music, should not be left out simply for the reason that they do not fit any particular occasions. This is true for example, with the first three Scriptural Songs of Brahms whose texts present a sombre picture rather than a triumphant outlook. They are, of course, excellent songs for sacred concerts or programs in the church and elsewhere.

(c) Solos for weddings include those which were found to be in good taste and suitable for performance in the church sanctuary. The so-called "traditional wedding songs", composed of love ballads and pop music, have no place whatsoever in the church sanctuary! They belong to the social event that follows the main activity. There a whole concert of light and secular music could be given and thoroughly enjoyed. The wedding ritual in the church is a sacred occasion - one which reaffirms the sincere dedication of the bride and groom to each other with God's blessings. A few settings of the much-used text from Ruth 1 are included here although the original quotation has nothing to do with a wedding. It is, however, a widely-accepted text for weddings because of its literary merit. In other words, the verse is suitable because it is so beautifully expressed without sounding cheap.

(d) Certain arias from cantatas and oratorios are useful for occasions not directly related to the title of the entire work. For example, Bach's "My heart ever faithful" from Cantata 68 is useful for any joyous occasion.

(e) Any song or aria in this reference may be used as teaching material or repertoire for concert. Sacred music enriches recitalists' repertoires and helps provide a wide range of vocal expression and experience.

In addition to the above, a few other observations may be noted.

1.   The articles "A", "An" and "The" are alphabetized with the song titles. These words must never be omitted, for if they were not part of the titles, they would not be there. Inaccuracy and carelessness in drafting church bulletins and concert programs are partly due to the neglect of this detail.

2.   A few unison anthems useful as solos are included.

3.   Very short one-verse songs may be sung twice. Two short songs may be sung in direct succession if their general mood and theme are compatible. For example, Beethoven's "The might of God" and "Nature's praise of God", numbers five and four in that order, in "Six Sacred Songs", make an admirable and useful pair.

4.   Although Negro Spirituals would naturally fall under Traditional Music, they are classified separately due to the special nature of their music and texts. Almost all hymnals now include spirituals, and for this reason hymnals are also used as references here. Spirituals do not require fancy keyboard accompaniments due to their simple beauty and unsophisticated sincerity. They may even be sung without accompaniment.

5.   All references to Bach mean Johann Sebastian Bach.

6.   A short supplement of selected choral works has been appended to this reference.

For the improvement of music in the
church and for THE GLORY OF GOD!

New York City, 1984

DR. NONI ESPINA

C O D E S

Pitches

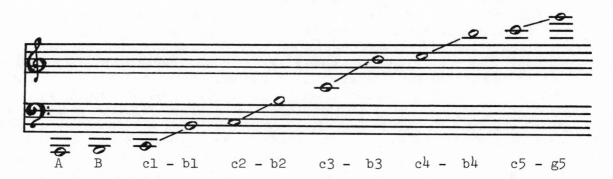

A   B   c1 - b1   c2 - b2   c3 - b3   c4 - b4   c5 - g5

Each song or aria has two pairs of pitches for each key. The first pair indicates the range and the second the tessitura. Example: c3-a4 e3-f4. Tessituras are only approximate. Some songs, especially contemporary works, almost defy tessitura designations. In using the above chart, one only needs to remember the combination 1-3-5 which stands for Bass low c, Middle c, and Soprano high c, respectively.

Other Codes

A 2-letter code, in capitals, stands for the name of a publisher.
 Example: CO means Concordia Publishing House.
A 3-member code of capital letters or a combination of letters and numbers stands for the title of a collection. Example: ASS means "Anthology of Sacred Song" published by G. Schirmer, Inc.
(S) Sheet music. This is followed by a publisher's code. Example: (S)ES means sheet music published by E. C. Schirmer Music Co.
(VS) Vocal-Piano score. This is followed by a publisher's code.
(SC) Score. Any music score, usually of a song cycle or set of songs. This is followed by a publisher's code.
Tess Tessitura or where most notes lie.
Acc Accompaniment. This is followed by one or two numbers indicating the degree of difficulty, from 1 to 5. Example: Acc 3 means moderate difficulty.
R Recitative.
A Aria.
O-S Original scoring. This refers to the instrumentation of an excerpt.
dnk Date-not-known.

CODES OF PUBLISHERS
A code in parentheses means the U.S. or principal affiliate.

AM Associated Music Publishers, New York (GS)

AH Augsburg Publishing House, Minneapolis

BA Bärenreiter-Verlag, Kassel

B-M Belwin-Mills Publishing Corp., Melville, NY

BL Berandol Music Ltd., Toronto

B-H Boosey & Hawkes, New York, London

BM Boston Music Co., Boston

BC Bosworth & Co. Ltd., London

BH Breitkopf & Hartel, Wiesbaden

BD Brodt Music Co., Charlotte, NC

AB Broude Bros., New York

CY Chantry Music Press, Springfield, OH

CC Chappell Music Ltd., London

CH J. & W. Chester, London

CM Coburn Press (TP)

CO Concordia Publishing House, St. Louis

JC J. Curwen & Sons, Ltd., London

OD Oliver Ditson (TP)

EV Elkan-Vogel (TP)

EL Elkin & Co. Ltd., London (GA)

EN Enoch & Sons, London (B-H)

CF Carl Fischer, New York

JF J. Fischer & Bro. (B-M)

FS H. T. FitzSimons, Chicago

HF Harold Flammer (SP)

GA Galaxy Inc., Boston

HG H. W. Gray (B-M)

HI Hinrichsen Editions Ltd., London (CP)

RH R. L. Huntzinger (WM)

IM International Music Co., New York

EK Edwin F. Kalmus (B-M)

NK Neil A. Kjos, Park Ridge, IL

LG Lawson-Gould Music Publishers (GS)

LK Alfred Lengnick Ltd., London

EM Edward B. Marks Music Corp. (B-M)

MM Mercury Music Co. (TP)

MG Verlag Carl Merseburger, Berlin

GM Gordon Myers, 31 Bayberry Rd., Trenton, NJ 08618

NW New Music Society (TP)

NO Novello & Co., London (TP)

OX Oxford University Press, New York & London

PP Paterson's Publications, London (CF)

PI Peer International (SM)

CP C. F. Peters Corp., New York

TP Theodore Presser, Bryn Mawr, PA

GR G. Ricordi & Co. (GS, B-M)

RR R. D. Row Music Co., (CF)

SA Editions Salabert, Paris (GS)

ES E. C. Schirmer Co., Boston

GS G. Schirmer Inc., New York

SC Schott & Co., London

SP Shawnee Press, Inc., Delaware Water Gap, PA

NS N. Simrock (LK)

SM Southern Music Publishers, New York

SB Stainer & Bell Ltd., London (GA)

CL Summy-Birchard, Evanston, IL

VA Vita d'Arte, New York

JW Joseph Williams Edition, London (SB)

WM Willis Music Co., Cincinnati

MW M. Witmark & Sons, New York

BIBLIOGRAPHY OF GENERAL COLLECTIONS

AEI Folk Songs American-English-Irish. Two sets: high, low. Edited by John Edmunds. NY: R. D. Row Music Co.

ARB The Aria. Renaissance and Baroque. High, low. From the Alessandro Parisotti collection, revised by Estelle Liebling. Italian texts, with English version. Melville, NY: Belwin-Mills.

ASS Anthology of Sacred Song. 4 vols: Soprano, Alto, Tenor, Bass. English and English versions. Ed. by Max Spicker. NY: G. Schirmer.

CON Contemporary American Songs. High, low. Ed. by Bernard Taylor. Evanston, IL: Summy-Birchard Publishing Co.

CPS Classic Period Songs. Medium high, Medium low. Original texts with English versions. Dubuque: William C. Brown Co. (Has some over-editing and awkward prosody.)

CSV Christmas Carols for Solo Voice. Compiled by G. Winston Cassler. Minn: Augsburg Publishing House.

EAE English Ayres Elizabethan and Jacobean. 6 volumes, original keys. Edited by Peter Warlock & Philip Wilson. London: Oxford University Press, 1931. (Expensive, but highly recommended.)

ELS Elizabethan Love-Songs. 2 volumes. Edited by Frederick Keel. English texts. London: Boosey & Hawkes, 1909.

ESL English School of Lutenist Song-Writers. Edited by Dr. Edmund H. Fellowes. Single books available. (Scholarly, highly recommended.) London: Stainer & Bell.

ESS Eleven Scriptural Songs from the Twentieth Century. Medium voice, organ or piano. Bryn Mawr, PA: Coburn Press, 1975, Th. Presser.

FSS Fifty Selected Songs by Schubert, Schumann, Brahms, Wolf, Strauss. High, low. Original German, with English by F. Easton. NY: GS

GAS Great Art Songs of Three Centuries. High, low. New York: G.Schirmer.

MHL The Methodist Hymnal. Edited by Austin Lovelace. Nashville: The Methodist Publishing House, 1966.

NOR Norway Sings. English-Norwegian edition. Oslo: Norsk Musikforlag.

OAS Old American Songs. 2 sets, edited and arranged by Aaron Copland. 3 songs in each set, one key. London, New York: Boosey & Hawkes.

PEH The Hymnal of the Protestant Episcopal Church in the U.S.A., 1940. New York: The Church Pension Fund.

PHD The Hymnal. First edition edited by Dr. Clarence Dickinson; second
or edition by Hugh Jones. Philadelphia: The Presbyterian (Christian)
PHJ Board of Christian Education. (PHD means the edition by Dickinson.)

PHP Pilgrim Hymnal. Revised edition by Dr. and Mrs. Hugh Porter. Boston: The Pilgrim Press, 1958.

POS Pathways of Song. 4 volumes, high, low. Edited by Frank LaForge and Will Earhart. Original texts and English versions. New York: M. Witmark & Sons.

SCS Seven Centuries of Solo Song. 6 volumes, high, low. Edited by James Woodside. Boston: Boston Music Co.

SCV Songs for Children's Voices by Ludwig Lenel. Springfield, OH: Chantry Music Press.

SCY   Solos for the Church Year. Compiled by Lloyd Pfautsch. New York: NY: Lawson-Gould Music Publishers, c/o G. Schirmer.

SEA   Six Songs of Early Americans. Edited by Gordon Myers. Available from Dr. Myers, 31 Bayberry Rd., Trenton, NJ 08618

SHC   Songs for Holy Communion by Borghild Jacobson. St. Louis: Concordia Publishing House, 1982.

SHS   The Sacred Hour of Song. High, low. English adaptations by Mack Harrell. NY: Carl Fischer.

SMM   The Solo Song, 1580-1730. Edited by Carol MacClintock. Original texts with English translations, original keys. NY: W. W. Norton & Co., 1973. Paper edition available.

SPC   Songs of Praise by Contemporary Composers. Edited and compiled by Darwin Wolford. Delaware Water Gap, PA: Harold Flammer, 1975. (Designated "for medium solo voice", but most are for high voice.)

SVR   Standard Vocal Repertoire. 2 volumes: high, low. Edited by Richard D. Row. NY: R. D. Row Music Co., c/o Carl Fischer.

TMB   A Third Morning Star Choir Book. Edited by Paul Thomas. St. Louis: Concordia Publishing House. (Has several unison pieces useful as solos.)

TSL   Three Solos for High Voice. Songs by Lovelace and Pelz. Oboe or violoncello obbligato. Minneapolis: Augsburg Publishing House.

TSM   Three Solos for Medium Voice. Songs by Engel, Held, Lovelace. Minneapolis: Augsburg Publishing House, 1979.

TSS   Ten Sacred Songs. Moravian music edited by Hans T. David. English texts. Organ (or piano) and strings ad lib. NY: C. F. Peters.

TWB   The Worshipbook. Philadelphia: The Westminster Press. 1972.

TWS   Three Wedding Solos. High voice and organ. Edited by G. W. Cassler. Minneapolis: Augsburg Publishing House, 1968.

WBB   Wedding Blessings. Edited by Paul Bunjes. St. Louis: Concordia Publishing House.

3SS   Three Sacred Songs for Soprano. Music by Moravians Johann Peter and David Michael. Edited by Thor Johnson and Donald McCorkle, Original German texts and English versions. New York:Boosey & Hawkes.

24I   Twenty-four Italian Songs and Arias of the Seventeenth and eighteenth Centuries. Medium high, medium low. NY: G. Schirmer, 1948.

52S   52 Sacred Songs You Like To Sing. A general collection for different voices. NY: G. Schirmer, 1939.

56S   56 Songs You Like To Sing. A general collection which has only three sacred songs. NY: G. Schirmer.

THE SACRED SOLO LITERATURE

ADOLPHE ADAM
1803-1856, France

Christmas song (Cantique de Noel)   All Voices
    Text: Anonymous, English by Carl Deis.
    Range & Tess: high, d3-bb4(a4) a3-eb4 low, b2-f4(g4) g3-c4
    Remarks: Popular title - O holy night. Sustained in moderate slow
        tempo. Long, sweeping lines with high, strong passages. Climactic
        high ending. Showy, now performed in most churches. 3 verses.
        Acc 3-4 (S)CF-2 keys; GS-4 keys. 52S-high key.
    Occasions: Christmas and Christmas Day.

SAMUEL ADLER
United States

In Thine own image   Medium Voice
    Text: Fania Kruger.
    Range & Tess: bb2-f4 eb3-c4
    Remarks: Sustained in slow tempo. Generally on MF level. Has high,
        climactic passages, frequent meter changes. Melody moves with flow
        of text. Subdued, low ending. Dissonant, textually strong. Acc 3-4
        (S)OX
    Occasions: General use. Special use with sermon theme: racial equali-
        ty.

ANONYMOUS

A joyous song of Easter   All Voices
    Text: English version by Elizabeth M. Lockwood.
    Range & Tess: high, f3-f4 f3-f4 low, eb3-eb4 eb3-eb4
    Remarks: Source - Geistliche Kirchengesang, Cologne, 1623. Arr. by
        Heinrich Reimann. Sustained in lively tempo. Generally strong and
        full-sounding. All 3 verses end with "Alleluia". Same melody used
        in hymnals: All creatures of our God and King. Acc 3 (S)LK
    Occasions: Easter and Sundays after Easter.

Music thou soul of heaven   All Voices
    Text: Robert Herrick.
    Range & Tess: d3-eb4 f3-d4
    Remarks: From Ms 87, Christchurch College, Oxford. Realized and edit-
        ed by John Edmunds. Sustained in moderate tempo. Irregular meter,
        follows flow of text. Generally on MF level; requires fine P & PP.
        Very subdued ending. Acc 3 (S)RR
    Occasions: Dedication of music facilities. Installation of church
        musician.

JOHN ANTES
1740-1811, United States
Moravian Composer

And Jesus said: It is finished   Soprano
   Text: John 19:30.
   Range & Tess: b♭2-g4 f3-e♭4
   Remarks: Very sustained in slow tempo. Generally subdued and dark;
     requires fine P & PP. Very subdued, descending ending line. Has
     some agitated accompaniment. Acc 3 (S)B-H
   Occasion: Good Friday.

Go, congregation, go   High Voice
   Text: Christian Gregor.
   Range & Tess: b2-a♭4 e♭3-f4
   Remarks: Very sustained in slow tempo. Short; in the style of late
     Baroque. Acc 3 TSS
   Occasions: General use.

Loveliest Immanuel   Soprano
   Text: John Antes.
   Range & Tess: f3-g4 a3-e♭4
   Remarks: Sustained in moderate slow tempo. Requires fine P & PP. Ge-
     nerally subdued, gentle. Gently climactic ending. Slightly agitated
     accompaniment and extended postlude. Acc 3(organ or piano) (S)B-H
   Occasions: Advent. General use.

VIOLET ARCHER
Canada

The twenty-third psalm   Medium Voice
   Text: Psalm 23.
   Range & Tess: b2-f4 d3-d4
   Remarks: Recitative-style first section, somewhat subdued. Sustained
     second section. Requires some flexibility.Has florid passages, dra-
     matic high ending. Acc 4 (S)BL
   Occasions: General use. New Year's Eve. Evening services. Memorial
     services. Massed religious gatherings. Evangelistic services.

JOHN ATTEY
dnk-c.1640, Great Britain

Sweet was the song   High Voice
   Text: Traditional verse.
   Range & Tess: e3-a4 a3-f4
   Remarks: Sustained in moderate tempo. Subdued, gentle, delicate. Re-
     quires some flexibility and fine PP. A lullaby. Best for light
     voices. May also be transposed. Acc 2-3 ELS-2
   Occasions: Christmas Eve programs and services.

CARL PHILIPP EMANUEL BACH
1714-1788, Germany

Christmas song (Weihnachtslied)   All Voices
   Text: Anonymous, English version by Van A. Christy.
   Range & Tess: high, c3-f4 f3-f4 low, bb2-eb4 eb3-d4
   Remarks: Animated in lively tempo. Requires some flexibility, 2 vers-
     es. Original key: 1 step higher than high voice. Acc 3 CPS
   Occasions: Christmas & Sunday after Christmas. Christmas Eve prog-
     rams and services.

R: Friends of our Master
A: I follow Thee   Tenor
   Work: THE RESURRECTION AND ASCENSION OF JESUS (Die Auferstehung und
     himmelfahrt Jesu), text by Karl Wilhelm Ramler, English by R. Brew-
     er.
   Range & Tess: d3-a4 g3-f#4
   Remarks: Extended recitative in moderate tempo, and animated aria in
     lively tempo. Bright, exultant, has florid passages and climactic
     passages. Gently climactic ending. Agitated accompaniment. Acc 3-4
     (VS)SP
   Occasions: Easter & Sunday after Easter. The aria alone, funerals.

Lord, who art worthy   Mezzo-Soprano, Contralto
   Work: HOLY IS GOD, text by Martin Luther, English by H. S. Drinker.
   Range & Tess: d3-f4 e3-c4
   Remarks: Animated, joyous. The score is edited by Karl Geiringer.
    Acc 4-5 (VS)CO
   Occasions: General use. Trinity Sunday & Sundays after.

R: Eleven true disciples
A: My Lord, my God!   Tenor
   Work: THE RESURRECTION AND ASCENSION OF JESUS (See first entry).
   Range & Tess: d3-g4 f3-e4
   Remarks: Extended recitative and sustained aria in moderate slow tem-
     po. Generally on MF level with some fine P. Contemplative, subdued
     ending. Has florid figures. Acc 3 (VS)SP
   Occasions: General use. Sunday after Easter. Special use with sermon
     theme: doubting Thomas.

R: Judea trembles
A: My soul in fear and joy   Baritone, Bass
   Work: THE RESURRECTION AND ASCENSION OF JESUS (See first entry).
   Range & Tess: g1-f3 eb3-eb4
   Remarks: Dramatic recitative and generally sustained aria in alternat-
     ing moderate and moderate slow tempi. Joyous, florid, requires flex-
     ibility. Quite tessitura in some passages. Difficult. Agitated ac-
     companiment. Acc 4-5 (VS)SP
   Occasions: Easter. Ascension Sunday.

C. P. E. BACH

Prayer (Bitten)   All Voices
   Text: Anonymous, English version by Van A. Christy.
   Range & Tess: high, f3-f4 g3-eb4 low, d3-d4 e3-c4
   Remarks: Sustained in moderate slow tempo. Generally subdued, re-
      quires fine P. Descending ending. Original key ½ step lower.
      Acc 3 CPS
   Occasions: General use. Evening services. Special use in services of
      personal dedication.

Ye gates of heaven   Baritone, Bass
   Work: THE RESURRECTION AND ASCENSION OF JESUS (See first entry).
   Range & Tess: a1-f3 eb2-d3
   Remarks: Animated in lively tempo. Strong, dramatic, has some florid
      figures. Dramatic ending. Agitated accompaniment. Acc 4 (VS)SP
   Occasions: Ascension Sunday. Easter.

JOHANN CHRISTOPH BACH
1732-1795, Germany

Softly rest within a manger   Mezzo-Soprano, Contralto
(Schlummre sanft in deiner Krippe)
   Work: THE CHILDHOOD OF CHRIST (Die Kindheit Jesu), text by Johann G.
      Herder, English version by Lowell P. Beveridge.
   Range & Tess: b2-e4(f#4) e3-d4
   Remarks: Sustained and graceful, in lullaby style. Generally on MF
      level. High tessitura. The beautiful recitative before it may also
      be sung. Acc 3 (VS)JF
   Occasions: Christmas Eve programs and services.

JOHANN SEBASTIAN BACH
1685-1750, Germany

ACC   Arias from Church Cantatas for Soprano. With obbligato instrument
      and piano or organ. Vol. I, J. S. Bach. German texts with English
      versions by Jane May. Opa-Locka: Edwin F. Kalmus.
BAS   Bach Arias for Soprano. Compiled by Barnard Taylor. German texts
      with English versions. New York: G. Schirmer.
BSS   J. S. Bach Sacred Songs. High, Low. 69 songs from the Schemelli
      Gesangbuch. English texts: H. S. Drinker & T. Lau. St. Louis:
      Concordia Publishing House. A very fine collection, highly recom-
      mended.
FSS   Five Sacred Songs. J. S. Bach. Issued in octavo. German with Eng-
      lish texts. Realization for organ by M. Lundquist. Boston: E. C.
      Schirmer Music Co.
SSB   Sacred Songs. J. S. Bach. High voice, 25 songs. Edited by Herman
      Roth. German texts with English versions by Herbert Grossman. New
      York: International Music Co.
TSB   Twelve Songs from Schemelli's Gesangbuch. Johann Sebastian Bach.
      Springfield, OH: Chantry Music Press.

Note: The excellent Bach collection "40 Songs and Airs", English ver-
       sions by Ebenezer Prout, published by Augener Ltd., and reviewed
       in the first two editions of this book is out-of-print.

The Songs

Ah, happy are ye, steadfast spirits BWV442   All Voices
(Beglückter Stand getreuer Seelen)
  Text: Ulrich B. von Bonin, English by H. S. Drinker & T. Lau.
  Range & Tess: high, d3-d4 e3-c4 low, d3-d4 e3-c4
  Remarks: Sustained in moderate tempo. Slow, with subdued ending. 3
     verses. Acc 3 BSS
  Occasions: Baptism. Installation for missionary service. Installation
     of church officers or pastor. Evangelistic services. Services of
     personal dedication

All ye stars, ye winds of heaven BWV476   All Voices
(Ihr Gestirn', ihr hohen Lüfte)
  Text: Johann Franck, English by H. S. Drinker & T. Lau.
  Range & Tess: high, d3-f4 f3-e4 low, b2-d4 d3-c#4
  Remarks: Sustained in moderate tempo. Bright, joyful song of praise.
     Requires some flexibility. Climactic ending. 3 verses. Acc 3 BSS
  Occasions: Christmas and first Sunday after Christmas.

Awake, my heart, with gladness BWV441   All Voices
(Auf, auf! mein Herz, mit Freuden)
  Text: P. Gerhardt, English by J. Kelly.
  Range & Tess: high, e3-f4 f3-e♭4 low, c#3-d4 d3-c4
  Remarks: Sustained in lively tempo. Bright, joyful, graceful. Climac-
     tic high ending. Melody by J. Cruger, 1648. 3 verses. Acc 3 BSS,
     TSB
  Occasion: Easter.

Be thou contented and rest quiet BWV510   All Voices
(Gib dich zufrieden und sei stille)
  Text: Paul Gerhardt.
  Range & Tess: d#3-g4 g3-d4
  Remarks: From Anna Magdalena Bach's "Notenbuch", 1725. Sustained in
     moderate slow tempo. Requires some flexibility. Short. Acc 3 TSB
  Occasion: General use.

Be Thou with me BWV508   All Voices
(Bist du bei mir)
  Text: J. S. Bach(?), English sacred words by Mack Harrell.
  Range & Tess: high, e♭3-a♭4 a♭3-g4 medium, a#2-e4 e3-d#4
  Remarks: From Anna Magdalena Bach's "Notenbuch", 1725. Very sustained
     in moderate slow tempo. Gentle, requires simplicity. Acc 3 SHS
  Occasions: General use. New Year's Eve. New Year's Day.

BACH

Beside Thy manger here I stand BWV469   All Voices
(Ich steh' an deiner Krippe hier)
   Text: Paul Gerhardt, English by W. M. Czamanske.
   Range & Tess: high, d3-e♭4 g3-d4 low, b2-c4 e3-b3
   Remarks: Sustained in moderate tempo. Gentle. Has running bass melody
      in the accompaniment. 3 verses. Acc 3 BSS, TSB, FSS
   Occasions: Christmas and Sunday after Christmas.

Bridegroom of my soul BWV496   All Voices
(Seelenbräutigam)
   Text: A. Dresse, English by J. T. Mueller.
   Range & Tess: high, a2-f4 a3-d4 low, f#3-d4 f#3-b3
   Remarks: Sustained in moderate tempo. 3 verses. Acc 2-3 BSS
   Occasions: General use. Special use with sermon theme - love of God.
      Palm Sunday.

Cloudless, serene, and splendid BWV448   All Voices
(Der Tag mit seinem Lichte)
   Text: Paul Gerhardt, English by H. S. Drinker & T. Lau.
   Range & Tess: high, d3-e4 f3-d4 low, c3-d4 e♭3-c4
   Remarks: Sustained in moderate tempo. Climactic ending. An evening
      song of praise. 3 verses. Acc 3 BSS
   Occasions: Evening services and prayer meetings.

Come, gentle death, come blessed peace BWV478   All Voices
(Komm, süsser Tod, komm, sel'ge Ruh'!)
   Text: J. S. Bach, English by H. S. Drinker & T. Lau.
   Range & Tess: high, c3-g4 g3-e♭4 low, a2-e4 e3-c4
   Remarks: Very sustained in slow tempo. Subdued and gentle. 2 verses.
      Acc 3 BSS, (S)SC
   Occasions: Special use with sermon theme - death in Christ's care,
      sacrifice. Maundy Thursday.

Come praise the Lord BWV479   All Voices
(Kommt, Seelen, dieser Tag)
   Text: Valentin Ernst Loescher, English by Mack Harrell.
   Range & Tess: high, d3-a4 g3-e4 medium, b♭2-f4 e♭3-c4
   Remarks: Sustained in moderate slow tempo. Slightly majestic, joyful.
      Requires some flexibility. Title in BSS: Come, souls, behold today.
      Also known as: Come, Christians, greet this day. One step lower for
      both keys in BSS. Acc 3 SHS, BSS, TSB, FSS
   Occasions: Whitsunday (Pentecost). General use.

Dearest Immanuel BWV485   All Voices
(Liebster Immanuel)
   Text: A. Fritsch, English by H. S. Drinker & W. E. Buszin.
   Range & Tess: high, f3-f4 a3-f4 low, c3-c4 e3-c4
   Remarks: Sustained in moderate tempo. 3 verses. A song of faith,
      comfort, and love for Christ. Acc 3 BSS, TSB
   Occasions: General use. Communion. Evening services.

6

Fount of every blessing BWV445   All Voices
(Brunnquell aller Güter)
   Text: Johann Franck, English by H. S. Drinker & T. Lau.
   Range & Tess: high, f#3-f4 g3-d4 low, d#3-d4 e3-b3
   Remarks: Sustained in moderate tempo. Descending ending line. 2 vers-
      es. Acc 3 BSS
   Occasions: General use. Whitsunday (Pentecost).

Fret not, soul, that God give thee BWV489   All Voices
(Nicht so traurig, nicht so sehr)
   Text: Paul Gerhardt, English by H. S. Drinker & T. Lau.
   Range & Tess: high, d3-f#4 f#3-d#4 low, bb2-d4 d3-b3
   Remarks: Sustained in moderate tempo. Requires some flexibility.
      Short; 2 verses. Acc 3 BSS
   Occasions: General use. Evening services.

God liveth yet BWV461   All Voices
(Gott lebet noch)
   Text: J. F. Zihn, English by H. S. Drinker & W. E. Buszin.
   Range & Tess: high, d3-f4 g3-e4 low, b2-d4 e3-c#4
   Remarks: Slightly animated in moderate tempo. A graceful 3/4 time. 2
      verses. Acc 3 BSS
   Occasions: Funerals. Evening services and prayer meetings. General use.

I hold Thee fast BWV467   All Voices
(Ich lass dich nicht)
   Text: W. C. Dessler, English by H. S. Drinker & T. Lau.
   Range & Tess: high, f3-f4 a3-d4 low, d3-d4 f#3-b3
   Remarks: Sustained in moderate tempo, 3 verses. A song of faith and
      comfort. Acc 3 BSS
   Occasions: Lent. Funerals. Evening services.

I love my Jesus every hour BWV468   All Voices
(Ich liebe Jesum alle Stund')
   Text: Anonymous, English by H. S. Drinker & T. Lau.
   Range & Tess: high, f#3-e4 g3-d4 low, e3-d4 f3-c4
   Remarks: Sustained in moderate tempo. Semi-climactic ending. 3 verses.
      Theme - love of Jesus. Acc 3 BSS
   Occasions: Funerals. Memorial services. Evening services. Communion.

I would live my life for Jesus BWV490   All Voices
(Nur mein Jesus ist mein leben)
   Text: Anonymous, English by H. S. Drinker & T. Lau.
   Range & Tess: high, d3-eb4 g3-d4 low, b2-c4 e3-b3
   Remarks: Sustained in moderate tempo. Descending ending line. 2 vers-
      es. Theme - Affirmation of Faith. Acc 3 BSS
   Occasions: Baptism. Special use in services of personal dedication.
      General use.

BACH

If I to God be true BWV503   All Voices
(Steh' ich bei meinem Gott)
   Text: Johann D. Herrenschmidt, English by H. S. Drinker & T. Lau.
   Range & Tess: high, e3-g4 g3-d4 low, b2-d4 d3-a3
   Remarks: Sustained in moderate tempo. Generally on MF level. Gentle,
      with low ending. 3 verses. A song of faith. Acc 3 BSS
   Occasions: Memorial services. Services of personal dedication. Gene-
      ral use.

In quiet faithfulness BWV466   All Voices
(Ich halte treulich still)
   Text: J. H. Till, English by T. Lau.
   Range & Tess: high, f3-g4 g3-d4 low, d3-e4 e3-b3
   Remarks: Very sustained in moderate slow tempo. Gentle, 3 verses.
      Theme: affirmation of faith. See this melody on text by H. Bonar,
      O love that casts out fear in WBB. Acc 3 BSS
   Occasions: Evening services.Funerals. Memorial services. General use.

It is fulfilled! BWV458   All Voices
(Es ist vollbracht!)
   Text: Johann E. Schmidt, English by H. S. Drinker & T. Lau.
   Range & Tess: high, d3-f#4 a3-d4 low, bb2-d4 f3-bb3
   Remarks: Sustained in moderate slow tempo. Generally on MF level, 3
      verses. Acc 3 BSS
   Occasion: Good Friday.

Jesus is a jewel fair BWV474   All Voices
(Jesus ist das schönste Licht)
   Text: C. F. Richter, English by H. S. Drinker & T. Lau.
   Range & Tess: high, c3-g4 g3-e4 low, a2-e4 e3-c#4
   Remarks: Slightly animated in moderate lively tempo. Joyous, bright,
      semi-climactic ending. 2 verses. Theme - love of God. Acc 3 BSS
   Occasions: General use. Baptism. Services of personal dedication.

Jesus, is my heart's delight BWV473   All Voices
(Jesu, meines Herzens Freud')
   Text: J. Flitner, English by W. E. Buszin.
   Range & Tess: high, d#3-e4 a3-c4 low, c#3-d4 g3-bb3
   Remarks: Slightly animated in moderate lively tempo. 3 verses. Theme -
      love of Christ, an affirmation of faith. Acc 3 BSS
   Occasion: General use.

Jesus, Jesus, Thou art mine BWV470   All Voices
(Jesu, Jesu, du bist mein)
   Text: Anonymous, English by H. S. Drinker & T. Lau.
   Range & Tess: high, c3-f4 g3-d4 low, b2-e4 f#3-c#4
   Remarks: Sustained in moderate tempo. Has climactic passages and a
      descending ending line. 3 verses. Theme: love for Christ, a song of
      comfort. Acc 3 BSS, FSS
   Occasions: Evening services. Funerals.

8

Jesus, Thou my soul's delight BWV472   All Voices
(Jesu, meines Glaubens Zier)
   Text: G. W. Sacer, English by H. S. Drinker & T. Lau.
   Range & Tess: high, d3-e4 g3-d4 low, c3-d4 f3-c4
   Remarks: Sustained in moderate tempo. 2 verses. A "song of justifica-
     tion". Acc 3 BSS
   Occasion: General use.

Jesus, Thy humiliation BWV471   All Voices
(Jesu, deine Liebeswunden)
   Text: C. Wegleiter, English by T. Lau.
   Range & Tess: high, e3-c4 g3-b3 low, e3-c4 g3-b3
   Remarks: Sustained in moderate slow tempo. 3 verses. A song of faith.
     Acc 3 BSS
   Occasions: Communion. Lent. Evening services.

Jesus, who salvation gave us BWV475   All Voices
(Jesus, unser Trost und Leben)
   Text: E. C. Homburg, English by H. S. Drinker & W. E. Buszin.
   Range & Tess: high, f3-eb4 g3-d4 low, d3-c4 e3-b3
   Remarks: Slightly animated in moderate lively tempo. Bright, joyous,
     graceful. Ends with Alleluias. Melody in Freyingshausen Gesangbuch,
     1714. 3 verses. Acc 3 BSS, TSB
   Occasions: Easter. Evangelistic services. General use.

Let us strive to be like our Savior BWV481   All Voices
(Lasset uns mit Jesu ziehen)
   Text: J. Schop, English by Mack Harrell.
   Range & Tess: high, e3-g4 g3-f#4 medium, c3-eb4 eb3-d4
   Remarks: Sustained in moderate tempo. An invitation to faith. See
     "Let us walk with Jesus" in BSS, useful also for Lent. Acc 3 SHS,
     BSS
   Occasions: General use. Evangelistic services.

Lord, how plenteous is Thy bounty BWV462   All Voices
(Gott, wie gross ist deine Güte)
   Text: G. C. Schemelli, English by H. S. Drinker & W. E. Buszin.
   Range & Tess: high, a3-g4 b3-f4 low, e3-d4 f3-c4
   Remarks: Slightly animated in moderate lively tempo. Requires some
     flexibility. Acc 3 BSS
   Occasions: Whitsunday (Pentecost). General use.

Lord, remember Thou the Savior BWV463   All Voices
(Herr, nicht schikke deine Bache)
   Text: M. Opitz, English by H. S. Drinker & T. Lau.
   Range & Tess: high, d3-d4 f#3-bb3 low, d3-d4 f#3-bb3
   Remarks: Sustained in moderate slow tempo. 2 verses. A "hymn of con-
     fession". Acc 3 BSS
   Occasions: Lent. Special use with sermon theme - day of humiliation
     and prayer.

BACH

My joy is all in Thee BWV465   All Voices
(Ich freue mich in dir)
   Text: Kaspar Ziegler, English by H. S. Drinker & T. Lau.
   Range & Tess: high, e♭3-e4 g3-e♭4   low, c3-d4 e3-c4
   Remarks: Sustained in moderate tempo. Moving bass line in the accompa-
      niment. Acc 3 BSS
   Occasions: Christmas and Sunday after Christmas.

O Saviour sweet, O Saviour mild BWV493   All Voices
(O Jesulein süss, O Jesulein mild)
   Text: Anonymous, English by Mack Harrell.
   Range & Tess: high, g3-f4 a3-d4   medium, e♭3-d♭4 f3-b♭3
   Remarks: Very sustained in moderate slow tempo. 3 verses.See "O Jesus
      so gentle, Jesus so sweet" in BSS, suitable for Christmas and the
      Sunday after. Acc 3 SHS
   Occasions: Advent. General use.

O slaughtered Lamb BWV455   All Voices
(Erwürgtes Lamm)
   Text: U. B. von Bonin, English by H. S. Drinker & T. Lau.
   Range & Tess: high, f3-f4 a3-e4   low, d3-d4 f#3-c#4
   Remarks: Sustained in moderate tempo. Slightly climactic ending. 2
      verses. Acc 3 BSS
   Occasion: Special use with sermon theme - discipleship.

O soul beloved BWV494   All Voices
(O liebe Seele)
   Text: Anonymous, English by H. S. Drinker & T. Lau.
   Range & Tess: high, d3-e4 g3-d4   low, c3-d4   f3-c4
   Remarks: Sustained in moderate slow tempo. Gentle, generally on MF
      level. Requires some flexibility. 3 verses. Acc 3 BSS
   Occasions: General use. Evangelistic services.

One thing's needful BWV453   All Voices
(Eins ist not)
   Text: J. H. Schroeder, English by F. E. Cox.
   Range & Tess: high, c3-e4 f3-d4   low, b♭2-d4 e♭3-c4
   Remarks: Sustained in moderate tempo. Low ending line. 2 verses. A
      "song of justification". Acc 3 BSS
   Occasion: Lent

Return from gloomy caves of death BWV480   All Voices
(Kommt wieder aus der finstern Gruft)
   Text: V. E. Loescher, English by T. Lau.
   Range & Tess: high, e3-g4 a3-e4   low, c3-e♭4 f3-c4
   Remarks: Animated in lively tempo. Joyful. Requires some flexibility.
      2 verses. Acc 3 BSS, TSB, FSS
   Occasions: Easter and Sunday after Easter. General use.

Rise up! The hour will not await BWV440   All Voices
(Auf, auf! Die rechte Zeit ist hier)
   Text: M. Opitz, English by H. S. Drinker & T. Lau.
   Range & Tess: high, e3-f4 g3-d4 low, c#3-d4 e3-b3
   Remarks: Sustained in moderate tempo. Stately, 3 verses. Acc 3 BSS
   Occasions: Advent. General use. New Year's Eve.

Take courage now, my weary soul BWV454   All Voices
(Ermuntre dich, mein schwacher Geist)
   Text: J. Rist, English by T. Lau.
   Range & Tess: high, f3-f4 g3-c4   low, d3-d4 e3-a3
   Remarks: Sustained in moderate lively tempo. Bright, joyful. Descend-
      ing ending line. 2 verses. Acc 3 BSS
   Occasion: Christmas.

The Holy Passiontide now brings to mind again BWV450   All Voices
(Die bittre Leidenszeit beginnet abermal)
   Text: H. Elmenhorst, English by T. Lau.
   Range & Tess: high, c3-g4 g3-eb4   low, a2-e4 e3-c4
   Remarks: Sustained in slow tempo. Descending, low ending phrases.
      Ends on the lowest note of the song. 2 verses. Acc 3 BSS
   Occasions: Lent. Maundy Thursday.

The sun is sinking in the west BWV446   All Voices
(Der lieben Sonne Licht und Pracht)
   Text: Christian Scriver, English by H. S. Drinker & T. Lau.
   Range & Tess: high, f3-g4 a3-f4 low, c3-d4 e3-c4
   Remarks: Sustained in moderate tempo. 3 verses. Useful as a solo in-
      troit in an evening service. Acc 3 BSS
   Occasion: Evening service.

The sun's bright splendor BWV451   All Voices
(Die güldne Sonne)
   Text: Paul Gerhardt, English by T. Lau.
   Range & Tess: high, eb3-f4 ab3-eb4 low, c3-d4 f3-c4
   Remarks: Sustained in moderate tempo. Has climactic passages and a
      climactic ending. 3 verses. A song of hope and joy. Acc 3 BSS,
      POS-4
   Occasions: General use, especially morning services. New Year's Day
      and the Sunday after.

The wise confine their choice in friends BWV443   All Voices
(Beschränkt, ihr Weisen dieser Welt)
   Text: C. Wegleiter, English by T. Lau.
   Range & Tess: high, d3-f#4 f#3-e4   low, bb2-d4 d3-c4
   Remarks: Sustained in moderate tempo. Slightly climactic ending. 2
      verses. Theme - longing for Christ, affirmation of faith. Acc 3
      BSS
   Occasions: General use. Evangelistic services.

BACH

Think, dear heart, on Jesus now BWV482   All Voices
(Liebes Herz, bedenke doch)
   Text: C. J. Koitsch, English by H. S. Drinker & T. Lau.
   Range & Tess: high, d3-g4 g3-e4   low, bb2-eb4 eb3-c4
   Remarks: Sustained in moderate tempo. Slightly majestic. 3 verses.
      Theme: Grace of God. Acc 3 BSS
   Occasions: General use. Advent.

To be a Christian, great the cost BWV459   All Voices
(Es costet viel, ein Christ zu sein)
   Text: C. F. Richter, English by T. Lau.
   Range & Tess: high, e3-e4 a3-e4   low, c3-c4 f3-c4
   Remarks: Sustained in moderate tempo. 2 verses. Acc 3 BSS
   Occasions: Special use with sermon theme - duties of a Christian. Bap-
      tism. General use.

To Thee, Jehovah, will I sing praises BWV452   All Voices
(Dir, dir, Jehova, will ich singen)
   Text: Bartholomaeus Crasselius, English by H. S. Drinker & T. Lau.
   Range & Tess: high, f3-g4 a3-eb4   low, c3-d4 e3-bb3
   Remarks: Animated in moderate tempo. A joyful song of praise. Requires
      some flexibility. 2 verses Acc 3 BSS, TSB, FSS
   Occasions: New Year's Day. Trinity Sunday. General use.

When seraphim must hide their faces BWV486   All Voices
(Mein Jesu, dem die Seraphinen)
   Text: W. C. Dessler, English by H. S. Drinker & T. Lau.
   Range & Tess: high, c3-d4 f3-c4   low, c3-d4 f3-c4
   Remarks: Sustained in moderate tempo. 3 verses. A song of faith or "a
      song of justification". Acc 3 BSS
   Occasions: General use.

Why art thou, soul, discouraged and dejected BWV506   All Voices
(Was bist du doch, o Seele, so Betrübet)
   Text: R. F. von Schultt, English by T. Lau.
   Range & Tess: high, g3-f4 b3-f4   low, d3-c4 f#3-c4
   Remarks: Sustained in moderate tempo. 3 verses. A "song of comfort".
    Acc 3 BSS
   Occasions: Funerals. Evening services. General use.

                    Solos From The Cantatas

Cantata numbers correspond with W. Schmieder's "Bach-Werke-Verzeichnis"
(BWV). Entries are listed alphabetically by the English version of the
aria.

                            Soprano

And though with muted, feeble voices   Soprano
(Auch mit gedämpften, schwachen Stimmen)

Work: CANTATA 36 - Schwingt freudig euch empor. Text by Christian
    Friedrich Henrici.
Range & Tess: d3-g4   f#3-e4
Remarks: With violin obbligato. Animated in moderate tempo. Graceful
    and rhythmic, has florid passages, requires flexibility. Climactic
    passages. Acc 4 ACC-1
Occasions: General use. New Year's Day. Festivals.

Blessed morn, when Jesus was born   Soprano
(Süsser Trost, mein Jesus kommt)
  Work: CANTATA 151 - Susser Trost, mein Jesus kommt. Text, anonymous.
  Range & Tess: e3-a4   a3-f#4
  Remarks: Very sustained in slow tempo. Delicate. Has some florid pas-
    sages and an animated middle section. Requires flexibility. Acc 4
    (VS)BH
  Occasions: Christmas and the Sunday after.

God my shepherd walks beside me   Soprano
  Work: CANTATA 208 - Was mir behagt (Jagdkantate). Text by Salomo
    Franck, English by Helen A. Dickinson.
  Range & Tess: f3-a4   g3-ab4
  Remarks: Sustained in moderate tempo. In pastoral style. Generally on
    MF level. See also "Jesus shepherd, be Thou near me" in WBB and
    "Sheep may safely graze" (S)OX, both medium high, d3-f4 e3-e4;
    (S)GA-2 keys. Acc 4 (S)HG. WBB.
  Occasions: General use. Weddings. Installation services. New Year's
    Eve. Evening services. Memorial services.

God provides for all the living (Gott versorget alles Leben)   Soprano
  Work: CANTATA 187 - Es wartet alles auf dich (Everything is awaiting
    you). Text, anonymous.
  Range & Tess: d3-ab4   f3-f4
  Remarks: Animated vocal part in slow tempo. Has some short florid fig-
    ures, some wide intervalic skips, descending ending line. Requires
    flexibility. With solo oboe. Acc 3 ACC-1
  Occasions: Thanksgiving. General use. Evangelistic services.

Great One, what I treasure (Höchster, was ich habe)   Soprano
  Work: CANTATA 39 - Brich dem Hungrigen dein Brot (Break bread for the
    hungry). Text, anonymous.
  Range & Tess: d3-ab4   g3-f4
  Remarks: Animated in moderate lively tempo. Has some short florid fig-
    ures, some high tessitura, slightly climactic passages. Graceful.
    With flute obbligato. Acc 3 ACC-1
  Occasion: General use.

He who holds nought within his soul (Es halt' es mit der   Soprano
    blinden Welt)
  Work: CANTATA 94 - Was frag' ich nach der Welt (What do I ask of the
    world). Text, anonymous.

13

Range & Tess: c#3-g4   f#3-e4
Remarks: Animated in moderate tempo. Has some florid passages and a
   descending ending line. Requires flexibility. Acc 3-4 ACC-1
Occasions: General use. Advent.

Hear, ye people (Hört, ihr Volker)   Soprano
   Work: CANTATA 76 - Die Himmel erzahlen die Ehre Gottes (The heavens
      declare the glory of God). Text by Christian Weise(?), English by
      Mevanwy Roberts.
   Range & Tess: d3-g4   g3-e4
   Remarks: Gracefully animated in moderate tempo. Requires flexibility.
      Has some florid passages and wide intervalic skips. Acc 3-4 (VS)BH
   Occasions: Massed religious gatherings. Evangelistic services. Second
      Sunday after Trinity (Bach).

How precious are the gifts of the Holy Sacrament?   Soprano
(Wie theuer sind des heil'gen Mahles Gaben?)
   Work: CANTATA 180 - Schmücke dich, o liebe Seele (Beautify thyself,
      my spirit). Text by Johann Franck, English by J. M. Stein and Ifor
      Jones.
   Range & Tess: d3-a4   f3-d4
   Remarks:A recitative followed by a sustained arioso. Has slightly cli-
      mactic passages. Acc 3-4 (VS)GS, BH
   Occasions: Communion. 20th Sunday after Trinity (Bach).

How sweetly in mine ear is singing   Soprano
(Wie lieblich klingt es in den Ohren)
   Work: CANTATA 133 - Ich freue mich in dir. Text by Kaspar Ziegler.
   Range & Tess: e3-a4   a3-g4
   Remarks: Sustained in moderate tempo. Slower middle section. Requires
      some flexibility and fine high notes. Acc 4 (VS)BH
   Occasion: Christmas.

I carry my sorrow with joy in my heart   Soprano
(Ich nehme mein Leiden mit Freuden auf mich)
   Work: CANTATA 75 - Die Elenden sollen essen (The afflicted shall eat).
      Text by Christian Weise(?).
   Range & Tess: c3-a4   f3-f4
   Remarks: Animated vocal part in moderate slow tempo. Has florid pas-
      sages. Generally graceful. With oboe obbligato. Acc 3 ACC-1
   Occasions: Funerals. General use.

Lord, as Thy name is, so Thy praise resounds   Soprano
(Jesus soll mein erstes Wort)
   Work: CANTATA 171 - Gott, wie dein Name, so ist auch dein Ruhm. Text
      by Georg Christian Eilmar.
   Range & Tess: d3-g4   e3-f4
   Remarks: Sustained in moderate tempo. Has some florid passages and
      figures. Extended instrumental prelude and postlude. O-S: solo
      violin and continuo. Acc 4 (VS)BH

Occasion: New Year's Day or the Sunday after.

My heart ever faithful (Mein gläubiges Herze)　　　　　　　Soprano
 Work: CANTATA 68 - Also hat Gott die Welt geliebt. Text translated by
  Mariane von Ziegler.
 Range & Tess:　f3-a4　　a3-f4
 Remarks: Animated in lively tempo. Requires some flexibility. Bright,
  joyous, generally on MF level. Slightly climactic ending.　Acc 4
  ASS-1, 52S. (VS)GS, BH. (S)GS, NO.
 Occasions: Advent. Whitsunday (Pentecost). Massed religious gatherings.
  New Year's Day or the Sunday after.

My soul shall rest in Jesus' keeping　　　　　　　　　　　　Soprano
(Die Seele ruht in Jesu Händen)
 Work: CANTATA 127 - Herr Jesu Christ, wahr'r Mensch und Gott. Text by
  Paul Eber.
 Range & Tess:　c3-ab4　　g3-f4
 Remarks: Sustained in slow tempo. Has some short florid passages, re-
  quires some flexibility.　Acc 4　(VS)BH
 Occasions: Funerals. Evening services.

My soul's delight in God's own word　　　　　　　　　　　　Soprano
(Mein Seelenschatz ist Gottes Wort)
 Work: CANTATA 18 - Gleich wie der Regen und Schnee von Himmel fällt.
  Text by Erdmann Neumeister.
 Range & Tess:　eb3-ab4　　g3-f4
 Remarks:　Sustained in moderate slow tempo. Has some slightly animat-
  ed passages and climactic ending. Extended prelude and postlude.
  O-S: 2 flutes in unison, 4 violas in unison, continuo.　Acc 3-4
  (VS)BH
 Occasions: General use, best before and after reading of Scriptures.

O God how long afflict ye　　　　　　　　　　　　　　　　　Soprano
(Mein Gott, wie lang', ach, lange?)
 Work: CANTATA 155 - Mein Gott, wie lang', ach, lange. Text by Salomo
  Franck.
 Range & Tess:　d3-g4　　f3-f4
 Remarks: Animated in moderate tempo. Majestic, with some short florid
  passages.　Acc 3-4　(VS)BH
 Occasions: Lent. Evening services.

Rejoice! the old year now is ended　　　　　　　　　　　　Soprano
(Gottlob! Nun geht des Jahr zu Ende)
 Work: CANTATA 28 - Gottlob! Nun geht das Jahr zu Ende. Text by Erdmann
  Neumeister.
 Range & Tess:　d3-a4　　g3-f4
 Remarks: Sustained in moderate slow tempo. Has florid passages,　re-
  quires flexibility. Extended instrumental prelude　and postlude.
  O-S: 2 oboes, tenor oboe, 2 violins, viola and continuo. Acc 3-4
  (VS)BH
Occasion: New Year's Eve.　　　　　　15

BACH

Sun of life, my spirit's radiance (Lebens Sonne, Licht der   Soprano
  Sinnen)
    Work: CANTATA 180 - Schmücke dich, o liebe Seele (Beautify thyself,
      my spirit). Text by Johann Franck, English by J. M. Stein and Ifor
      Jones.
    Range & Tess: d3-g4   f3-f4
    Remarks: Animated, florid, joyous. Requires some flexibility. Theme:
      Jesus, the light of life. Acc 3-4 (VS)BH
    Occasion: General use.

The Lord gives love, and grants His blessing   Soprano
(Die Armen will der Herr umarmen)
    Work: CANTATA 186 - Argre dich, o seele nicht (Be not annoyed, oh my
      soul). Text, anonymous, adapted by Salomo Franck.
    Range & Tess: d3-g4   g3-eb4
    Remarks: Sustained in slightly slow tempo. Has some slightly florid
      passages and some wide intervalic skips. Violin obbligato. Acc 3
      ACC-1
    Occasion: General use.

Think, Lord, on us, Thy grace bestowing   Soprano
(Gedenk' an uns mit deiner Liebe)
    Work: CANTATA 29 - Wir danken dir, Gott, wir danken dir. Text, anony-
      mous.
    Range & Tess: f#3-a4   a3-f#4
    Remarks: Gently animated vocal line in moderate slow tempo. Graceful;
      requires flexibility. O-S: 1 oboe, 2 violins, viola, continuo. Acc
      3-4 (VS)BH
    Occasions: Special use with sermon theme - love of country. National
      holidays.

Up! arouse thee! (Wirf, mein Herze)   Soprano
    Work: CANTATA 155 - Mein Gott, wie lang, ach, wie lange. Text by Sa-
      lomo Franck.
    Range & Tess: c3-a4   g3-f4
    Remarks: Animated in lively tempo. Has some high tessitura. Abounds
      in triplet figures, has florid passages, and a descending ending
      line. Acc 3 (VS)BH
    Occasions: General use. Special use with sermon theme - Jesus' lov-
      ing mercy.

Within my heart of hearts (Komm in mein Herzenshaus)   Soprano
    Work: CANTATA 80 - Ein' feste Burg ist unser Gott. Text by Martin Lu-
      ther.
    Range & Tess: e3-a4   g3-g4
    Remarks: Sustained in moderate tempo. Florid. Requires fine high
      notes and flexibility. Acc 3-4 BAS. (VS)GS, BH
    Occasions: General use. Reformation Sunday. Advent. Palm Sunday.

Mezzo-Soprano and Contralto

Ah, slumbering watchman, why?   Mezzo-Soprano, Contralto
(Ach, schläfrige Seele)
  Work: CANTATA 115 - Mache dich, mein Geist bereit. Text by Johann Bur-
    chard Freystein.
  Range & Tess: a2-d4   e3-c4
  Remarks: Sustained in moderate slow tempo. Has a rapid and florid mid-
    dle section. Extended instrumental interludes. Acc 3-4 (VS)BH
  Occasion: Lent

Christian, ne'er let sin o'erpower thee   Contralto
(Widerstehe, doch der Sunde)
  Work: CANTATA 54 - Widerstehe, doch der Sünde. Text, anonymous.
  Range & Tess: f2-bb3   c3-f4
  Remarks: Sustained vocal part in slow tempo. Grave, dark, warm. Has
    florid figures. A solo cantata. Acc 3-4 (VS)BH, EK
  Occasions: General use. Special use with sermon theme - overcoming sin.

Christians, hold this rite for comfort   Mezzo-Soprano, Contralto
(Menschen, glaubt doch dieser Gnade)
  Work: CANTATA 7 - Christ unser Herr zum Jordan kam. Text by Martin Lu-
    ther(?).
  Range & Tess: b2-e4   e3-c#4
  Remarks: Very vigorous and dramatic. Has some florid passages. Acc 3-4
    (VS)BH
  Occasions: General use. Special use with sermon theme - sin, faith,
    and baptism. Baptism. Evangelistic services.

R: My spirit doth rejoice
   (Ich fühle schon im Geist)
A: Christians, show your lovely deeds
   (Liebt, ihr Christen, in der Tat)   Mezzo-Soprano, Contralto
  Work: CANTATA 76 - Die Himmel erzählen die Ehre Gottes (The heavens
    declare the glory of God). Text by Christian Weise(?). English by
    Mevanwy Roberts.
  Range & Tess: b2-d4   e3-c4
  Remarks: Sustained in slow tempo. Grave, dark, subdued. Theme: broth-
    erhood. Acc 3 (VS)BH
  Occasions: World Brotherhood Sunday. Installation for missionary ser-
    vice. Evangelistic services.

God is still our sun and shield   Mezzo-Soprano, Contralto
(Gott ist unser Sonn' und Schild)
  Work: CANTATA 79 - Gott, der Herr, ist Sonn' und Schild. Text, anony-
    mous.
  Range & Tess: c#3-e4   e3-d4
  Remarks: Animated in moderate tempo. Has florid figures. Acc 3-4
    (VS)BH
  Occasions: General use. Reformation Sunday (Bach).

Hallelujah! power and might   Mezzo-Soprano, Contralto
(Hallelujah! Stärk und Macht)
  Work: CANTATA 29 - Wir danken dir, Gott, wir danken dir. Text, anony-
    mous.
  Range & Tess: a2-e4   c#3-b3
  Remarks: Same text as the tenor aria earlier in the cantata. Animated
    in lively tempo, with florid passages. Exultant song of praise,
    short. Repetitive text. Requires fine a2. Acc 4 (S)PP. (VS)BH
  Occasions: Easter. Festivals. Trinity Sunday.

Highly honored Son Divine   Mezzo-Soprano, Contralto
(Hochgelobter Gottes)
  Work: CANTATA 6 - Bleib bei uns, denn es will Abend werden. Text, an-
    onymous.
  Range & Tess: bb2-eb4   eb3-c4
  Remarks: Animated in moderate lively tempo. Graceful, generally on MF
    level. Requires some flexibility. Acc 3-4 (VS)BH
  Occasions: General use. Evening services.

In Jesus is my hope and trust   Mezzo-Soprano, Contralto
(In Jesu Demuth kann ich Trost)
  Work: CANTATA 151 - Süsser Trost, mein Jesus kommt. Text, anonymous.
  Range & Tess: a2-e4   d3-d4
  Remarks: Sustained in moderate tempo. Requires flexibility. Has some
    florid figures and a subdued ending. Acc 4 (VS)BH
  Occasions: Epiphany. General use.

R: Immanuel! O give to me (Immanuel! Du wollest dir gefallen)
A: Lord, I sing Thy name (Jesu, dir sei Preis)Mezzo-Soprano, Contralto
  Work: CANTATA 142 - Uns ist ein Kind geboren (For us a Child is born).
    Text by Erdmann Neumeister, English by Sydney Biden.
  Range & Tess: c3-c4   e3-c4
  Remarks: Recitative and sustained air in moderate slow tempo. General-
    ly on MF level. Requires some flexibility. Acc 3-4 (VS)GA, BH, GS.
    (S)GA-aria only.
  Occasions: Christmas. Christmas Eve programs and services. General use
    (the aria alone).

O well for you, all bliss possessing   Mezzo-Soprano, Contralto
(Wohl euch, ihr auserwählten Seelen)
  Work: CANTATA 34 - O ewiges Feuer, o Ursprung der Liebe. Text by J.
    S. Bach(?).
  Range & Tess: b2-e4   e3-d4
  Remarks: Sustained in moderate slow tempo. Requires some flexibility.
    Acc 3-4 (VS)BH
  Occasions: Thanksgiving . Whitsunday (Pentecost). General use.

Sound your knell, blest hour of parting   Mezzo-Soprano, Contralto
(Schlage doch, gewünschte Stunde)

Work: CANTATA 53 - Schlage doch, gewünschte Stunde. Text, anonymous.
Range & Tess: b2-e4   e3-c#4
Remarks: Very sustained in moderate slow tempo. Grave, dark, general-
  ly subdued. From a solo cantata for Contralto. Acc 3 (VS)BH
Occasions: Funerals. Evening services.

Tenor

All pitch indications for Tenor are understood to sound one octave lower.

Arise, my soul! (Ermunt're dich)   Tenor
  Work: CANTATA 180 - Schmücke dich, o liebe Seele (Beautify thyself, my
    spirit). Text by Johann Franck.
  Range & Tess: d3-a4   g3-g4
  Remarks: Animated in moderate tempo. Joyful. Requires considerable
    flexibility. Has a wide range and generally high tessitura. Florid
    passages. Acc 3-4 (VS)BH
  Occasions: Massed religious gatherings. Evangelistic services. Mis-
    sions Sunday. General use.

Christ Jesus, God's only Son (Jesus Christus, Gottes Sohn)   Tenor
  Work: CANTATA 4 - Christ lag in Todesbanden. Text by Martin Luther.
  Range & Tess: d#3-f#4   g3-e4
  Remarks: Sustained in moderate lively tempo. Majestic. A sustained
    chorale melody. Ends with "hallelujah" passage. Florid final line.
    Acc 4 (VS)BH
  Occasions: Easter and the Sunday after.

Christ Jesus now is risen (Mein Jesus ist erstanden)   Tenor
  Work: CANTATA 67 - Halt im Gedächtnis Jesus Christ. Text by Christian
    Weise(?).
  Range & Tess: e3-a4   a3-g#4
  Remarks: Animated in moderate lively tempo. Spirited, majestic, rhyth-
    mically strong. Requires flexibility. Very high tessitura. Climactic
    ending. Acc 4 (VS)BH
  Occasions: Easter and the two Sundays after.

R: Ah, why hast Thou, my God (Wie hast du dich, mein Gott)
A: From my eyes the salt tears showering (Bäche von gezalznen   Tenor
  Zähren)
  Work: CANTATA 21 - Ich hatte viel Bekümmernis. Text by Salomo Franck
    (?).
  Range & Tess: c3-g4   g3-f4
  Remarks: Sustained aria in slow tempo. Slightly faster 2nd section.
    Has florid passages. Acc 3-4 (VS)BH
  Occasion: Lent.

BACH

Hallelujah! Power and might (Hallelujah! Stärk und Macht)   Tenor
    Work: CANTATA 29 - Wir danken dir, Gott, wir danken dir. Text, anony-
        mous.
    Range & Tess: e3-b4   g#3-f#4
    Remarks: Animated in moderate lively tempo. Spirited, vigorous, joy-
        ous. Has florid passages, requires flexibility. Broader 2nd section.
        Has climactic high spots. Same text as the alto aria from the same
        cantata. Acc 4 (VS)BH
    Occasions: Easter. Festivals. Trinity Sunday.

I know that my Redeemer liveth (Ich weiss, dass mein Erlöser lebt)Tenor
    Work: CANTATA 160 - Ich weiss dass mein Erlöser. Text by Erdmann Neu-
        meister.
    Range & Tess: d3-g4   g3-e4
    Remarks: Animated in lively tempo. Majestic. Has some short florid
        passages; requires flexibility. A solo cantata. Acc 3-4 (VS)BH
    Occasions: Easter and the Sunday after. Massed religious gatherings.
        Funerals. Memorial services. General use.

Jesu, on Thy features gazing (Jesu, lass uns auf dich sehen)   Tenor
    Work: CANTATA 6 - Bleib bei uns, denn es will Abend werden. Text, an-
        onymous.
    Range & Tess: d3-a4   g3-eb4
    Remarks: Sustained in moderate slow tempo. Generally on MF level. Has
        some wide intervalic skips, high tessitura, and florid passages.
        Acc 3-4 (VS)BH
    Occasions: General use. Advent. New Year's Eve.

Lord, my thanks to Thee (Jesu, dir sei Dank)   Tenor
    Work: CANTATA 142 - Uns ist ein Kind geboren (For us a Child is born).
        Text by Erdmann Neumeister.
    Range & Tess: g3-g4   a3-f4
    Remarks: Sustained in moderate slow tempo. Has some florid figures,
        requires flexibility. Generally on MF level. Acc 3 (VS)GA, BH, GS
    Occasions: Advent. Christmas. Christmas Eve programs and services.
        Thanksgiving. General use, except Lent.

So be thou still (Man halte nur ein wenig stille)   Tenor
    Work: CANTATA 93 - Wer nur den lieben Gott lässt walten. Text by
        Georg Neumark.
    Range & Tess: eb3-bb4   ab3-f4
    Remarks: Sustained in moderate slow tempo. Graceful and generally sub-
        dued. Somewhat meditative. Florid closing passage. Acc 3 (VS)BH
    Occasions: Holy Week. Lent.

Take me, Saviour, for Thine own (Nimm mich dir zu eigen hin)   Tenor
    Work: CANTATA 65 - Sie werden aus Saba all kommen. Text by Christian
        Weise(?).
    Range & Tess: d3-a4   g3-e4

Remarks: Sustained in moderate tempo. Has florid passages. Acc 3-4
   (VS)BH
Occasions: Baptism. Epiphany (Bach). Special use in services of per-
   sonal dedication. Installation of church officers or pastor.

R: Ah, I am a child of evil (Ach! ich bin ein Kind der Sunden)
A: Thy blood, which doth my guilt redeem (Dein Blut, so meine
   Schuld durch-streicht)   Tenor
   Work: CANTATA 78 - Jesu, der du meine Seele (Jesus, Thou my wearied
      spirit). Text by Johann Rist, English by J. M. Stein and Ifor Jones.
   Range & Tess: c3-a4   g3-f4
   Remarks: A recitative and a sustained and graceful air. Has some flor-
      id passages. Acc 3-4 (VS)GS, BH
   Occasion: General use.

Undaunted stand and bold (Hebt euer Haupt empor)   Tenor
   Work: CANTATA 70 - Wachet, betet, seid bereit allezeit. Text by Salo-
      mo Franck.
   Range & Tess: c3-g4   g3-e4
   Remarks: Sustained in moderate slow tempo. Requires some flexibility.
      Acc 3-4 (VS)BH
   Occasion: General use.

Baritone and Bass

Ah, when upon that last great day   Bass-Baritone, Bass
(Ach, soll nicht dieser grosse Tag)
   Work: CANTATA 70 - Wachet, betet, seid bereit allezeit. Text by Salo-
      mo Franck.
   Range & Tess: g1-f3   c2-d3
   Remarks: Sustained recitative and aria in moderate slow tempo. Majes-
      tic. Very florid and animated middle section. Requires flexibility.
      Ends with a florid passage. Acc 4 (VS)BH
   Occasion: General use.

Despiseth thou the riches of His goodness?   Baritone, Bass
(Verachtest du den Reichthum seiner Gnade?)
   Work: CANTATA 102 - Herr, deine Augen sehen nach dem Glauben. Text by
      Christian Friedrich Henrici(?).
   Range & Tess: g1-e♭3   e♭2-d3
   Remarks: Spirited, has strongly marked sections. Generally animated.
      Climactic ending. Acc 3-4 (VS)BH
   Occasion: General use.

Here in my Father's house   Bass-Baritone, Bass
(Hier, in meines Vaters Stätte)
   Work: CANTATA 32 - Liebster Jesu, mein Verlangen. Text, anonymous.
   Range & Tess: g1-e3   d2-d3
   Remarks: Sustained in moderate slow tempo. Graceful, gentle, generally
      subdued. Requires flexibility. Acc 3-4 (VS)BH

BACH

Occasions: Epiphany. General use.

I with my cross-staff gladly wander   Bass-Baritone, Bass
(Ich will den Kreutzstab gerne tragen)
  Work: CANTATA 56 - Ich will den Kreutzstab gerne tragen. Text by J. S.
    Bach(?).
  Range & Tess: g1-e3   c2-d3
  Remarks: Sustained in moderate tempo. Requires some flexibility and
    fine high notes. High tessitura in some passages. Florid. From the
    bass solo cantata. Acc 3-4 (VS)BH
  Occasion: General use.

Let trumpets clear resound   Bass-Baritone, Bass
(Auf, auf, mit hellem Schall)
  Work: CANTATA 128 - Auf Christi Himmelfahrt allein. Text by Mariane
    von Ziegler.
  Range & Tess: f#1-e3   c#2-d3
  Remarks:Animated in moderate lively tempo. Vigorous, majestic, florid.
    The final section is a short recitative followed by an instrumental
    ritornel. Acc 4-5 (VS)BH
  Occasions: Ascension Sunday. Easter or the Sunday after.

R: Ah, human will, perverse art thou (Ach, unser Wille bleibt verkehrt)
A: Lord, as Thou wilt (Herr, so du willt)   Baritone, Bass
  Work: CANTATA 73 - Herr, wie du willt, so schicke mit mir. Text by
    Christian Friedrich Henrici(?).
  Range & Tess: g1-e♭3   d2-d3
  Remarks: Recitative and sustained air in moderate slow tempo. Grave and
    generally subdued. Acc 3-4 (VS)BH
  Occasions: Lent. General use.

R: The wounds, nails, thorns (Die Wunden, Nagel, Kron')
A: O Lord, my conscience wilt Thou quiet   Bass-Baritone, Bass
    (Nun du wirst mein Gewissen stillen)
  Work: CANTATA 78 - Jesu, der du meine Seele (Jesus, Thou my wearied
    spirit). Text by Johann Rist, English by J. M. Stein and Ifor Jones.
  Range & Tess: g1-e♭3   c2-c3
  Remarks: A recitative and a sustained, florid air. A song of assurance
    and hope. Acc 3-4 (VS)GS, BH
  Occasion: General use.

Slumber on, oh weary spirit   Baritone, Bass
(Schlummert ein, ihr matten Augen)
  Work: CANTATA 82 - Ich habe genug. Text, anonymous.
  Range & Tess: b♭1-e♭3   c2-c3
  Remarks: Sustained in moderate slow tempo. Subdued, gentle, warm. Re-
    quires some flexibility. From the bass solo cantata. Acc 3-4 (VS)BH
  Occasions: Lent. Evening services.

So appears Thy natal day   Baritone, Bass
(Dein Geburtztag ist erschienen)
  Work: CANTATA 142 - Uns ist ein Kind geboren (For us a Child is born).
    Text by Erdmann Neumeister.
  Range & Tess: al(el)-d3   e2-b2
  Remarks: Sustained in moderate tempo. Has some florid figures, requires
    some flexibility. el is the final note. Acc 3-4 (VS)GA, BH, GS
  Occasions: Christmas. Christmas Eve programs and services. Advent.

So farewell, earth's vain distractions   Bass-Baritone, Bass
(Gute Nacht, du Weltgetümmel)
  Work: CANTATA 27 - Wer weiss, wie nahe mir mein Ende. Text by Johann
    G. Albinus and J. S. Bach.
  Range & Tess: gl-e♭3   c2-d3
  Remarks: Very sustained in slow tempo. Grave. Has some short florid
    passages and a descending ending line. Acc 3 (VS)BH
  Occasion: Lent, especially evening services during the season.

Thine enemies shall all be scattered   Baritone, Bass
(Ja, ja, ich kann die Feinde schlagen)
  Work: CANTATA 57 - Selig ist der Mann. Text by Christian Friedrich
    Henrici.
  Range & Tess: gl-e♭3   d2-d3
  Remarks: Animated in very lively tempo. Vigorous, florid, outgoing.
    Requires flexibility and fluent enunciation. Acc 4-5 (VS)BH
  Occasion: General use, especially the Sunday after Christmas.

'Tis finished! The strife is over   Baritone, Bass
(Es ist vollbracht, das Leid ist alle)
  Work: CANTATA 159 - Sehet, wir geh'n hinauf gen Jerusalem. Text by
    Christian Friedrich Henrici.
  Range & Tess: gl-e♭3   d2-d3
  Remarks: Very sustained in slow tempo. Has florid passages. General-
    ly gentle. Acc 3-4 (VS)BH
  Occasions: Evening services. General use.

Adaptation

Jesu, joy of man's desiring   High, Medium Voices
(Wohl mir, das ich Jesum habe)
  Work: CANTATA 147 - Herz und Mund und Tat und Leben. Text, anonymous.
    English by R. Bridges.
  Range & Tess: g3-f4   a3-d4
  Remarks: The famous chorale for SATB arranged for solo voice by Gor-
    don Jacob. Sustained in moderate tempo. A few variations in dyna-
    mics are suggested. Acc 3-4 (S)OX-English only. (VS)BH
  Occasions: General use. World Brotherhood Sunday. Children's Day.

BACH

Excerpts From Passions and Oratorios

Soprano

Ah, my Saviour (Flösst, mein Heiland)   Soprano
  Work: CHRISTMAS ORATORIO, BWV248. Texts arranged from Luke & Matthew.
  Range & Tess: d3-g4   g3-e4
  Remarks: Graceful, gently moving in moderate tempo. Has florid pas-
    sages; requires flexibility. Has occasional chorus entrances, but
    useful as a straight solo. No. 19 in the score. May also be sung by
    Tenor. Acc 3-4 (VS)GS, NO, BH
  Occasions: General use. Christmas. May also be used in Lent.

I follow Thee also (Ich folge dir gleichfalls)   Soprano
  Work: ST. JOHN PASSION, BWV245. Texts by Barthold Heinrich Brockes,
    after the Bible. English by H. S. Drinker and H. Officer.
  Range & Tess: d3-ab4   g3-g4
  Remarks: Animated in moderate lively tempo. Florid, bright, gently
    joyous. Requires flexibility. Acc 3-4 (VS)GS-Mendel, NO
  Occasions: Lent. General use.

Nought against Thy power (Nur ein Wink von seinen Händen)   Soprano
  Work: CHRISTMAS ORATORIO, BWV248. Texts, see first entry.
  Range & Tess: c#3-a4   a3-f#4
  Remarks: Sustained in moderate slow tempo. Requires considerable
    flexibility and fine command of high notes. Has some florid figures.
    Acc 3-4 (VS)GS, NO, BH
  Occasion: Christmas. General use.

Release, O my spirit thy torrents (Zerfliesse, mein Herze)   Soprano
  Work: ST. JOHN PASSION, BWV245. Texts, see first entry.
  Range & Tess: c3-ab4   g3-g4
  Remarks: Generally sustained in moderate slow tempo. Quite florid. Re-
    quires flexibility and a fine command of high notes. Acc 4-5
    (VS)GS-Mendel, NO
  Occasion: Good Friday.

Mezzo-Soprano and Contralto

From the tangle of my transgressions   Mezzo-Soprano, Contralto
(Von der Stricken meiner Sünden)
  Work: ST. JOHN PASSION, BWV245. Texts by Barthold Heinrich Brockes, af-
    ter the Bible.
  Range & Tess: bb2-eb4   d3-c4
  Remarks: Sustained in moderate slow tempo. Has some short florid fig-
    ures; requires some flexibility. Generally subdued; subdued, low
    ending. Acc 3-4 (VS)GS-Mendel, NO
  Occasions: Lent. Maundy Thursday.

It is fulfilled (Es ist vollbracht)   Mezzo-Soprano, Contralto
  Work: ST. JOHN PASSION, BWV245. Texts, see first entry.
  Range & Tess: b2-d4   d3-d4
  Remarks: A sustained, subdued, quite slow section, followed by a vig-
    orous, animated, joyful, and florid section. Requires flexibility.
    Acc 5 (VS)GS-Mendel, NO
  Occasion: Good Friday.

Keep, O my spirit (Schliesse, mein Herze)   Mezzo-Soprano, Contralto
  Work: CHRISTMAS ORATORIO, BWV248. Texts arranged from Luke & Matthew.
  Range & Tess: b2-e4   e3-d4
  Remarks: Sustained in moderate tempo. Rather vigorous, has climactic
    and strong passages. Descending ending line. Acc 3 (VS)GS,NO,BH
  Occasions: General use. Christmas.

Look ye, Jesus waiting stands   Mezzo-Soprano, Contralto
(Sehet, sehet, Jesus hat die Hand)
  Work: ST. MATTHEW PASSION, BWV244. Texts arranged from the Bible by
    Christian Friedrich Henrici.
  Range & Tess: g2-e♭4   e♭3-d♭4
  Remarks: Very sustained in slow tempo. Intense and warm. Has florid
    passages; requires flexibility. Acc 3-4 (VS)GS, NO
  Occasions: Special use in services of personal dedication. Evangelis-
    tic services.

R: See now the Bridegroom (Nun wird mein liebster Bräutigam)
A: Prepare thyself Zion (Bereite dich, Zion) Mezzo-Soprano, Contralto
  Work: CHRISTMAS ORATORIO, BWV248. Texts, see first entry.
  Range & Tess: b2-e4   e3-c4
  Remarks: Animated in moderate lively tempo. Has one florid passage.
    Acc 3-4 (VS)GS, NO, BH
  Occasion: Advent.

Slumber, beloved (Schlafe, mein Liebster)   Mezzo-Soprano, Contralto
  Work: CHRISTMAS ORATORIO, BWV248. Text, see first entry.
  Range & Tess: e3-a4   g3-g4
  Remarks: Sustained in moderate slow tempo. Has florid passages; re-
    quires very fine high notes. Difficult. Acc 4 (VS)GS-Mendel, NO
  Occasion: Christmas. Christmas Eve programs and services.

Tenor

Behold then how each living stripe   Tenor
(Erwäge, wie sein blutgefärbter Rücken)
  Work: ST. JOHN PASSION, BWV245. Texts by Barthold Heinrich Brockes,
    after the Bible.
  Range & Tess: e3-a4   g3-g4
  Remarks: Sustained in moderate slow tempo. Has florid passages. Re-
    quires very fine high notes and some flexibility. Difficult. Acc 4

(VS)GS-Mendel, NO
Occasion: Lent.

Haste, ye shepherds (Froh, Hirten, eilt, ach eilet)   Tenor
  Work: CHRISTMAS ORATORIO, BWV248. Texts arranged from Luke & Matthew.
  Range & Tess: d3-a4   g3-e4
  Remarks: Animated in moderate tempo. Graceful and very florid. Re-
    quires flexibility. Ends with florid passage. Acc 4 (VS)GS,NO,BH
  Occasions:Christmas and the Sunday after.

O my soul, where wilt thou find thy goal   Tenor
(Ach, mein Sinn, wo willt du endlich hin)
  Work: ST. JOHN PASSION, BWV245. Texts, see first entry.
  Range & Tess: e3-a4   g3-g4
  Remarks: Sustained in moderate tempo. Requires some flexibility and
    fine command of high notes. Generally subdued. Acc 3-4 (VS)GS-
    Mendel, NO
  Occasion: Lent.

Peaceful shall be my departure (Sanfte soll mein Todeskummer)   Tenor
  Work: EASTER ORATORIO, BWV249. Texts, anonymous.
  Range & Tess: c#3-a4   d3-f#4
  Remarks: Sustained in slow tempo. Subdued. Has some long-held notes.
    Requires flexibility. Acc 4-5 (VS)BH
  Occasion: Lent

'Tis Thee I would be praising (Ich will nur dir zu Ehren leben)   Tenor
  Work: CHRISTMAS ORATORIO, BWV248. Texts, Luke 2:1,3-12; Matthew 2: 1-
    12.
  Range & Tess: c3-g4   f3-d4
  Remarks: Animated in moderate lively tempo. Quite florid, requires
    flexibility. Climactic ending. Acc 4 (VS)GS, NO, BH
  Occasions: Christmas. General use.

Ye foes of man (Nun mögt ihr stolzen Feinde schrecken)   Tenor
  Work: CHRISTMAS ORATORIO, BWV248. Texts, see first entry.
  Range & Tess: d3-a4   a3-f#4
  Remarks: Rather vigorous. Has florid figures, requires flexibility.
    Acc 3-4 (VS)GS, BH, NO. ASS-T
  Occasions: Christmas. Advent. General use.

Baritone and Bass

At evening, hour of calm and rest   Baritone, Bass
(Am Abend da es kühle war)
  Work: ST. MATTHEW PASSION, BWV244. Texts arranged from the Bible by
    Christian Friedrich Henrici.
  Range & Tess: g1-eb3   c2-c3
  Remarks: A sustained arioso in moderate slow tempo. Tranquil and sub-
    dued. Acc 3-4 (VS)GS, NO

Occasions: Evening services. Good Friday.

Bethink thee, O my soul (Betrachte, meine Seel')   Baritone, Bass
   Work: ST. JOHN PASSION, BWV245. Texts by Barthold Heinrich Brockes,
      after the Bible.
   Range & Tess: bb1-eb3   eb2-d3
   Remarks: Sustained in moderate slow tempo. Contemplative, mainly lyr-
      ic in style. The words "Bethink thee" may be substituted with "Con-
      sider". Acc 3-4 (VS)GS-Mendel, NO
   Occasion: Lent.

R: The Saviour, low before His Father bending   Baritone, Bass
      (Der Heiland fallt von seinem Vater nieder)
A: Gladly would I be enduring (Gerne will ich mich beqeumen)
   Work: ST. MATTHEW PASSION, BWV244. Texts, see first entry.
   Range & Tess: g1-eb3   d2-c3
   Remarks: Sustained in moderate slow tempo. Requires some flexibility
      and fine command of high notes. Generally on MF level. Acc 3 (VS)
      GS, NO
   Occasions: Maundy Thursday. Good Friday.

Make thee clean, my heart from sin   Baritone, Bass
(Mache dich mein Herze rein)
   Work: ST. MATTHEW PASSION, BWV244. Texts, see first entry.
   Range & Tess: a1-eb3   c2-c3
   Remarks: Sustained in moderate slow tempo. Requires some flexibility,
      and a fine command of high notes. Has climactic passages. Acc 3-4
      (VS)GS, NO
   Occasions: Special use in services of personal dedication. Evening
      services. General use.

Mighty Lord, and King all glorious   Baritone, Bass
(Grosser Herr und starker König)
   Work: CHRISTMAS ORATORIO, BWV248. Texts arranged from Luke & Matthew.
   Range & Tess: a1-e3   e2-d3
   Remarks: Animated in moderate tempo. Vigorous and majestic. Requires
      flexibility and solid tone. Has some short florid passages. Acc 3-
      4 (VS)GS, BH, NO. ASS-B
   Occasions: Christmas. Festivals. General use.

O Lord, my darkened heart enlighten   Baritone, Bass
(Erleucht' auch meine finstre)
   Work: CHRISTMAS ORATORIO, BWV248. Texts, see above entry.
   Range & Tess: b1-e3   e2-d3
   Remarks: Sustained in moderate slow tempo. Has many florid passages.
      Requires flexibility. Acc 3 (VS)GS, BH, NO. ASS-B
   Occasions: Christmas. Advent. Evening services. General use.

ERNST BACON
United States

FSB Fifty Songs by Ernst Bacon. Original keys, mostly high. Repro-
     duced manuscript, not easy to read. Georgetown, CA: Dragon's
     Teeth Press, 1974.

Ancient carol   Medium, Low Voices
   Text: Traditional poem.
   Range & Tess: b#2-e4   e3-c#4
   Remarks: Sustained in moderate slow tempo. Generally subdued. Starts
      and ends on low notes. Short. First line: He came so still where
      His mother was.   Acc 3 FSB
   Occasions: Christmas Eve. Christmas or the Sunday after.

Christmas Eve   All Voices
   Text: Alfred Tennyson.
   Range & Tess: e3-f4   g3-d4
   Remarks: Moderate slow tempo, sustained. Short song, 42 measures in-
      cluding extended piano ending. Subdued throughout, requires simpli-
      city. Acc 3 FSB
   Occasions: Christmas Eve programs and services.

Christ's Sunday morn   Medium Voice
   Text: Old English poem.
   Range & Tess: c3-e4   eb3-d4
   Remarks: Animated in moderate slow tempo, graceful, rhythmic with a
      "broad swing", in 6/8 time. Lines end with strong, exultant Allelu-
      ias. Acc 3-4 FSB
   Occasions: Christmas or Sunday after. New Year's Day or the Sunday
      after.

Little Boy   Soprano, Mezzo-Soprano
   Text: 17th century English poem.
   Range & Tess: e3-g#4   e3-c#4
   Remarks: Sustained in slow tempo, subdued, simple. Gentle, in lullaby
      style. First line: Upon my lap my sov'reign sits. Low ending line.
      Acc 3 FSB
   Occasions: Christmas Eve. Christmas.

RICHARD BALES
United States

Mary's gift   Mezzo-Soprano, Contralto
   Text: Dorothy Callaway.
   Range & Tess: b2-e4   e3-d4
   Remarks: Sustained in moderate tempo, in the style of a carol. Requires
      fine P & PP. Strong middle section and ending phrase. Acc 3 (S)PI
   Occasions: Christmas Eve programs and services.

28

SAMUEL BARBER
1910-1981, United States

CSO Collected Songs. Samuel Barber. High, Low. New York: G. Schirmer.

Lord Jesus Christ!   Soprano
    Text: Soren Kierkegaard. From "Prayers of Kierkegaard".
    Range & Tess: e3-a4   f#3-f#4
    Remarks: Very sustained in slow tempo. Requires fine high PP. Very
        tranquil. Has some slightly climactic passages. Acc 3 (SC)GS.
        SGO-S
    Occasions: Easter. General use.

The crucifixion   All Voices
    Text: The Speckled Book, 12th century, anonymous.
    Range & Tess: d3-f4   e3-d4
    Remarks: Sustained and generally subdued. Unmetered or in free rhythm.
        Has dissonances. 5th song in the cycle "Hermit Songs".
    Occasion: Lent

JOSEPH BARNBY
1838-1896, England

O perfect love   All Voices
    Text: Dorothy Frances Gurney.
    Range & Tess: c3-e♭4   e♭3-c4
    Remarks: A sustained hymn in moderate tempo, useful as a solo. In
        most hymnals. PHD-J, PHP, MHL, PEH. See the solo arrangement in
        TWS, high and low; (S)SP by Hutson. See the settings by Nystedt,
        Sowerby, Wetherill. Acc 3
    Occasions: Weddings. General use.

MARSHALL H. BARNES
United States

The gate of the year   All Voices
    Text: M. Louise Haskins.
    Range & Tess: c3-d4(L)   e3-a4
    Remarks: Sustained in moderate slow tempo. Irregular meter, in the
        style of a gentle recitative. Chant-like, contemplative, short,
        subdued. Low key is original; also issued for high voice. Acc 2-3
        (S)CY
    Occasions: New Year's Day. General use.

LaMAR BARRUS
United States

Consolation   High Voice
    Text: Oliver Wendell Holmes.

29

BARRUS

Range & Tess: e♭3-g#4   a3-e♭4
Remarks: Sustained in slow tempo. Contrasting dynamics. Requires
   flexibility. High, subdued ending. Acc 3 SPC
Occasion: Funerals.

Praise   Medium Voice
   Text: Psalm 106:1,47,48; 108:3-5
   Range & Tess: d3-e4   a3-d4
   Remarks: Mostly animated in lively tempo. Joyful, exultant. Starts
      with majestic, recitative-style passage. Dramatic high ending.
      Full-sounding chords in accompaniment. Acc 3 SPC
   Occasions: General use. New Year. Festivals. Massed religious gath-
      erings.

Prayer   High Voice
   Text: Christina G. Rosetti
   Range & Tess: c3-f4   f3-d4
   Remarks: Sustained in moderate slow tempo. Subdued ending. Has climac-
      tic high passages and soft high ending. Syncopated accompaniment.
      Acc 3 SPC
   Occasions: Evening services and prayer meetings. General use. Special
      use with sermon theme: nature.

                           JOHN BARTLET
                        16th century, England

O Lord, Thy faithfulness   High Voice
   Text: John Bartlet(?)
   Range & Tess: g3-g4   a3-e4
   Remarks: Sustained in moderate tempo. A song of praise in the minor
      key. May be transposed for lower voices. Acc 3 ESL-3 2nd series.
   Occasions: Dedication of music facilities. Installation of church
      musician. General use.

                        H. LEROY BAUMGARTNER
                          United States

BWM Behold What Manner of Love. Op. 49. H. Leroy Baumgartner. St.
       Louis: Concordia Publishing House, 1955.
OLM O Lord, My God, Thou Art Very Great. Four songs, Op. 48. H. Leroy
       Baumgartner. St. Louis: Concordia Publishing House.

Behold what manner of love   High Voice
   Text: I John 3:1-3
   Range & Tess: d3-g4   g3-e♭4
   Remarks: Sustained first and last sections, animated middle with
      strong passages. Has meter changes. Organistic accompaniment. Acc 3
      BWM
   Occasions: Evening services. Special use with sermon theme - God's
      love, sons of God. General use.

He that dwelleth in the secret place of the most high   High Voice
   Text: Psalm 91:1,2,5,6,9,10,14-16 .
   Range & Tess: d3-g4(a4)   f#3-e4
   Remarks: Has both sustained and agitated sections, bold contrasts in
     dynamics, dramatic high passages. Strong final section with de-
     scending line. Acc 3-4 OLM
   Occasions: General use. Special use with sermon theme - faith and
     assurance. Festivals. Evening services.

Lord, I have loved the habitation of Thy house   High Voice
   Text:Psalm 26:8; 27:4-6b, 1b.
   Range & Tess: d3-g4   f3-eb4
   Remarks: Generally sustained in four tempi indications. Starts with
     joyful exultation. Has some strong climactic passages, frequent me-
     ter changes. Very strong descending ending line. Acc 3-4 OLM
   Occasions: Dedication of church building. Special use with sermon
     theme - confidence in God. General use.

Love is of God   High Voice
   Text: I John 4:7-12,18,19,21.
   Range & Tess: d3-f#4   g3-d4
   Remarks: Moderate slow tempo; faster middle section. Subdued beginning
     and ending. Has some short climactic passages. Organistic accompa-
     niment has moving lines complimenting the voice part. Acc 3 BWM
   Occasions: Special use with sermon theme - love. General use.

O Lord, my God, Thou art very great   High Voice
   Text: Psalm 104:1-3,24; 147:3,4; 145:9; Romans 11:33-36.
   Range & Tess: d3-g4   f#3-e4
   Remarks: Sustained vocal part in lively tempo. Slower, more tranquil
     middle section. Has climactic passages, dramatic ending. Organistic
     accompaniment. Acc 3 OLM
   Occasions: Massed religious gatherings. Reformation Sunday. Festivals.
     Evangelistic services. General use.

This is the victory, even our faith   High Voice
   Text: I John 5:4,5,11,14,15.
   Range & Tess: c3-g4   f3-d4
   Remarks: Sustained in moderate tempo. Majestic. Strong unaccompanied
     beginning. Dramatic high passages and ending. Theme: affirmation of
     faith. Acc 3 BWM
   Occasions: Easter. Festivals. Evangelistic services. Massed religious
     gatherings. General use.

ARNOLD BAX
1883-1953, England

A Christmas carol   High Voice
   Text: 15th century manuscript.

J. N. BECK

    Range & Tess: d3-a4   f3-f4
    Remarks: First line - There is no rose of such virtue. Sustained in
        moderate tempo. Majestic. Has florid passages, climactic high
        ending. Requires flexibility. Acc 3 In: Seven Bax Songs (CH)
    Occasions: Christmas Eve programs and services.

                        JOHN NESS BECK
                        United States

Song of joy   High Voice
    Text: Psalm 40.
    Range & Tess: bb2-g4   f3-d4
    Remarks: Animated, exultant; has many held notes at ends of phrases.
        Dramatic high passages and contrasting dynamics. High, climactic
        final note held 15½ beats. Acc 4 (S)CP
    Occasions: General use. Festivals. Massed religious gatherings.

                        W. LEONARD BECK

An Easter carillon   High Voice
    Text: Traditional German, 1623, translated.
    Range & Tess: eb3-eb4(f4)   ab3-eb4
    Remarks: Animated in lively tempo. Joyous, starts strongly. Has "al-
        leluia" interjections. Bell-type tones from accompaniment. Issued
        octavo size. Acc 3 (S)OX
    Occasions: Easter and the Sunday after. General use.

                    LUDWIG VAN BEETHOVEN
                    1770-1827, Germany
BES Ludwig van Beethoven Songs. Complete, 66 songs, mostly in high and
    medium keys. German texts with English versions. Opa-Locka: Edwin
    F. Kalmus, c/o B-M. These songs may be transposed. The fine com-
    plete edition of Boosey & Hawkes is out-of-print.
See "30 Lieder for Mezzo-Soprano or Baritone", only in German, C.F. Pe-
ters.

                        Six Sacred Songs
                    Sechs geistliche Lieder

A set of six songs with texts by Christian F. Gellert. Unidentified
English version. May be transposed for lower voices.

(1) A prayer (Bitten)   All Voices
    Range & Tess: e3-f#4   f#3-e4
    Remarks: A short sustained solo. Majestic, hymn-like. Low, subdued
        ending. Useful as a solo introit for regular Sunday services,
        massed religious gatherings, and festivals. Acc 3
    Occasions: General use. Evening services.

(2) Love of one's neighbor (Die Liebe des Nächsten)   All Voices
    Range & Tess: d3-f4   g3-c4
    Remarks: A short, sustained song useful as a solo introit or solo
       response to the reading of the Scriptures on the brotherhood
       theme. Stately. Acc 3
    Occasions: World Brotherhood Sunday. Missions Sunday. General use.

(3) Death (Vom Tod)   All Voices
    Range & Tess: c#3-g4   f#3-c#4
    Remarks: Very sustained in moderate tempo. Somber, short, subdued.
       Low ending phrase. Acc 2
    Occasion: Special use with sermon theme - death.

(4) Nature's praise of God (Die Ehre Gottes aus der Natur)   All Voices
    Range & Tess: c3-g4   e3-e4
    Remarks: Sustained in moderate tempo. Vigorous, majestic. Climactic
       ending. This song moves in two beats per measure, not in four as
       indicated in some editions. Acc 3 (S)GS-2 keys. 52S-high, CPS.
    Occasions: Massed religious gatherings. Festivals. New Year's Day.
       Thanksgiving. General use.

(5) The might of God (Gottes Macht und Vorsehung)   All Voices
    Range & Tess: e3-g4   g3-f4
    Remarks: A short, sustained, stately song. Full sounding and dramat-
       ic. This song and No. 4 make a suitable pair for performance due
       to the sameness in character. Acc 3
    Occasions: Massed religious gatherings. Festivals. New Year's Day
       and the Sunday after. General use.

(6) Song of penitence (Busslied)   All Voices
    Range & Tess: d#3-g4   g3-e4
    Remarks: Sustained, slow first half, and animated, joyful second
       section. Climactic ending. Acc 4 CPS
    Occasions: Lent. General use.

Excerpt and Single Songs

R: Now tremble, nature?
A: Praise the Redeemer's goodness   Soprano
  Work: CHRIST ON THE MOUNT OF OLIVES (CHRISTUS AM OELBERG). Text by
    Franz Xaver Huber, English by J. Troutbeck.
  Range & Tess: e3-d5   g3-g4
  Remarks: A slow, extended recitative and a generally sustained aria.
    Has florid and dramatic passages, and animated, fairly fast, ju-
    bilant sections. Requires flexibility; vocally demanding. Dramatic
    ending. See the editions entitled ENGEDI. Acc 3-4 (VS)NO, HG
  Occasions: Maundy Thursday. Good Friday.

The quail (Der Wachtelschlag)   All Voices
  Text: S. F. Sauter.

BEETHOVEN

    Range & Tess: e♭3-a4   g3-f4
    Remarks: Animated vocal part in varied tempi. Has some recitative-
      like sections, contrasts in tempi, dramatic passages, and impos-
      ing climaxes. Acc 3-4 BES
    Occasion: Thanksgiving.

To an infant (An einen Säugling)   All Voices
    Text: Wirths.
    Range & Tess: e3-a4   g3-e4
    Remarks: Sustained in moderate slow tempo. Requires simplicity and
      lightness. Folk-like. 2 verses. Best for high or medium-high
      voice. Acc 3 BES
    Occasion: Epiphany.

Note: The fine Beethoven collection in two keys, high and low, German
        and English, published by Augener Ltd. and reviewed in the second
        edition of this book, is permanently out-of-print.

SUPPLY BELCHER
dnk-1836, United States

While shepherds watched their flocks by night   Medium, Low Voices
    Text: Nahum Tate, 1652-1715.
    Range & Tess: b♭2-e♭4   e♭3-c4
    Remarks: Sustained in slow tempo. Generally on MF level. Joyous, has
      short florid passages. May be transposed for high voice. Transcribed
      and edited by Gordon Myers. Acc 3 (S)GM
    Occasions: Christmas. Christmas Eve programs and services.

JAN BENDER
United States

Let the children come to me   High Voice
    Text: Mark 10:14.
    Range & Tess: e3-f#4   a3-d4
    Remarks: In: Two Solos for Baptism. Sustained in moderate lively tem-
      po. Starts strongly; generally strong throughout. Scored for voice,
      keyboard, and a solo instrument - recorder, flute, oboe or violin.
      High ending line. Acc 3 (S)CY
    Occasions: Baptism (child). Children's Day.

Whosoever does not receive the kingdom   High Voice
    Text: Mark 10:14-15.
    Range & Tess: e3-f#4(g4)   g3-d4
    Remarks: In: Two Solos for Baptism. Sustained in moderate slow tempo,
      followed by faster tempo. Has some strong passages, and a climactic
      and high ending. Scored for voice, keyboard, and a solo instrument
      as above. Acc 3 (S)CY
    Occasion: Baptism (child). Children's Day.

SIR WILLIAM STERNDALE BENNETT
1816-1875, England

Abide with me   All Voices
  Work: THE WOMAN OF SAMARIA, oratorio. Text in SHS by Mack Harrell.
  Range & Tess: high, f3-g♭4 b♭3-f4   low, d3-e♭4 g3-d4
  Remarks: Recitative in slow tempo, sustained air in moderate slow
    tempo. Has climactic passages. Majestic, vigorous ending. A solo
    arrangement from a chorale in the oratorio, texts from the hymn.
    Acc 3 SHS
  Occasion: General use.

WILLIAM BERGSMA
United States

Lullee, lullay   High Voice
  Text: Janet Lewis.
  Range & Tess: e3-g4   g3-e4
  Remarks: Sustained in moderate slow tempo. Gentle, subdued throughout
    except for the short high climax. Requires flexibility and sensiti-
    vity to pitch. Acc 3 (S)CF
  Occasions: Christmas. Christmas Eve programs and services.

CHRISTOPH BERNHARD
1627-1692, Germany

Create in me a clean heart, O God   High Voice
(Schaffe in mir, Gott, ein reines Herz)
  Text: Psalm 51:10,11 and C. Bernhard.
  Range & Tess: b2-a4   e3-e4
  Remarks: A sacred cantata for high voice, 2 violins, organ and violon-
    cello. Generally sustained in moderate tempo. Has climactic passages,
    florid figures, and quasi-recitative phrases. Subdued ending. Acc 3
    (SC)CO
  Occasions: Special use in services of personal dedication. Baptism.
    Installation of church musician. Installation of church officials
    or Pastor. Installation for missionary service.

WILLIAM BILLINGS
1746-1800, United States

When Jesus wept   Medium Voice
  Text: William Billings(?).
  Range & Tess: b2-e4   e3-b3
  Remarks: Sustained in moderate tempo. Generally on MF level. Descend-
    ing ending line. A solo transcription of the well-known canon by
    Gordon Myers. Acc 2 (S)GM
  Occasions: Lent. General use.

GORDON BINKERD
United States

Song of praise and prayer   High Voice
   Text: William Cowper, 1731-1800.
   Range & Tess: e♭3-f4   g3-e♭4
   Remarks: Subtitle: Children's hymn. Sustained in moderate tempo, has
      flowing lines. Requires simplicity. Subdued first half, strong sec-
      ond half with subdued ending. Acc 3 (S)B-H
   Occasions: Children's Day. Evening services.

What sweeter musick   All Voices
   Text: Robert Herrick.
   Range & Tess: high, c3-g♭4   f#3-e♭4   low, a2-e♭4   d3-c4
   Remarks: Sustained in slow tempo. Subdued first and last sections. Has
      some climactic high passages in the middle section. Mild dissonances
      and organistic accompaniment. Acc 3 (S)B-H
   Occasions: Christmas. Christmas Eve programs and services.

ROBERT FAIRFAX BIRCH
United States

Blessed be He who is Lord   High, Medium Voices
   Text: Anonymous Arabic.
   Range & Tess: e3-f4   a3-e4
   Remarks: Sustained in moderate tempo. Majestic; powerful after an MF
      start. Not for light, high voices. Climactic ending. Acc 3 (S)TP
   Occasions: General use. Festivals. Massed religious gatherings.

Entreat me not to leave thee   High Voice
   Text: Ruth 1:16,17.
   Range & Tess: e3-f#4   g3-e4
   Remarks: Sustained in slow tempo, with variations. Starts on MF level
      and moves into intense and dramatic sections. Climactic high end-
      ing. Acc 4 (S)TP
   Occasions: Weddings.

I will worship the Lord   All Voices
   Text: Psalm 18:1-6, 49.
   Range & Tess: high, c3(e♭3)-a♭4(b♭4)   g3-e♭4
              medium, a2(c3)-f4(g4)   e3-c4
   Remarks: Sustained in generally slow tempo. Rhythmically strong. Ef-
      fective climax. Best for high or medium voices. Acc 3 (S)TP
   Occasions: Memorial services. General use.

Love   All Voices
   Text: Song of Solomon 8:6,7.
   Range & Tess: d3-g4   g3-d4
   Remarks: Generally sustained, starts and ends in slow tempo. Slightly
      animated middle section. Has climactic high passages and dramatic
      high ending. Acc 4 (S)TP

Occasions: Weddings.

Music in heaven   High Voice
    Text: Isaak Walton.
    Range & Tess: ab3-ab4   ab3-f4
    Remarks: Sustained in slow tempo. Starts gently and builds toward a
        dramatic climax. High tessitura. Brief, only 12 measures. Acc 3-4
        (S)TP
    Occasions: General use. Dedication of music facilities. Installation
        of church musician.

Prayer to Jesus   Medium, Low Voices
    Text: Mosen Tallante, translated from Spanish by John Bowring.
    Range & Tess: c3-eb4   d3-bb3
    Remarks: Sustained in slow tempo. Solemn, deeply serious. Has some
        dramatic intensity. Includes Latin quotes "Agnus Dei" and "Memento
        mei". Acc 3 (S)TP
    Occasions: Lent. Maundy Thursday. Good Friday.

Note: See Birch's setting of "His voice, as the sound of the dulcimer
    sweet" in Traditional Songs.

GEORGES BIZET
1838-1875, France

Lamb of God (Agnus Dei)   All Voices
    Text: Agnus Dei, English by Olga Paul.
    Range & Tess: high, d3-bb4   a3-f4   med. high, c3-ab4 g3-eb4
                   medium, b2-g4 f#3-d4 low,   g2-eb3 d3-b3
    Remarks: An adaptation from the composer's L'Arlesienne Suite, No. 2.
        Very sustained in moderate slow tempo. Has effective climaxes.
        Dramatic high ending. A showy piece. Latin text and English version.
        Acc 3-4 (S)GS-4 keys, CF-3 keys. 52S-medium, not high as indicated.
    Occasions: Lent. General use.

ERNEST BLOCH
1880-1959, United States

Psalm 22 (Elohim! Why hast Thou forsaken me?)   Baritone
    Range & Tess: b1-f3   e2-d3
    Remarks: Generally sustained in various tempi. Has dramatic high cli-
        maxes. Many parts in recitative style. Animated and fast final sec-
        tion with high tessitura and dramatic ending. A reduction of the
        orchestral score. Acc 5 (S)GS
    Occasions: General use. Massed religious gatherings.

JOHANNES BRAHMS
1833-1897, Germany

Four Scriptural Songs
(Vier Ernste Gesange)
Four songs for Baritone or Bass-Baritone. Sometimes sung by Mezzo-Soprano or Contralto. The title above: GS edition. Also issued "Four Serious Songs" with original German and the English by Paul England, in
four keys published by N. Simrock.

(1) For it befalleth man (Denn es gehet dem Menschen)
Text: Ecclesiastes 3:19-22.
Range & Tess: e1-f3   d2-d3
Remarks: Sustained in slow tempo. Somber and dark. Has animated
    sections. Musically and interpretatively not easy. Acc 4
Occasion: Special use with sermon theme - Death.

(2) I turned 'round (Ich wandte mich)
Text: Ecclesiastes 4:1-3.
Range & Tess: g1-e3   d2-d3
Remarks: Very sustained, grave, slow. Has some high tessitura. High
    and subdued ending, requires fine high P. Musically and interpre-
    tatively not easy. Acc 4
Occasion: Special use with sermon theme - suffering of the wronged.

(3) O death, O death, how bitter (O Tod, wie bitter bist du)
Text: Ecclesiastes 41.
Range & Tess: b1-f#3   c#2-c#3
Remarks: Very sustained, grave, slow. Requires fine high P. Intense
    with subdued drama. Musically and interpretatively not easy. Acc 4
Occasion: Special use with sermon theme - death.

(4) Though I speak with the tongues of men
(Wenn ich mit Menschen und mit Engelszungen)
Text: I Corinthians 14:1-3, 12-13.
Range & Tess: a1(ab1)-f3(g3)   c2-c#3
Remarks: Slightly animated, vigorous, joyful. Requires flexibility.
    Has some very sustained and slow sections, as well as dramatic
    passages. Musically and interpretatively not easy. Acc 4-5
Occasions: Weddings. General use, especially Sundays after Easter.

EDWIN CARTER BREEZE
United States

God the Architect   High Voice
  Text: Harry Kemp.
  Range & Tess: f3-f4   ab3-eb4
  Remarks: Sustained in moderate slow tempo. Requires smooth, unhurried
    delivery. Rising, slightly climactic ending line. May be transposed
    for low voice. Acc 3 (S)CY
  Occasions: General use. New Year's Day or the Sunday after. Special
    use with sermon theme. Whitsunday (Pentecost).

BENJAMIN BRITTEN
1913-1976, England

Corpus Christi carol   Low Voice
   Text: Anonymous 15th century poet.
   Range & Tess: high, f3-g4 a3-f4   low/medium, c3-d4 e3-c4
   Remarks: Sustained in moderate slow tempo. Very subdued beginning and
      ending, with "Lully. lullay" refrains. Low key is original. From
      the composer's "A Boy is Born", arranged by him from his "Choral
      Variations for Mixed Voices". Acc 2-3 (S)OX
   Occasions: Christmas. Christmas Eve programs and services.

The birds   Medium, Low Voices
   Text: Hilaire Belloc.
   Range & Tess: b2-f4   d#3-e4
   Remarks: Sustained in moderate slow tempo. Folk-like, requires simpli-
      city. Very subdued final section. Uses some ostinato figures in the
      accompaniment. Fictionized sacred texts. See V. Persichetti's
      "Thou Child so wise". Acc 3 (S)B-H
   Occasions: Epiphany. General use.

The Canticles
Published by Boosey & Hawkes

Canticle I: My beloved is mine and I am His   High Voice
   Text: Francis Quarles, 1592-1644.
   Range & Tess: c#3-g4   g3-f#4
   Remarks: An extended solo in different tempi, moods, musical devices.
      Starts in moderate slow, graceful tempo. Very subdued ending. Re-
      quires considerable flexibility. Difficult. Mystic poetry. Acc 4
   Occasion: Special use with sermon theme - Dedication.

Canticle II: Abraham and Isaac   Alto & Tenor
   Text: from The Chester Miracle Play.
   Range & Tess: alto, ab2-eb4 d3-c4   tenor, c#3-ab4 a3-eb4
   Remarks:An extended song for alto, tenor and piano. Dramatic piece on
      the sacrifice of Isaac. In recitative style, varied tempi, dynamics,
      etc. Acc 3-4
   Occasion: Special use with sermon theme: Abraham and Isaac.

Canticle III: Still falls the rain   Tenor
   Text: Edith Sitwell.
   Range & Tess: c3-g4   b3-eb4
   Remarks: An extended song for tenor, horn and piano. A florid recita-
      tive in the style of Henry Purcell. Difficult, vocally demanding,
      requires flexibility and agility. Ending is quiet and subdued. Acc
      4 Horn: 3-4
   Occasions: Lent. General use.

BRITTEN

The Holy Sonnets of John Donne (1572-1631)
Published by Boosey & Hawkes

For practical use in church services only sonnets 2,5,7,8,9 are included. High Voice and Piano.

(2) Batter my heart
    Range & Tess: c#3-a4   g3-f4
    Remarks: Animated in very fast tempo. Strong, dramatic. Requires
      flexibility and crisp articulation. Has high climactic passages.
      Difficult. Agitated accompaniment. Acc 4-5
    Occasion: Special use with sermon theme - renewal.

(5) What if this present
    Range & Tess: d3-bb4   g3-eb4
    Remarks: Animated in moderate tempo. In march style with marked
      chords in left hand accompaniment. Starts strongly, generally
      strong throughout. Very subdued ending. Acc 4
    Occasion: Lent.

(7) At the round earth's imagined corners
    Range & Tess: d3-a4   a3-e4
    Remarks: Sustained in very slow tempo. Slightly declamatory; majes-
      tic, dramatic. Ends with unaccompanied passage. Acc 4-5
    Occasions: Lent. General use.

(8) Thou hast made me
    Range & Tess: d3-ab4   eb3-eb4
    Remarks: Animated in very rapid tempo. Vigorous for the most part.
      Requires precise diction. Dramatic and accented. Requires flex-
      ibility. Acc 4
    Occasions: General use. Massed religious gatherings.

(9) Death be not proud
    Range & Tess: d#3-g4   f#3-e4
    Remarks: Sustained, full-sounding vocal part in moderate lively
      tempo. Has many dramatic high passages. Requires very fine PP &
      PPP, flexibility, and crisp diction. Emphatic ending. Acc 4
    Occasions: Memorial services. Good Friday. Special use with sermon
      theme - conquering death.

"BROTHER JAMES"
Real name: James Leith Macbeth Bain, dnk, England

Brother James' air   All Voices
  Text: Psalm 23.
  Range & Tess: high, e3-f4 f3-f4   low, c#3-d4   d3-d4
  Remarks: Sustained in slow tempo. Generally gentle, serious. Acc 3
    (S)OX
  Occasions: General use. Weddings.

40

ANTON BRUCKNER
1824-1896, Germany

Jesus, Redeemer, our loving Savior   All Voices
   Text: English by Walter E. Buszin.
   Range & Tess: high, c3(a♭2)-a4 f3-e4   low, a2(f2)-g♭4 d3-d♭4
   Remarks: Sustained. Has imposing, dramatic high climaxes. wide vo-
      cal range and wide range of dynamics. Not for light voices. Or-
      ganistic accompaniment. Acc 3 (S)CP
   Occasions: General use. Lent.

GEOFFREY BURGON
England

Nunc dimittis   All Voices
   Text: Luke 2:29-32; Gloria Patri.
   Range & Tess: e3-e4   f3-c#4
   Remarks: For voice and organ, with optional B♭ trumpet. English text.
      Sustained in moderate slow tempo. Chant style, requires easy and
      slightly free delivery. Requires flexibility. Has some strong pas-
      sages. Acc 3 Trumpet: 3 (S)CH
   Occasions: Epiphany. Special use with sermon theme.

DIDERIK (DIETRICH) BUXTEHUDE
1637-1707, Denmark

Behold! I come   Bass
   Work: REJOICE, BELOVED CHRISTIANS. English text by Helen Dickinson.
   Range & Tess: a1-c#3   c#2-b2
   Remarks: Sustained in slow tempo. Generally on MF level. Has florid
      passages. From the composer's series "Twilight Music". Organ ac-
      companiment. Acc 3 (VS)HG
   Occasions: General use. Special use with sermon theme.

Beloved Christians   Soprano
   Work: REJOICE, BELOVED CHRISTIANS. Text, see first entry.
   Range & Tess: b2-g4   b3-g4
   Remarks: Sustained in moderate tempo. High tessitura. Organ accom-
      paniment. A short solo suitable as an introit. From the compos-
      er's series "Twilight Music". Acc 3 (VS)HG
   Occasion: Advent.

Rejoice, earth and heaven   Various Voices
   Work: REJOICE, EARTH AND HEAVEN. Text by Gustaf Duben, English by
      Walter E. Buszin.
   Remarks: Four very short solo excerpts. The range of each is given.
      (1) Joy is God's great gift (Soprano, e3-g4)
      (2) Grace brings peace to all believers (Contralto, a2(g2)-a3)
      (3) Peace brings joy beyond all measure (Tenor, e2-g3)
      (4) Truth divine our God hath pledged us (Bass, g1-c3)
      Acc 3 (SC)CP

41

Occasions: General use. Suitable as solo introits.

Sing to the Lord a new song   Soprano
   (Singet dem Herrn ein neues Lied)
   Text: Psalm 33:3 and various small fragments.
   Range & Tess: c3-g4   e3-e4
   Remarks: A solo cantata for soprano (or tenor), violin, basso contin-
      uo. Not for light voices. In varied tempi and moods. Has recitative
      and cantabile sections, many florid passages, ornamentations, and a
      climactic ending. German text and English version. Acc 3 (SC)CO
   Occasions: Massed religious gatherings. General use.

MARY E. CALDWELL
United States

A lute carol   Medium Voice
   Text: Robert Herrick.
   Range & Tess: db3-f4   eb3-c4
   Remarks: Sustained in moderate tempo. Has climactic passages, very
      subdued ending, some arpeggiated accompaniment. With flute or viol-
      in obbligato. Acc 3 (S)HG
   Occasions: Christmas. Christmas Eve programs and services.

THOMAS CAMPIAN (CAMPION)
1562-1620, England

From "First Booke of Ayres", Vol. I, English Lute Songs, 2nd series,
Dr. Edmund H. Fellowes, editor. London: Stainer & Bell.

Author of light   All Voices
   Text: Thomas Campian(?).
   Range & Tess: d3-eb4   f#3-d4
   Remarks: Sustained in slow tempo. Requires flexibility. 2 verses. Acc
   3
   Occasions: General use. Funerals.

Never weather-beaten sail   All Voices
   Text: Thomas Campian(?).
   Range & Tess: d3-e4(L)   f3-c4
   Remarks: Sustained in slow tempo. 2 verses. Originally for four parts.
      From "Divine and Moral Songs". Acc 2-3 SCS-1, ESB
   Occasion: General use.

Out of my soul's depth to Thee   All Voices
   Text: Thomas Campian(?).
   Range & Tess: f#3-f4   g3-eb4
   Remarks: Sustained in moderate tempo. Hymn-like, short. 4 verses. Acc
   2-3
   Occasions: General use. Evening services. Communion.

Seek the Lord   All Voices
   Text: Thomas Campian(?).
   Range & Tess: d3-d4   g3-d4
   Remarks: Sustained in slow tempo. Climactic ending. 4 verses. Acc 2-3
   Occasions: General use. Evangelistic services.

Sing a song of joy   All Voices
   Text: Thomas Campian(?).
   Range & Tess: g3-e4   a3-d4
   Remarks: Animated in moderate lively tempo. Bright and spirited. Short
     melody. 7 verses. Acc 2-3
   Occasions: General use. New Year's Day.

To music bent   All Voices
   Text: Thomas Campian(?).
   Range & Tess: f#3-c4   g3-c4
   Remarks: Sustained in moderate tempo. Generally on MF level. Narrow
     range. Climactic ending. Acc 3
   Occasions: Dedication of music facilities. Installation of church mu-
     sician. General use.

View me, Lord, a work of Thine   All Voices
   Text: Thomas Campian(?).
   Range & Tess: d3-d4   d3-bb3
   Remarks: Very sustained in moderate tempo. Hymn-like. Strong ending.
     5 verses. Acc 2-3
   Occasion: General use.

G. WINSTON CASSLER
United States

Christ was born on Christmas Day   All Voices
   Text: Traditional.
   Range & Tess: c3-e4   g3-c4
   Remarks: Animated in lively tempo. Strong beginning. Joyous and outgo-
     ing. Acc 3-4 CSV
   Occasions: Christmas. Christmas Eve programs and services.

Lord, who at Cana's wedding   All Voices
   Text: Adelaide Thrupp.
   Range & Tess: high, eb3-g4 eb3-eb4   medium, c3-e4 c3-c4
   Remarks: Sustained in moderate tempo. Has climactic passages and a
     climactic ending. Requires some flexibility. Acc 3 TWS
   Occasions: Weddings.

Whither thou goest   All Voices
   Text: Ruth 1:16,17.
   Range & Tess: medium, c3-f4 f3-d4   low, a2-d4 d3-b3
   Remarks: Sustained in various moderate tempi. Has some slightly strong

passages. Strong descending ending line.See the settings by Birch, Engel, Gore, Peeters, Schutz. Acc 3 (S)AH
Occasions: Weddings.

FREDERIC FRANCOIS CHOPIN
1810-1849, Poland

Christ be with me!   All Voices
  Text: Attributed to St. Patrick, Arr. & English text by Carl Deis.
  Range & Tess: c3-eb4   eb3-c4
  Remarks: Arranged from the composer's "Prelude No. 20", Op. 28. Solemn and sustained, meditative and introspective. Generally subdued with highlights no stronger than MF. Acc 3 52S
  Occasions: General use. Evening services.

CLAY R. CHRISTIANSEN
United States

Celestial home   High Voice
  Text: Anonymous.
  Range & Tess: d3-g4   f#3-d4
  Remarks: Sustained in moderate slow tempo. Starts and ends subdued. Has strong, high climaxes. Subdued ending section, descending final line. Organistic accompaniment. Acc 2-3 SPC
  Occasions: Funerals.

JOHN CLEMENTS
England

Blessed is the man   Medium, Low Voices
  Text: Psalm 1:1-3.
  Range & Tess: bb2-f4   d3-c4
  Remarks: Sustained in moderate tempo. Has some animated passages and some high climaxes. Subdued, low ending on f3. Acc 3 (S)LK
  Occasion: General use.

PETER CORNELIUS
1824-1874, Germany

Six Christmas Songs
Texts by Peter Cornelius. Edited by Henry Clough-Leighter. Boston: Boston Music Co. Editions with German and English versions: CP, BH. These songs may also be performed singly. For all voices.

(1) The Christmas tree (Christbaum)
     Range & Tess: high, e3-f#4 g#3-e4   low, d3-e4 f#3-d4
     Remarks: Animated in moderate lively tempo. Spirited, graceful, joyous. Generally on MF level. Acc 3
     Occasions: Christmas Eve programs and services.

(2) The shepherds (Die Hirten)
     Range & Tess: high, e3-g♭4 g3-f4   low, c#3-e♭4 e3-d4
     Remarks: Sustained in moderate slow tempo. Graceful. Has some cli-
        mactic passages. Acc 3
     Occasions: Christmas Eve programs and services.

(3) The kings (Die Könige)
     Range & Tess: high, d3-g4 g3-e4   low, b2-e4 e3-c#4
     Remarks: Sustained in slow tempo. The accompaniment is based on the
        chorale "How brightly shines the morning star" by P. Nicolai, 1599,
        see Bach chorales edited by H. S. Drinker. Acc 3
     Occasions: Epiphany. Christmas.

(4) Simeon (Simeon)
     Range & Tess: high, d3-g4 f3-e♭4   low, b2-e4 d3-c4
     Remarks: Gently animated in moderate slow tempo. A narrative, quasi-
        declamatory. Acc 3
     Occasion: Epiphany.

(5) Christ, the friend of children (Christus der Kinderfreund)
     Range & Tess: high, e3-e4 g3-d4   low, c3-c4 e♭3-b♭3
     Remarks: Gently animated vocal part in slow tempo. Rather delicate.
        Requires fluent enunciation. Acc 3
     Occasions: Christmas Eve programs and services. Children's Day.

(6) The Christ Child (Christkind)
     Range & Tess: high, e3-g4 g3-e4   low, c3-e♭4 e♭3-c4
     Remarks: Animated in moderate lively tempo. Has climactic passages
        and a descending, low ending. Acc 3
     Occasion: Christmas.

PAUL CRESTON
United States

Psalm 23 (The Lord is my shepherd)   All Voices
   Range & Tess: high, f3-a♭4 a3-f4   medium, d3-f4 f#3-d4
   Remarks: Very sustained in moderate slow tempo. Builds up to a dra-
     matic climax. Vocally not easy; not for light voices. Has dissonan-
     ces. Orchestration available. Acc 3-4 (S)GS
   Occasions: General use. Festivals. New Year's Eve. Evening services.
     Memorial services.

JOHANN CRÜGER
1598-1662, Germany

Awake, my heart, with gladness   All Voices
   Text: Anonymous, translation by Paul Gerhardt.
   Range & Tess: c#3-d4 f#3-c#4
   Remarks: Sustained in moderate tempo. Climactic ending. Trumpet obbli-
     gato ad lib. 3 verses. Acc 3 TMB

CUNDICK

Occasions: Easter. General use.

ROBERT CUNDICK
United States

Thou, whose unmeasured temple stands   High, Medium Voices
  Text: William Cullen Bryant.
  Range & Tess: e♭3-f4   g3-d♭4
  Remarks: Sustained in slow tempo. Starts and ends subdued. Strong,
    full-sounding middle section with high tessitura. Descending end-
    ing line. Has meter and key changes. Organistic accompaniment. Acc
    3 SPC
  Occasion: Dedication of church building.

JOHN DANYEL
c.1565-c.1630, England

If I could shut the gate against my thoughts   All Voices
  Text: Anonymous.
  Range & Tess: e3-e4   g3-c4
  Remarks: Sustained in very slow tempo. Has some rhythmic complexities.
    3 verses. Acc 3 EAE-5
  Occasions: Evening services. Special use in services of personal dedi-
    cation.

NEWELL DAYLEY
United States

The Lamb   Medium Voice
  Text: William Blake.
  Range & Tess: c3-e♭4(f4)   e3-c4
  Remarks: Sustained in moderate slow tempo. Generally on MF level with
    variations. Has one short climactic passage. Subdued, descending
    ending. Simple, transparent accompaniment. Acc 3 SPC
  Occasion: General use.

REGINALD DE KOVEN
1859-1920, United States

Recessional   All Voices
  Text: Rudyard Kipling.
  Range & Tess: high, c3-g♭4 g3-d4   low, a2-e♭4 e3-b3
  Remarks: Animated in moderate tempo. Majestic, marked, full-sounding.
    Descending ending line. Same text as "God of our fathers, known of
    old" in most hymnals. Acc 3 (S)TP
  Occasions: Massed religious gatherings. General use. National holi-
    days.

NORMAN DELLO JOIO
United States

A Christmas carol   High, Medium Voices
  Text: Gilbert Keith Chesterton.
  Range & Tess: c3-e4   f#3-d4
  Remarks: First line - "The Christ Child lay on Mary's lap". Sustained
    in slow tempo. Gentle and graceful, generally on MF level. Has some
    climactic, strong passages. Very subdued, low ending. Also issued
    in higher key. Acc 3 (S)EM
  Occasions: Christmas. Christmas Eve programs and services.

Bright star   High, Medium Voices
  Text: Anonymous.
  Range & Tess: f3(eb3)-g4   g3-eb4
  Remarks: Sustained in moderate slow tempo. Requires simplicity. Starts
    gently on high tessitura. Graceful with one climactic passage. Acc 3
    (S)EM
  Occasions: Christmas. Christmas Eve programs and services.

The Holy Infant's lullaby   All Voices
  Text: Anonymous.
  Range & Tess: high, f3-f4 a3-e4   medium, d3-d4 f#3-c#4
  Remarks: Sustained in moderate slow tempo. Subdued throughout, gentle.
    Uses "a la ru" refrain. Final note is hummed. Acc 3 (S)EM
  Occasions: Christmas. Christmas Eve programs and services.

JEREMIAH DENCKE
1725-1795, Selisian-American
Moravian Composer

Go ye forth in His Name   High Voice
  Text: Matthew 25:1-6; 45:11; Philippians 4:7.
  Range & Tess: f3-f4   a3-eb4
  Remarks: Sustained, stately first half; slow, sustained second. Has
    climactic passages. Acc 3 TSS
  Occasions: Installation for missionary service. General use. Fine as
    a solo benediction after "And the peace of God ... through Christ
    Jesus".

I speak of the things   High Voice
  Text: Psalm 45:1,2; 8:4.
  Range & Tess: e3-f4   f3-d4
  Remarks: Animated in moderate lively tempo. Light and bright. Semi-
    climactic ending. Acc 3 TSS
  Occasion: General use.

My soul doth magnify the Lord   High Voice
  Text: Luke 1:46,47; Dencke(?).

47

DELLO JOIO

    Range & Tess: f3-f4   b♭3-d4
    Remarks: Sustained in moderate tempo. Short, majestic. Climactic end-
      ing. Acc 3 TSS
    Occasion: General use. Advent.

O, be glad, ye daughters of His people   High Voice
    Text: Jeremiah Dencke(?).
    Range & Tess: f3-f4   a3-e4
    Remarks: Sustained in moderate slow tempo. Bright and joyful. Extended
      instrumental introduction. Acc 3 TSS
    Occasion: General use.

DAVID DIAMOND
United States

David mourns for Absalom   Tenor
    Text: II Samuel 18:33
    Range & Tess: d3-g4(a4)   f3-e♭4
    Remarks: Sustained in moderate slow tempo. Heavy and solemn, intense.
      Has dramatic climaxes. Subdued ending on c4.
    Occasion: Special use with sermon theme - King David's lament.

Let nothing disturb thee   Medium Voice
    Text: St. Theresa of Avila, English by Henry W. Longfellow.
    Range & Tess: a3-f4   f3-c4
    Remarks: Sustained in slow tempo. Subdued, tranquil, gentle. Has dis-
      sonances. Subdued ending. Acc 3   (S)AM
    Occasions: General use. Funerals. Evening services.

The shepherd boy sings in The Valley of Humiliation   High Voice
    Text: John Bunyan.
    Range & Tess: c#3-g#4(b4)   f3-e4
    Remarks: Sustained in moderate lively tempo. Graceful. Has climactic
      passages, frequent meter changes, and a subdued ending. See Vaughan
      Williams' "The woodcutter's song". Acc 3 (S)SM
    Occasion: Special use with sermon theme - contentment.

RICHARD DICKSON
United States

Praise, praise the Lord   High Voice
    Text: Richard Dickson.
    Range & Tess: e3-g4   g3-e4
    Remarks: Animated in various lively tempi. Exultant, bright, with "al-
      leluia" verse endings. Requires flexibility for fast-moving figures.
      Strong ending with alleluia section. Acc 4 SPC
    Occasions: Festivals. Massed religious gatherings. Easter and the Sun-
      day after.

STANLEY DICKSON
England

Thanks be to God   All Voices
  Text: P. J. O'Reilly.
  Range & Tess in 4 keys: (1) e♭3-a♭4 g3-e♭4 (2) d♭3-g♭4 f3-d♭4
                       (3)   c3-f4   e3-c4   (4) b♭2-e♭4 d3-b♭3
  Remarks: Sustained in moderate tempo. Majestic final section with
    dramatic high passages and climactic high ending. Full chords in
    the accompaniment. Issued also as a duet for Soprano and Baritone.
    Acc 3 (S)B-H
  Occasions: Thanksgiving. General use.

HUGO DISTLER
1908-1942, Germany

TSD Three Sacred Concertos. English version. High Voice and Keyboard.
    St. Louis: Concordia Publishing House, 1969. Written with the same
    idea as Schutz's sacred concertos.

It is a precious thing to thank our God   High Voice
  Text: Psalm 92:1-3.
  Range & Tess: b2-g4   g3-e4
  Remarks: Sustained vocal part in moderate fast tempo, with variations.
    Starts strongly. Subdued middle section and ending. Has some long-
    sustained passages. Acc 3 TSD
  Occasions: Thanksgiving. General use.

My dear brethren, meet the demands of this time   High Voice
  Text: Romans 12:11,12,18.
  Range & Tess: c3-a4   e3-e4
  Remarks: Sustained in moderate slow tempo. Very fast and florid mid-
    dle section. Requires some flexibility. Joyous and bright. Subdued
    high ending. Acc 3 TSD
  Occasions: General use. Funerals. Memorial services.

O rejoice in the Lord at all times   High Voice
  Text: Philippians 4:4; Isaiah 9:2,6,7.
  Range & Tess: c3-g4   g3-g4
  Remarks: Generally sustained vocal part in various tempi. Has climac-
    tic high passages & high tessitura, long phrases, and climactic end-
    ing. Joyous, bright. Acc 3 TSD
  Occasions: General use. New Year's Day. Massed religious gatherings.

JOHN DOWLAND
1563-1626, England

The first and fourth songs are from "Fifty Songs", Book II. The second
and third are from "Fourth Book of Airs" and "A Pilgrimes Solace",

1612, first series. Edited by Dr.Edmund H. Fellowes, published by Stainer & Bell. Also available separately. The texts are probably by Dowland himself.

If that a sinner's sighs   All Voices
   Range & Tess: high, f#3-g4 g3-f4   low, c#3-d4 d3-c4
   Remarks: Sustained in slow tempo. Rhythmically complex. A beautiful
      setting in the minor key. Theme: penitence. Acc 3
   Occasions: Evening services.

In this trembling shadow cast   High, Medium Voices
   Range & Tess: g#3-f4   a3-e4
   Remarks: Sustained in slow tempo. Rhythmically complex. A song of
      praise. Has climactic passages. 3 verses. Best for darker voices.
      Acc 3
   Occasion: General use.

Thou mighty God   All Voices
   Range & Tess: c3-d4   eb3-d4
   Remarks: Sustained in slow tempo. Rhythmically complex, requires flex-
      ibility. Has dramatic passages and varied moods. Interpretatively
      not easy. Not for light, high voices. Originally a 3-part song.Acc 3
   Occasion: General use.

Where sin sore wounding   All Voices
   Range & Tess: high, g3-g4 ab3-eb4   low, e3-e4 f3-c4
   Remarks: Sustained in slow tempo. Short, rhythmically complex. Not for
      light, high voices. Theme: supplication. Acc 3
   Occasions: Lent. Evening services.

JOHN DUKE
United States

Calvary (Text: E. A. Robinson)   Medium, Low Voices
   Range & Tess: g2-f4   e3-d4
   Remarks: Sustained in moderate tempo. Intensely dramatic. Requires an
      excellent pianist. Acc 4-5 (S)CF
   Occasions: Lent. Good Friday.

ANTONÍN DVOŘÁK
1841-1904, Czechoslovakia

Biblical Songs, Op. 99
A set of ten songs issued in two books, five songs in each. In Czech, with English versions by Astra Desmond. High, Low. Surrey, England: Alfred Lengnick & Co., 1949. Other recommended edition: N. Simrock, with Czech, English and German. Texts in the G. Schirmer edition correspond with N. Simrock.

FFS   Four Favorite Songs. A.Dvořák. High, Low. New York: R. D. Row Music Co. Texts correspond with N. Simrock.

(1)   Clouds and darkness   All Voices
       Text: Psalm 97:2-6
       Range & Tess: high, d#3-f#4 g#3-d#4   low, b2-d4 e3-b3
       Remarks: Same title in Simrock edition. Sustained in generally
          moderate slow tempo. Declamatory and dramatic. Best for heav-
          ier voices. Acc 3-4
       Occasions: General use. Special use with sermon theme - Judge-
          ment Day or The Power of God.

(2)   Thou, O Lord, art my hiding-place and shield   All Voices
       Text: Psalm 119:114,115,117,120.
       Range & Tess: high, e3-f4 a3-e4   low, b2-c4 e3-b3
       Remarks: Title in Simrock ed. - Lord, Thou art my refuge. Sus-
          tained in moderate slow tempo. Has some slightly climactic pas-
          sages. Subdued ending. Acc 3-4
       Occasions: General use. Special use in services of personal ded-
          ication. Evening services.

(3)   Hear my prayer, O God   All Voices
       Text: Psalm 55:1-8.
       Range & Tess: high, e♭3-a4 g3-e♭4   low, b♭2-e4 d3-b♭3
       Remarks: Title in Simrock ed. - Hear my prayer, O Lord. Sustained
          in generally slow tempo. Has dramatic passages. Strong descend-
          ing ending line. Acc 3-4 (S)LK
       Occasions: General use. Evening services.

(4)   The Lord is my shepherd   All Voices
       Text: Psalm 23.
       Range & Tess: high, e3-f#4 f#3-e4   low, b2-c#4 c#3-b3
       Remarks: Title in Simrock ed. - God is my shepherd. Very sustained
          in moderate slow tempo. Subdued, gentle, requires fine P & PP.
          Acc 3
       Occasions: General use. Evening services. Funerals. Memorial ser-
          vices. Baptism. New Year's Day.

(5)   I will sing a new song unto Thee   All Voices
       Text: Psalm 144:9; 145:2,3,5,6.
       Range & Tess: high, g3-g4 g3-e4   low, e♭3-e♭4 e♭3-c4
       Remarks: Title in Simrock ed. - I will sing new songs of gladness.
          Animated in moderate tempo. Majestic, bright. Has dramatic pas-
          sages and an impressive, climactic ending. An exultant song of
          praise. Acc 3-4 TMB-in E major.
       Occasions: General use. Massed religious gatherings. Weddings.
          New Year's Day. Dedication of music facilities. Installation
          of church musician.

(6)   Hear my crying, O Lord   All Voices
        Text: Psalm 61:1,3,4; 63:1,4,5.
        Range & Tess: high, e3-g4 g3-e4   low, b2-d4 d3-b3
        Remarks: Title in Simrock ed. - Hear my prayer, O Lord. Sustained
            in moderate slow tempo. Has climactic passages and a descending
            ending line. Requires fine PP & PPP. Acc 3
        Occasions: General use. Evening services.

(7)   By the waters of Babylon   All Voices
        Text: Psalm 137:1-5.
        Range & Tess: high, d3-g4 g3-e4   low, bb2-eb4 eb3-c4
        Remarks: Same title in the Simrock edition. Sustained in moderate
            slow tempo. Starts gently. Has some dramatic passages and a sub-
            dued ending. Agitated accompaniment. Acc 4
        Occasion: Special use with sermon theme.

(8)   Turn Thee to me and have mercy   All Voices
        Text: Psalm 25:16-18,20.
        Range & Tess: high, f3-f4 g3-c4   low, db3-db4 eb3-ab3
        Remarks: Same title in the Simrock edition. Sustained in moderate
            slow tempo. Subdued ending phrase. Grave and intense. Acc 3
        Occasion: General use.

(9)   I will lift mine eyes   All Voices
        Text: Psalm 121:1-4.
        Range & Tess: high, f#3-g4 a3-e4   low, d3-eb4 f3-c4
        Remarks: Same title in the Simrock edition. Sustained in moderate
            tempo. Subdued, slightly declamatory, requires fine P & PP. See
            Gober, Sowerby, and Vaughan Williams' "Watchful's Song". Acc 3
        Occasions: General use. New Year's Eve. New Year's Day.

(10) O sing unto the Lord   All Voices
        Text: Psalm 98:1,7,8; 96:12.
        Range & Tess: high, f3-g4 bb3-f4   low, c3-d4 f3-c4
        Remarks: Title in Simrock ed. - Sing ye a joyful song. Animated in
            moderate lively tempo. Joyous and bright. Has some dramatic pas-
            sages and a climactic and strong ending. Agitated accompaniment.
            Acc 4
        Occasions: General use. New Year's Day.

PAUL EARLS
United States

The Lord's Prayer   High Voice
    Text: Matthew 6:9-13.
    Range & Tess: db3-f4   g3-d4
    Remarks: Sustained in slow tempo. Mostly syllabic treatment of the
        text, in quasi-speech movement. Generally subdued. Descending end-
        ing line. In octavo format. Acc 3 (S)ES

Occasions: General use. Evening services.

JOHN EDMUNDS
United States

HJE Hesperides. Fifty songs by John Edmunds. Original keys. Texts by earlier poets. Georgetown, CA: Dragon's Teeth Press, 1975.

Behold, how good   Medium Voice
    Text: Psalm 133.
    Range & Tess: c3-f4   e3-c4
    Remarks: Sustained in moderate tempo. In broad style, has one high
        climax. f4 is passing note. Chordal accompaniment. Descending
        ending line. Acc 3 HJE
    Occasions: Installation of church officers or Pastor. Special use
        with sermon theme.

Hallelujah   High Voice
    Text: Hallelujah.
    Range & Tess: c#3-a4   g3-f4
    Remarks: Animated in fast tempo. Joyous, bright, requires flexibili-
        ty. Generally strong. Fine for light, high voices. Climactic high
        ending. Acc 3 HJE
    Occasions: Christmas. Easter. Festivals. Massed religious gather-
        ings.

O Lord, my heart is fixed   High Voice
    Text: Psalm 108:1-5.
    Range & Tess: e3-a4   a3-f#4
    Remarks: Animated in lively tempo. Joyous, exultant song of praise.
        Has high climaxes, frequent meter changes, extended piano intro-
        duction. Agitated accompaniment. Acc 3-4 HJE
    Occasions: General use. Festivals. Massed religious gatherings.

Praise ye the Lord   High Voice
    Text: Psalm 113:1-5
    Range & Tess: c3-a4   g3-e4
    Remarks: Sustained in moderate tempo. Has some high climaxes. De-
        scending ending line from highest note - 13 notes. One-line bass
        part in the accompaniment. Acc 3-4 HJE
    Occasion: General use.

The Lord is my shepherd   High Voice
    Text: Psalm 23.
    Range & Tess: c3-a4   f3-eb4
    Remarks: Sustained in moderate, easy (comodo) tempo. Generally on
        MF level. As in some other Edmunds songs, one-line bass accompani-
        ment moves unceasingly. Some awkward prosody in the voice part.
        Acc 3 HJE
    Occasion: General use.

EDMUNDS

When Israel went out of Egypt   Medium, High Voices
  Text: Psalm 114.
  Range & Tess: d3-f4   f3-c4
  Remarks: Sustained in slow tempo. Chromaticisms create interpretative
    melancholy. Generally on MF level. Subdued, "hanging" ending. Acc 3
    HJE
  Occasions: Special use with sermon theme. General use.

HERMENE WARLICK EICHHORN
United States

Prayer to the Trinity   Medium Voice
  Text: James Edmeston.
  Range & Tess: c3-e4   f#3-d4
  Remarks: Sustained in moderate slow tempo. Prayerful, there are no
    strong contrasts in dynamics. Slightly climactic high ending plus
    "amen". Organistic accompaniment. Acc 3 (S)BD
  Occasions: Trinity Sunday. New Year's Eve. General use.

EDWARD ELGAR
1857-1934, England

THE APOSTLES
Oratorio for soloists. choir and orchestra. The first part of the composer's intended trilogy of oratorios. Vocal score: Novello & Co.

Peace be unto you   Baritone, Bass
  Text: Luke 24:36c,49; Matthew 28:19,20.
  Range & Tess: c2-f3   eb2-c3
  Remarks: First part sustained in slow tempo, then moderate. Has reci-
    tative passages, a subdued section, and climactic phrases. Subdued
    ending. Acc 3
  Occasions: General use. Installation of church officers or Pastor.
    Installation for missionary service.

The voice of thy watchman   High Voice
  Text: Isaiah 52:9; Matthew 12:18-21.
  Range & Tess: eb3-g4   bb3-eb4
  Remarks: Sustained in moderate slow tempo. Starts very gently. Has
    dramatic passages. Requires fine P & PP. Gently climactic ending.
    Extended instrumental prelude and postlude. Acc 4
  Occasions: General use. Special use with sermon text. Installation of
    church officers or Pastor.

THE DREAM OF GERONTIUS
Oratorio for soloists, choir and orchestra. Texts by Cardinal Neuman.
Vocal score: Novello & Co.

Jesu, by that shuddering dread   Baritone, Bass
  Range & Tess: bb1-eb3   f2-c3

Remarks: Sustained in slow tempo. Starts strongly; has dramatic passages. Solemn, somewhat majestic. Requires some fine P. Acc 3-4
Occasions: Lent. Good Friday. General use.

My work is done, my task is o'er   Contralto, Baritone
   Range & Tess: d#3-e4   e3-c4
   Remarks: Sustained in moderate tempo. Subdued ending. Has passages
      with "alleluia" interjections. A "victorious song" for life's end.
      Acc 3-4
   Occasions: Funerals. Memorial services. Evening services.

Proficiscere, anima Christiana   Baritone, Bass
   Range & Tess: e2-e3   f#2-d3
   Remarks: Sustained in moderate, then slow tempo. Strong, dramatic
      first part in recitative style. Dramatic ending. The Latin text
      that starts the excerpt is later translated: Go forth upon thy
      journey, Christian soul! Acc 3
   Occasions: Installation for missionary service. Installation of
      church officers or Pastor. Evangelistic services. General use.

THE KINGDOM
Oratorio for soloists, choir and orchestra. The second part of the composer's intended trilogy of oratorios; the third was never finished.
Vocal score: Novello & Co.

The sun goeth down   High Voice
   Text: Psalm 63:6; Matthew 5:11; I Peter 4:14,13, etc.
   Range & Tess: eb3-bb4   ab3-f4
   Remarks: Sustained in moderate tempo. Starts gently. Requires fine
      high P & PP. Has dramatic passages and very subdued, high ending
      marked PP. Not for light voices. Acc 4
   Occasions: General use. Installation for missionary service. Evangelistic services. New Year's Day.

I have prayed for thee   Baritone, Bass
   Text: Acts 2:14b,16,17,21-23,32,33,36.
   Range & Tess: c2-f3   eb2-d3
   Remarks: Sustained in various tempi. Starts slowly, very gently on
      PPP. Has dramatic passages, recitative style, and climactic ending.
      Has several f3's. Acc 3-4
   Occasions: Sundays after Easter. Evangelistic services. Special use
      with sermon theme - The risen Lord.

THE LIGHT OF LIFE
Oratorio for soloists, choir and orchestra. Vocal score: Novello & Co.

I am the good shepherd   Baritone, Bass
   Text: John 10:14,10; 17:17,24.
   Range & Tess: c2-eb3   eb2-c3

ELGAR

Remarks: Sustained in moderate slow tempo, with variations. Starts gently; requires fine P & PP. Has climactic passages and a subdued ending. Acc 3
Occasion: General use.

Neither hath this man sinned   Baritone, Bass
Text: John 9:3-5.
Range & Tess: c#2-d3(g3)   e2-c3
Remarks: Sustained in slow tempo. Starts in quasi-recitative style. Requires fine P & PP. Has climactic passages near the end. Acc 3
Occasions: General use. Special use with sermon theme - The light of the world.

Thou only hast the words of life!   Mezzo-Soprano, Contralto
Text: E. Capel-Cure.
Range & Tess: c3(a2)-d4   e3-b3
Remarks: Sustained in moderate slow tempo. Requires fine P & PP. Has climactic passages and a low ending. Acc 3-4
Occasions: General use. Palm Sunday.

CARL ENGEL
1883-1944, United States

Christmas call   Medium Voice
Text: Carl Engel(?).
Range & Tess: d3-e4   g3-d4
Remarks: Sustained in moderate slow tempo. Bright and stately. Requires fine command of high P. A setting of a tune dated 1623. Acc 3 (S)BM
Occasions: Christmas Eve programs and services.

JAMES ENGEL
United States

Whither thou goest   High, Medium Voices
Text: Ruth 1:16,17.
Range & Tess: e3-e4   a3-c#4
Remarks: Flute obbligato. Sustained in moderate tempo. Easy, simplistic. Generally on MF level. Subdued ending passage. See Birch, Cassler, Gore, Peeters, Schutz. Acc 3 TSM
Occasions: Weddings.

NONI ESPINA
United States

Shepherd's psalm   High Voice
Text: Psalm 23.
Range & Tess: eb3-g#4   f3-f4
Remarks: Sustained in moderate slow tempo, with variations. Subdued starting and ending. Has climactic high passages, florid figures,

chromaticisms, and rhythmic complexities. Difficult. Original scoring: voice, flute, piano (organ). Also issued for voice and piano
(organ). Acc 4-5 (S)VA
Occasions: General use. New Year's Eve. New Year's Day. Evening services. Memorial services. Massed religious gatherings.

GABRIEL FAURÉ
1845-1924, France

Excerpts from Requiem Mass. Latin text, with English version by Mack
Evans. Vocal score: H. T. FitzSimons Co. Other edition: G. Schirmer.

Blessed Jesus (Pie Jesu)   Soprano (Tenor)
  Range & Tess: e3-f4   g3-eb4
  Remarks: Very sustained in very slow tempo. Gentle and delicate. Re-
    quires considerable control and fine P & PP. Deceptively easy. Acc
    3 (S)FS. (VS)FS,GS
  Occasions: Evening services. Funerals. Memorial services.

Deliver me, O Lord (Libera me)   Baritone
  Range & Tess: d2-d3   d2-d3
  Remarks: Sustained in moderate tempo. Has climactic passages. Starts
    subdued. The first part of Movement 6. Acc 3 (VS)FS,GS
  Occasion: Special use with sermon theme - The Judgement Day.

In Paradise (In paradisum)   Soprano (Tenor)
  Range & Tess: e3-f#4   d2-d3
  Remarks: Originally a unison piece for the soprano section, but use-
    ful as a solo. Very sustained, subdued, airy, floating. Requires
    fine P & PP. Requires considerable breath control. Acc 3-4 (VS)FS,
    GS
  Occasions: Good Friday. Funerals.

Unto Thee, we offer, Lord the sacrifice   Baritone
(Hostias, et preces Tibi)
  Range & Tess: d2-d3   g2-c#3
  Remarks: Sustained in slow tempo. Generally on MF level. A useful ex-
    cerpt. Acc 3 (VS)FS,GS
  Occasion: Memorial service.

JEAN-BAPTISTE FAURÉ
France

Crucifixus   High Voice
  Text: French text, with English by F. W. Rosier.
  Range & Tess: d#3-g#4(b4)   f#3-d4
  Remarks: Sustained in moderate slow tempo. Starts gently. Has strong,
    high passages. Very subdued, low ending phrase. Acc 3-4 52S (S)GS-
    high
  Occasions: General use. Funerals. Special use with sermon theme.

J. FAURE

The palms (Les rameaux)   All Voices
   Text: Jean-Baptiste Faure(?), English by Theodore T. Barker.
   Range & Tess: high, e3-g4 g3-e4 medium, d3-f4 f3-d4
                                       low, c3-e♭4 e♭3-c4
   Remarks: A festive song in moderate or moderate slow tempo. In three
      verses with climactic endings. Exultant, bright, rhythmic. In lush
      romantic style. Acc 3-4 (S)CF,GS. 52S-low
   Occasion: Palm Sunday.

                         DAVID FETLER
                        United States

O Father, all creating   All Voices
   Text: John Ellerton.
   Range & Tess: c3-f4   f3-e♭4
   Remarks: Sustained in moderate tempo. Has some climactic and strong
      passages. Subdued, low ending phrase. Acc 3 (S)CO
   Occasions: Weddings.

                         GERALD FINZI
                      1901-1956, England

                         Dies Natalis
A solo cantata in five movements for Soprano or Tenor and String Orchestra. Text by Thomas Traherne, c.1637-1674. Mystical poetry in
modern setting. Reduction for voice and piano available. London: Boosey & Hawkes. For practical use, three movements are given here. First
movement is instrumental.

(3) The rapture
   Range & Tess: d3-b♭4   b♭3-g4
   Remarks: Generally sustained vocal line over agitated accompani-
      ment. Brisk tempo, with variations. Joyous, outgoing, marked
      "Danza". Has dramatic high climaxes and long-sustained notes.
      Very strong ending section, dramatic ending. Text implies Mary's
      song. Acc 4-5
   Occasions. Christmas. Special use with sermon theme - The Magnifi-
      cat.

(4) Wonder
   Range & Tess: d3-a4   g3-e♭4
   Remarks: Generally sustained in moderate slow tempo. Starts gently.
      Has dramatic, high sections, frequent meter changes, climactic
      high ending. Mystical text implies a song of the boy Jesus.
      Acc 3-4
   Occasions: Epiphany. Special use with sermon theme.

                              58

(5) The salutation
   Range & Tess: d3-a4   g3-f4
   Remarks: Sustained in moderate slow tempo over agitated accompani-
      ment. Generally subdued, with climactic high passages in the mid-
      dle section. Requires fine command of soft high notes. Subdued
      low ending. Mystical text implies salutation to Spring. Acc 3-4
   Occasions: Sundays after Easter. Special use with sermon theme -
      Spring, nature.

IRWIN FISCHER
United States

Let the beauty of the Lord be upon us   High, Medium Voices
   Text: Psalm 90:1,16,17; 92:1,2,4,5.
   Range & Tess: e3-f#4   g3-d4
   Remarks: Generally sustained in moderate tempo. Alternating recita-
      tive and lyric sections. Strong climaxes and a descending, subdued
      ending line. Has dissonances. A song of praise. Organistic accom-
      paniment. Acc 3 ESS
   Occasion: General use.

Ye shall know the truth   High, Medium Voices
   Text: John 8:2,12,36,31,32.
   Range & Tess: c3-gb4   f3-d4
   Remarks: Sustained in varied moderate tempi. Starts in recitative
      style. Has climactic high passages and a forceful high ending. Or-
      ganistic accompaniment. Acc 3 ESS
   Occasions: General use. Evangelistic services. Massed religious gath-
      erings. Festivals. Special use with sermon theme.

GEOFFREY E. FLOWERS
United States

The Lord's my shepherd   Medium Voice
   Text: Psalm 23.
   Range & Tess: bb2-f4(g4)   g3-eb4
   Remarks: Sustained in varied tempi. Second half in march-like charac-
      ter, slightly animated. Ends strongly on high notes. Has phrases in
      gentle recitative. Acc 3 ESS
   Occasion: General use.

The Lord's Prayer   High, Medium Voices
   Text: Matthew 6:9-12.
   Range & Tess: f3-f4   a3-d4
   Remarks: Sustained in moderate tempo. Starts gently; ends very sub-
      dued on melismatic "Amens". Has one strong passage. Acc 3 ESS
   Occasions: General use. Evening services.

FLOYD

CARLISLE FLOYD
United States

Pilgrimage

Solo cantata for Low Voice and Piano (Orchestra). Score: Boosey &
Hawkes, Inc., New York. The composer states that the piano-vocal score
is a complete and true version and not merely an orchestral reduction.

(1) Man that is born of a woman
    Text: Job 14:1,2,7-12.
    Range & Tess: al-f3   d2-b2
    Remarks: Sustained in slow tempo, slightly faster middle section.
       In quasi-recitative style. Has dramatic high passages. Subdued,
       low ending on repeated notes: al.   Acc 3
    Occasion: Special use with sermon theme.

(2) Save me, O Lord, for the waters are come into my soul
    Text: Psalm 69:1-3,14-17,20.
    Range & Tess: g#1-f3   e2-e3
    Remarks: Generally sustained in moderate slow tempo. Dramatic, in
       declamatory style. Uses much of the opposite extremes of the vo-
       cal range. High tessitura and low passages. Subdued ending, with
       g#1 the final note sustained for 7 beats.   Acc 4
    Occasion: Special use with sermon theme.

(3) O Lord, Thou hast searched me and known me
    Text: Psalm 139:1-4,6-10,23-24.
    Range & Tess: b1-g♭3   c2-c3
    Remarks: Sustained in slow tempo. Has some slightly faster sec-
       tions and high tessitura. Requires some dramatic intensity. Dra-
       matic and imposing high ending - sustained f3.   Acc 4
    Occasion: General use.

(4) Praise the Lord, O my soul
    Text: Psalm 146:1,2; 148:1-3.
    Range & Tess: d2-f#3   g2-e3
    Remarks: Sustained vocal line in moderate tempo. Starts strongly.
       Heavy, with dramatic intensity and extremely high tessitura. Vo-
       cally difficult and demanding. Dramatic high ending - a whole
       passage of f#3's. Agitated accompaniment throughout.   Acc 4-5
    Occasions: General use. New Year's Day. Festivals.

(5) For I am persuaded   *Range & Tess:*
    Text: Romans 8:38,39; Numbers 6:24-26 (altered). *g1-f3(a3) c#2-d#3*
    Remarks: Sustained in slow tempo. Generally subdued and tranquil.
       In recitative style. Has several low passages with al. Subdued,
       low ending section with repeated al. Best as a benediction if
       used alone: May the Lord bless you and keep you .....   Acc 3
    Occasion: General use.

60

Note: The whole cantata was written for Baritone Mack Harrell, therefore, the pitch indications are in the bass-clef range.

CÉSAR FRANCK
1812-1890, France

O Lord most holy (Panis angelicus)   All Voices
   Work: MESSE SOLENNELLE. Latin text translated.
   Range & Tess: high, g3-f4 ab3-eb4 medium, e3-d4 f3-c4
                                       low, c3-bb3 db3-ab3
   Remarks: Sustained in moderate slow tempo. Has subdued as well as
      strong passages. After final strong, high climax, a descending line.
      Arr. by C. P. Scott. Acc 3 (S)CF
   Occasions: General use. Communion.

ISADORE FREED
1900-1960, United States

Psalm 8 (O Lord, how excellent is Thy name)   High, Medium Voices
   Range & Tess: c3-f4 f3-eb4
   Remarks: Mostly declamatory in moderate tempo. Requires fluent enun-
      ciation. Has dramatic passages and an imposing climax. Acc 3 (S)SM
   Occasion: General use.

ALFRED (ROBERT) GAUL
1837-1913,   England

THE HOLY CITY
Cantata for soloists, choir and orchestra. Vocal score: G. Schirmer.

Eye hath not seen   Contralto, Mezzo-Soprano
   Text: I Corinthians 2:9; Hebrews 11:10; 4:9.
   Range & Tess: b2-d4 d3-c4
   Remarks: Subdued in varied slow tempi. Generally solemn. Sparse cli-
      maxes; one strong passage in the middle. Subdued ending. GS vocal
      score includes the Mezzo-Soprano version which is the original, in
      Bb, d3-f4 f3-eb4. Acc 3 (VS)GS. 52S-contralto
   Occasions: General use. Special use with sermon theme: The Eternal
      City.

My soul is athirst for God   Soprano
   Text: Psalm 42:2,3; 25:17b.
   Range & Tess: e3-a4(f#4) g#3-e4
   Remarks: Sustained in moderate slow tempo. Has subdued, as well as
      strong, semi-dramatic passages. Subdued final section and ending
      phrase. Acc 3 (VS)GS. 52S
   Occasions:General use. Evening services. Lent.

These are they which came   Soprano

61

Text: Revelation 7:14,15.
Range & Tess: e3-g4(f#4)   g#3-e4
Remarks: Recitative and sustained air. Has climactic high passage.
   Subdued ending passages. Acc 3-4 (VS)GS. 52S
Occasions: General use. Special use with sermon theme - Revelation.

To the Lord our God   Tenor
   Text: Daniel 9:9; Psalm 103:13.
   Range & Tess: e3-g4   a3-g4
   Remarks: Sustained in moderate slow tempo. Has high tessitura. Re-
      quires fine high P. Strong descending ending line, with last two
      notes the lowest in the excerpt. Acc 3 (VS)GS
   Occasions: General use. Special use with sermon theme - God's mer-
      cies and forgiveness.

PATRICIA GENCHI
United States

The Lord's Prayer   High, Medium Voices
   Text: Matthew 6:9-13.
   Range & Tess: d3-f4   g3-c4
   Remarks: Sustained in slow tempo. Generally on MF level, with varia-
      tions. Free-flowing, speech-like with some short, florid figures
      suggesting eastern chant style. Requires flexibility. Acc 2-3 (S)
      Gilshafgen Music, Strongsville, OH
   Occasion: General use.

RICHARD W. GIESEKE
United States

Our Lord and King   Medium, Low Voice
   Text: Lutheran collect.
   Range & Tess: bb2-d4   eb3-bb3
   Remarks: Sustained in slow tempo. Subdued throughout. Low ending. Oc-
      tavo format. Acc 2 (S)CO
   Occasion: Lent.

CHRISTOPHER WILLIBALD (VON) GLUCK
1714-1789, Germany

O Saviour, hear me!   High Voice
   Text: Dudley Buck.
   Range & Tess: e3-f4   g3-e4
   Remarks: An adaptation from Act II Ballet in ORFEO. Sustained, gentle
      movement in moderate slow tempo. Generally on MF level. Descending
      and subdued ending. Violin, violoncello or flute obbligato. Acc 3
      52S
   Occasions: General use. Lent. Evening services.

BELLE BIARD GOBER
United States

I will lift up mine eyes   High, Medium Voices
  Text: Psalm 121.
  Range & Tess: d♭3-f4   f3-d♭4
  Remarks: Sustained in moderate tempo. Generally on MF level, with
    some high climaxes. Parlando style in some sections. Climactic high
    ending. Organistic accompaniment. See Vaughan Williams' "Watchful's
    Song" and "I will lift up mine eyes" by Dvorak and Sowerby. Acc 3
    (S)FS
  Occasions: General use. New Year's Day.

RICHARD T. GORE
United States

Entreat me not to leave thee   High Voice
  Text: Ruth 1:16,17.
  Range & Tess: high, d#3-g4 g3-d4   low, b2-e♭4 e♭3-b♭3
  Remarks: Sustained in moderate tempo. Has climactic high passages.
    Low, subdued ending. Organ accompaniment. See Birch, Cassler, Engel,
    Peeters, Schutz. Acc 3 (S)CO
  Occasions: Weddings.

O sing unto the Lord a new song   All Voices
  Text: Psalm 98; I Corinthians 15; Revelation 1 (Excerpts).
  Range & Tess: high, e3-a♭4 a3-g4   low, b2-e♭4 a3-d4
  Remarks: Sustained vocal part in very rapid tempo. Joyous, bright.Has
    quasi-recitative and climactic passages. Dramatic ending on "Amen".
    Acc 3 (S)JF
  Occasions: Easter. General use. Massed religious gatherings.

CHARLES (FRANÇOIS) GOUNOD
1818-1893, France

Ave Maria   All Voices
  Text: Latin hymn based on Luke 1:28,30,31, with English version.
  Range & Tess in 4 keys:
       high, d3-b4   g3-e4   medium, b♭2-g4   e♭3-c4
       high, c3-a4   f3-d4   low,   a2-f#4   d3-b3
  Remarks: An adaptation, uses for accompaniment the First Prelude by
    J. S. Bach. Sustained in moderate tempo. Has soaring lines. Starts
    gently and softly, then builds to a somewhat dramatic climax near
    the end. Acc 4 (S)GS-4 keys, CF-3 keys
  Occasions: Advent. General use.

MAURICE GREENE
1696-1755, England

SSG Seven Sacred Songs of the Early English School. Dr. Maurice Greene,

63

edited by E. Stanley Roper. High, Low. London: Bosworth & Co., Ltd.

Blessed are they that dwell in Thy house   All Voices
  Text: Psalm 84:4,5.
  Range & Tess: high, e3-g#4 g#3-f#4   low, d3-f#4 f#3-e4
  Remarks: Generally sustained in moderate lively tempo. Has florid pas-
    sages, climactic passages, climactic ending. Requires flexibility.
    Starts gently. Original key: D. Acc 3-4 SSG
  Occasions: Dedication of church building or facilities. New Year's
    Day. Dedication of music facilities. Installation for missionary
    service. Installation of church officers or Pastor. World Brother-
    hood Sunday. Weddings. Baptism.

I will lay me down in peace   All Voices
  Text: Psalm 4:8.
  Range & Tess: high, e3-f4 g3-f4   low, d3-eb4 f3-eb4
  Remarks: Sustained in moderate slow tempo. Generally on MF level. Re-
    quires some fine P & PP and flexibility. Melody abounds in descend-
    ing lines. Very subdued ending. Original key: Eb. Acc 3 SSG. (S)BC
  Occasions: Evening services or prayer meetings. General use.

O praise the Lord   All Voices
  Text: Psalm 103:20.
  Range & Tess: high, f#3-a4(bb4) a3-f4   low, eb3-gb4 gb3-d4
  Remarks: Animated in very rapid tempo. Requires crisp enunciation and
    flexibility. Brilliant, with climactic high passages. Climactic end-
    ing. Original key: G. Acc 3-4 SSG
  Occasions: Massed religious gatherings. Festivals. General use.

R: Thou hast charged that we
A: O that my ways were made so direct   All Voices
  Text: Psalm 119:4,5,18.
  Range & Tess: high, f3-ab4 g3-f4   low, db3-fb4 ab3-db4
  Remarks: Brief recitative and sustained air in moderate tempo. Has
    climactic passages. Requires fine P and some flexibility. Florid
    passages on triplet figures. Strong descending line at the end.
    Original key: B minor. Acc 3 SSG
  Occasions: General use. Whitsunday (Pentecost). Reformation Sunday.
    Special use in services of personal dedication. Baptism.

Praise the Lord, O my soul   All Voices
  Text: Psalm 103:1-4.
  Range & Tess: high, e3-g4 a3-f4   low, d3-f4 g3-eb4
  Remarks: Sustained in moderate slow tempo. Joyful, has climactic high
    passages. Requires fine P & PP. Strong descending ending line. Ori-
    ginal key: D. Acc 3-4 SSG
  Occasions: Evangelistic services. Festivals. General use.

Praise be the Lord   High, Medium Voices

Text: Psalm 68:19.
Range & Tess: c3-f4   eb3-d4
Remarks: Sustained in moderate tempo. Bright, exultant, generally
   strong. Falling ending. An excerpt from "O sing unto God", pub-
   lished as a unison anthem. Acc 3 (S)OX-octavo
Occasions: General use. Thanksgiving.

The Lord's name is praised   All Voices
   Text: Malachi 1:11.
   Range & Tess: high, e3-g4 g3-f4   low, c#3-e4 e3-d4
   Remarks: Sustained in moderate slow tempo. Generally on MF level. Has
      climactic passages, florid passages, climactic ending. Requires
      flexibility. Original key: E. Acc 3-4 SSG
   Occasions: Trinity Sunday. Ascension Sunday. Easter. Festivals. Na-
      tional holidays. World Brotherhood Sunday. Dedication of church
      building or facilities. General use.

The sun shall be no more thy light   All Voices
   Text: Isaiah 60:19.
   Range & Tess: high, e3-g4 a3-f4   low, d3-f4 g3-eb4
   Remarks: Sustained first part in moderate slow tempo; slightly slower
      second part. Requires flexibility and some fluent enunciation. Cli-
      mactic high ending. Original key: C minor. TMB: half step lower
      than low voice. Acc 3-4 SSG, TMB. (S)BC
   Occasions: Evangelistic services. New Year's Day. Funerals. Ascension
      Day. Installation of church officers or Pastor. Missions Sunday. Re-
      formation Sunday. World Brotherhood Sunday. Whitsunday (Pentecost).

JOHANN DANIEL GRIMM
1719-1760, Germany
Moravian Composer

HWA Two Holy Week Arias. Johann Grimm. High Voice and Piano or Organ.
   Charlotte, NC: Brodt Music Co.

For my transgressions   High Voice
   Text: Johann Grimm(?), English by Christian I. Latrobe(?).
   Range & Tess: d3-g4   g3-eb4
   Remarks: Sustained in slow tempo. Has some quasi-dramatic passages.
      In the harmonic style of late Baroque. May be transposed for lower
      voices. Acc 3 HWA
   Occasions: Lent. Maundy Thursday.

Lamb of God! Thou shalt remain forever   All Voices
   Text: Christian R. von Zinzendorf, 1727-1752.
   Range & Tess: high, eb3-g4 g3-eb4   low, c3-e4 e3-c4
   Remarks: Sustained in moderate slow tempo. Generally on MF level, with
      variations. Requires simplicity, flexibility, has some frequent
      large intervalic skips. Subdued descending ending. Edited by E. V.

65

Nolte. Acc 3 (S)BD
Occasions: Sunday after Easter. General use. Special use with sermon
   theme - Lamb of God.

O what love is here displayed   High Voice
   Text: Johann Grimm(?), English by Christian L. Latrobe(?).
   Range & Tess: e3-g4   g3-e4
   Remarks: Sustained in slow tempo. Has some intense and dramatic pas-
      sages. In the harmonic style of late Baroque.May be transposed for
      lower voices. Acc 3 HWA
   Occasions: Good Friday. Lent.

PAUL HAEUSSLER

Let not your heart be troubled   All Voices
   Text: John 14:1,2,27.
   Range & Tess: high, d3-f#4 g3-d4   low, c3-e4 f3-c4
   Remarks: Sustained in moderate slow tempo. Generally subdued with
      two climactic high passages. Has phrases with strong stresses. Sub-
      dued low ending. Acc 3 (S)B-H
   Occasions: Sunday after Easter. Ascension Sunday. Communion. Funerals.

RICHARD HAGEMAN
1882-1966, United States

Christ went up into the hills   High Voice
   Text: Katherine Adams.
   Range & Tess: d#3-ab4(gb4)   ab3-eb4
   Remarks: Sustained in generally slow tempo. Has several high, drama-
      tic passages. Very subdued and tranquil middle section, ab4 marked
      PP. Majestic, full-sounding ending. Written for John McCormack.
      Acc 4 (S)CF
   Occasions: Maundy Thursday. Lent. General use.

BERNARD HAMBLEN
England

Bless us, O Lord   All Voices
   Text: Bernard Hamblen.
   Range & Tess: high, eb3-f4(ab4) g3-eb4 low, bb2-c4(eb4) d3-bb3
   Remarks: Sustained in moderate slow tempo. Generally subdued. Has
      some climactic high passages. Strong, climactic high ending. Acc 3
      (S)B-H
   Occasions: Evening services and prayer meetings. General use. Funer-
      als.

ANDREAS HAMMERSCHMIDT
1612-1675, Germany

I am the Resurrection (Ich bin die Auferstehung)   Tenor
   Text: John 11:25,26.
   Range & Tess: d3-f4   e3-e4
   Remarks: A solo cantata for Tenor, string quartet, and continuo. Ge-
      nerally sustained in moderate tempo. Has florid figures, climactic
      passages, and a climactic ending. Not vocally demanding. Fine also
      for High Baritone. German text and English version. Acc 3 (SC)CO
Occasions: Easter. General use.

GEORGE FRIDERIC HANDEL
1685-1759, Germany-England

CHS   A Collection of Handel Songs. 7 volumes, one each for Light Sop-
      rano, Dramatic Soprano, Mezzo-Soprano, Contralto, Tenor, Baritone
      and Bass. Edited by Walter Ford and Rupert Erlebach. Original
      keys. London: Boosey & Hawkes. (CSH-1 means the volume for Light
      Soprano, etc.)
45A   45 Arias from Operas and Oratorios. G. F. Handel. 3 volumes, High
      and Low. Edited by Sergius Kagen. New York: International Music
      Co.
CF-C MESSIAH. G. F. Handel. Vocal score edited by Jacob Maurice Cooper-
      smith. New York: Carl Fischer, Inc. The Appendix consists of ver-
      sions of arias used in Handel's time. A fine, scholarly, authori-
      tative edition. Highly recommended.
NO-S MESSIAH. G. F. Handel. Vocal score edited by Watkins Shaw. Lon-
      don: Novello & Co. Ltd. Has notes, versions of arias and recita-
      tives, ornamentation, etc. with as little editing as possible. A
      fine, scholarly, and authoritative edition. Highly recommended.
      NO means the edition by Ebenezer Prout.
Note: Other editions of MESSIAH are published by G. Schirmer, C. F. Pe-
ters, and others.

Excerpts From Choral Works
Arranged alphabetically by title of the work. Remarks regarding text
sources appear only with the first excerpt.

Soprano

Choir of angels, all around thee   Dramatic, Lyric Soprano
   Work: DEBORAH, oratorio 1733, text by Samuel Humphreys.
   Range & Tess: f3-g4   a3-f4
   Remarks: Part of Deborah. Sustained in moderate lively tempo. Has two
      fast-moving, florid passages, and some climactic passages. Des-
      cending ending line. Acc 3 CHS-2
Occasion: General use.

HANDEL

In Jehovah's awful sight   Dramatic Soprano
  Work: DEBORAH.
  Range & Tess: f3-g4   g3-f4
  Remarks: Part of Deborah. Very sustained in slow tempo. Generally on
     MF level. Descending ending line. Chordal accompaniment throughout.
     Acc 3 CHS-2
  Occasion: General use.

O magnify the Lord   Dramatic, Lyric Soprano
  Work: EIGHTH CHANDOS ANTHEM, O come, let us sing. Aria text: Psalm
     99:9.
  Range & Tess: e3-g#4   g#3-e4
  Remarks: Animated in moderate tempo. Bright, joyous. Has florid pas-
     sages, dotted figures, climactic passages, and a descending end-
     ing line. Acc 3 CHS-2. (VS)NO
  Occasions: General use. Massed religious gatherings. Advent. New Year.

R: O King of Kings
A: Alleluia   Dramatic, Lyric Soprano
  Work: ESTHER, oratorio 1732, 2nd version. Texts by Alexander Pope,
     John Arbuthnot, after Racine. Other texts by Samuel Humphreys.
  Range & Tess: e3-a4   g3-g4
  Remarks: Part of Esther. Short and majestic recitative, and an animat-
     ed, florid alleluia in very rapid tempo. Joyous, bright, requires
     considerable flexibility. Climactic ending. Acc 3-4 CHS-2, 45A-3
     (High)
  Occasions: Easter. Christmas Day. Massed religious gatherings. Gen-
     eral use.

Praise the Lord, His power proclaim   Soprano
  Work: ESTHER.
  Range & Tess: e3-g4   a3-f4
  Remarks: Animated in lively tempo. Requires flexibility, has florid
     passages and some wide intervalic skips. Bright, joyful, ecstatic.
     Climactic ending. Acc 4 (S)PP
  Occasions: Festivals. Easter. Massed religious gatherings.

So shall the lute and harp awake   Soprano
  Work: JUDAS MACCABAEUS, oratorio 1747. Text by Thomas Morell, after
     the Bible.
  Range & Tess: d3-g4   g3-f4
  Remarks: Spirited aria in lively tempo. Light, florid, requires flex-
     ibility. Acc 3-4 (VS)GS,NO. 45A-2(High)
  Occasions: Dedication of music facilities. Installation of church mu-
     sician. Massed religious gatherings. Festivals. New Year's Day. Ge-
     neral use.

R: Thy rebuke....Behold and see....He was cut off
A: But Thou didst not leave His soul   Soprano

Work: MESSIAH, oratorio 1742. Text of excerpt: Psalm 69:20; Lamenta-
   tions 1:12; Isaiah 53:8; Psalm 16:10.
Range & Tess: d#3-g4   e3-e4
Remarks: Three short recitatives and a gently animated air. Air is
   graceful, incisive, vibrant. Agitated accompaniment. Acc 3-4
   (VS)CF-C, NO-S, NO, GS, CP
Occasions: Maundy Thursday. Good Friday.

But who may abide   Soprano
   Work: MESSIAH. Text of excerpt: Malachi 3:2.
   Range & Tess: c3-a4   g3-g4
   Remarks: Version C. The first part is very sustained, subdued, in slow
      tempo. Second part is very rapid, animated, florid, spirited. In the
      Appendix: CF-C, NO-S version II. Acc 5
   Occasions: Advent. Christmas.

Come unto Him   Soprano
   Work: MESSIAH. Text of excerpt: Matthew 11:28.
   Range & Tess: f3-g4   g3-f4
   Remarks: Version B, Part II. Sustained in slow tempo. Moves gently.
      Generally subdued. Acc 3 (VS)CF-C, NO-S, GS, NO, CP. ASS-S
   Occasions: General use. Evening services.

R: Comfort ye my people
A: Every valley   Soprano
   Work: MESSIAH. Text of excerpt: Isaiah 50:1-4.
   Range & Tess: e3-g#4   e3-e4
   Remarks: Sustained recitative and very florid aria in moderate slow
      tempo. Requires considerable flexibility. Has long lines and a cli-
      mactic ending. Acc 4 (VS)CF-C, NO-S, GS, NO, CP
   Occasions: Advent. Christmas.

R: Then shall the eyes
A: He shall feed His flock   Soprano
   Work: MESSIAH. Text of excerpt: Isaiah 35:5-6; 50:11.
   Range & Tess: f3-g4   g3-f4
   Remarks: Version A. Recitative and a sustained, gently-moving aria;
      incorporates all material in the more popular Contralto-Soprano
      version. Gentle, subdued. Acc 3 (VS)CF-C, NO-S
   Occasions: Epiphany. General use.

He was despised   Soprano
   Work: MESSIAH. Text of excerpt: Isaiah 53:3; 50:6.
   Range & Tess: f3-g4   g3-e4
   Remarks: Version B. Sustained, very slow first part; animated, rhyth-
      mic, dramatic second part. Acc 3 (VS)CF-C
   Occasions: Lent. Good Friday.

HANDEL

How beautiful are the feet   Soprano
    Work: MESSIAH. Text of excerpt: Romans 10:15.
    Range & Tess: Version A -   d3-a4   g3-g4
                     Version B -   f3-g4   g3-eb4
    Remarks: Sustained in moderate slow tempo. Often sung too slowly.
        Flowing lines, gentle movement. Generally on MF level. 2nd part of
        Version A uses different material and text: Their sound is gone
        out. Acc 3 (VS)CF-C, NO-S. Version B only: GS, NO, CP. ASS-S
    Occasions: General use. Missions Sunday. Installation for missionary
        service. Installation of church officers or Pastor.

I know that my Redeemer liveth   Soprano
    Work: MESSIAH. Text of excerpt: Job 19:25,26; I Corinthians 25:20.
    Range & Tess: e3-g#4   e3-e4
    Remarks: Sustained in moderate tempo. Has some long, sustained and
        florid passages. Textwise, one of the most dynamic solos in MES-
        SIAH. Acc 3 (VS)CF-C, NO-S, GS, NO, CP
    Occasions: Easter. Memorial services. Funerals. General use.

If God be for us   Soprano
    Work: MESSIAH. Text of excerpt: Romans 8:31,33,34.
    Range & Tess: eb3-ab4   g3-g4
    Remarks: Sustained in moderate slow tempo. Has some long, sustained
        and florid passages. Textwise, one of the most dynamic solos in
        MESSIAH. Acc 3 (VS)CF-C, NO-S, GS, NO, CP
    Occasions: Ascension Sunday. Missions Sunday. Massed religious gath-
        erings. General use.

Rejoice greatly   Soprano
    Work: MESSIAH. Text of excerpt: Zechariah 9:9-10.
    Range & Tess: Version A -   d3-ab4   g3-f4
                     Version B -   eb3-ab4   g3-f4
    Remarks: Animated in lively tempo. Bright, joyous, very florid. Re-
        quires considerable flexibility. Middle section is often sung too
        slowly and sentimentally. Version A: in 12/8 time, with triplet
        figures in the florid passages. Accompaniment is less involved.
        Version A accomp. 3-4; Version B accomp. 4-5. (VS)CF-C, NO-S.
        Version B only: (VS)GS, NO, CP. ASS-S
    Occasions: Advent. Christmas. Massed religious gatherings. Evangelis-
        tic services. General use.

Their sound is gone out   Soprano
    Work: MESSIAH. Text of excerpt: Romans 10:18.
    Range & Tess: f3-g4   f3-f4
    Remarks: Version C. Animated in moderate tempo. Short. Acc 3 (VS)CF-
        C
    Occasions: General use. Missions Sunday.

Thou art gone up on high   Soprano
   Work: MESSIAH. Text of excerpt: Psalm 68:18.
   Range & Tess: d3-a4   g3-f4
   Remarks: Version D. Sustained in moderate slow tempo. Long lines with
      slowly-moving melismas. One of the finest arias in MESSIAH. Appen-
      dix, Coopersmith and Shaw editions. Acc 3-4 (VS)CF-C,NO-S
   Occasions: Easter or the Sunday after. Ascension Sunday. Special use
      with sermon theme.

He through His chains will win   Soprano
   Work: SAINT JOHN PASSION, 1704, written when Handel was 19 years old.
      Text of the arias by Christian Heinrich Postel. English text in MG
      edition by R. Snell.
   Range & Tess   d3-ab4   f3-f4
   Remarks: Sustained, slow sections alternate with the animated and flor-
      id.Requires flexibility. Has some extended florid passages. Acc 3
      (VS)MG, EK.
Occasion: Lent.

Of the pains that He has borne   Soprano
   Work: SAINT JOHN PASSION. Text, see first entry.
   Range & Tess: c3-g4   g3-f4
   Remarks: Sustained in moderate tempo. Generally on MF level. Requires
      flexibility. The first aria in the work. Acc 3 (VS)MG, EK
   Occasions: Lent. Maundy Thursday.

Wherefore, Jesus, didst Thou thirst   Soprano
   Work: SAINT JOHN PASSION. Text, see first entry.
   Range & Tess: f3-g4   g3-f4
   Remarks: Sustained in slow tempo. Has a florid passage. Generally on
      MF level. Acc 3   (VS)MG, EK
   Occasions: Good Friday. Lent.

Let the bright seraphim   Soprano
   Work: SAMSON, oratorio 1743. Text by Newburgh Hamilton, adapted from
      John Milton's "Samson Agonistes" and other works.
   Range & Tess: d3-a4   a3-f#4
   Remarks: Animated in moderate tempo. Vigorous, quite florid, exultant,
      bright. Requires considerable flexibility. Has some recitative-like
      passages. Acc 3-4 (VS)GS. 45A-1(High)
   Occasions: Dedication of music facilities. Installation of church mu-
      sician. Festivals. General use.

Ah! the pains that now afflict Him   Dramatic Soprano
   Work: THE PASSION, 1716. Text by Barthold Heinrich Brockes, English
      by J. Troutbeck.
   Range & Tess: d3-f#4   f#3-e4
   Remarks: Part of Daughter of Zion. Sustained in slow tempo. Generally
      subdued. Has one florid passage. Acc 3 CHS-2

HANDEL

Occasions: Maundy Thursday. Good Friday. Lent.

Break, my heart   Lyric, Dramatic Soprano
   Work: THE PASSION.
   Range & Tess: eb3-g4   f3-f4
   Remarks: Part of Daughter of Zion. Very sustained in slow tempo. Ge-
     nerally subdued. Acc 3 (VS)NO, EK, OX
   Occasions: Maundy Thursday. Good Friday. Lent.

Mine offences   Soprano
   Work: THE PASSION.
   Range & Tess: d3-g4   g3-eb4
   Remarks: Sustained in slow tempo. Has florid passages. Generally sub-
     dued, somber. Acc 3 CHS-1. (VS) EK, OX
   Occasions: Maundy Thursday. Good Friday. Lent.

Our God, the heavenly circle filling   Soprano
   Work: THE PASSION.
   Range & Tess: f3-g4   g3-f4
   Remarks: Sustained in moderate tempo. The text is identical to No. 8
     which may be used as second verse. Acc 3 CHS-1. (VS)EK, OX
   Occasions: Communion. Lent.

Ye to whom God's grace extendeth   Soprano
(Die ihr Gottes Gnad' versäumet)
   Work: THE PASSION.
   Range & Tess: f3-g4   g3-f4
   Remarks: Part of Daughter of Zion. Very sustained in moderate slow
     tempo. Intense. Accompaniment mainly of full chords. Better known
     by its Italian text: Chi sprezzando. Acc 3 45A-1. (VS)EK, OX
   Occasions: Lent. Special use with sermon theme.

Mezzo-Soprano and Contralto

O God, who from the suckling's mouth   Mezzo-Soprano, Contralto
   Work: FOUNDLING HOSPITAL ANTHEM. Text adapted by G. F. Handel.
   Range & Tess: bb2-eb4   d3-d4
   Remarks: Sustained in moderate slow tempo. Requires flexibility. No.
     16 in the series" Blessed Are They". Acc 3 (VS)HI
   Occasions: General use. Children's Day.

Thou shalt bring them in   Mezzo-Soprano, Contralto
   Work: ISRAEL IN EGYPT, oratorio 1739. Text adapted from Exodus.
   Range & Tess: b2-c#4(e4)   e3-b3
   Remarks: Sustained in slow tempo. Requires some flexibility. Has some
     florid passages. Acc 3-4 (VS)GS. ASS-A
   Occasions: Installation for missionary services. Special use with
     sermon theme.

But who may abide   Mezzo-Soprano, Contralto
  Work: MESSIAH, oratorio 1742. Text of excerpt: Malachi 3:2.
  Range & Tess: g2-e4   c3-d4
  Remarks: Alternating slow-sustained and very rapid-animated sections.
    Florid, requires considerable flexibility and fluent enunciation.
    Climactic ending. This 3rd version was composed in 1750 for the
    male alto, Gaetano Guadagni. Handel had it sung also by a woman al-
    to, and also transposed it for soprano. Acc 5 (VS)NO-S
  Occasion: Advent.

R: Then shall the eyes of the blind
A: He shall feed His flock   Mezzo-Soprano, Contralto
  Work: MESSIAH. Text of excerpt: Isaiah 35:5,6; 40:11; Matthew 11:28,
    29.
  Range & Tess: c3-d4   d3-c4
  Remarks: Recitative and sustained air in slow tempo. Gentle, general-
    ly on MF level. Part II "Come unto Him" is sung by soprano. Version
    B, Part I. Acc 3 (VS)CF-C, NO-S, GS, NO, CP
  Occasions: Epiphany. General use.

He was despised   Mezzo-Soprano, Contralto
  Work: MESSIAH. Text of excerpt: Isaiah 53:3; 50:6.
  Range & Tess: bb2-c4   d3-bb3
  Remarks: Version A. Sustained in slow tempo. Faster and more agitated
    middle section, with dramatic energy, and incisive rhythm. Intense.
    Acc 3-4 (VS)CF-C, NO-S, GS, NO, CP. ASS-A
  Occasions: Lent. Good Friday.

How beautiful are the feet   Mezzo-Soprano, Contralto
  Work: MESSIAH. Text of the excerpt: Romans 10:15.
  Range & Tess: bb2-d4   c3-c4
  Remarks: Version C. Sustained in moderate slow tempo. Flowing, must
    not be sung too slowly. Gentle and graceful. Version II, Shaw edi-
    tion. Acc 3-4 (VS)CF-C, NO-S
  Occasions: General use. Missions Sunday. Installation for missionary
    service. Installation of church officers or Pastor.

If God be for us   Mezzo-Soprano, Contralto
  Work: MESSIAH. Text of this excerpt: Romans 8:31-34.
  Range & Tess: ab2-db4   c3-c4
  Remarks: Version II, for contralto. Sustained in moderate slow tempo.
    Has extended and florid passages. Textwise, one of the most dynamic
    solos in MESSIAH. Acc 3-4 (VS)NO-S
  Occasions: Ascension Sunday. Missions Sunday. Massed religious gather-
    ings. General use.

R: Behold, a Virgin shall conceive
A: O thou that tellest   Mezzo-Soprano, Contralto
  Work: MESSIAH. Text of this excerpt: Isaiah 7:14; 60:9,1.

73

Range & Tess: a2-b3   d3-a3
Remarks: Short recitative and sustained air. Has florid passages and
    graceful movement. If used as a solo, omit choral section. Acc 3-4
    (VS)CF-C, NO-S, GS, NO, CP. ASS-A
Occasion: Advent.

Thou art gone up on high   Mezzo-Soprano, Contralto
    Work: MESSIAH. Text of excerpt: Psalm 48:18.
    Range & Tess: Version B,   c3-f4   e3-e4
                       Version C,   a2-e4   d3-c4
Remarks: Sustained in moderate slow tempo. Long lines and slowly mov-
    ing melismas. One of the finest arias in MESSIAH. See Appendix of
    Coopersmith edition. Acc 3-4   (VS)CF-C, NO-S
Occasions: Sunday after Easter. Ascension Sunday. Special use with
    sermon theme.

Courage, my soul   Mezzo-Soprano, Contralto
    Work: SAINT JOHN PASSION, 1704. Texts of the arias by Christian Hein-
    rich Postel. English text in MG by R. Snell.
    Range & Tess: a2-d4   f3-c4
Remarks: Sustained in slow tempo. Generally on MF level. Has florid
    passages. Ends with a ritornello. Acc 3 (VS)MG, EK
Occasions: Lent. Good Friday. Funerals. General use.

O Lord, whose mercies numberless   Mezzo-Soprano, Contralto
    Work: SAUL, oratorio 1739. Text by Charles Jennens.
    Range & Tess: bb2-d4   f3-c4
Remarks: Very sustained in slow tempo. Has some short florid figures.
    The rest signs must be performed as written. Acc 3   (VS)GS. ASS-A
Occasions: Evening services. General use.

Lord, to Thee, each night and day   Mezzo-Soprano, Contralto
    Work: THEODORA, oratorio 1750. Text by Thomas Morell.
    Range & Tess: c#3-e4   f#3-d4
Remarks: Sustained, slow, solemn section followed by one that is ani-
    mated. Has florid passages. Acc 3-4 ASS-A
Occasions: General use. Massed religious gatherings.

Tenor

To God, who made the radiant sun   Tenor
    Work: ALEXANDER BALUS, oratorio 1748. Text by Thomas Morell.
    Range & Tess: e3-f4   f3-f4
Remarks: Part of Jonathan. Sustained in slow tempo. Generally on MF
    level. Bright, exultant. Descending ending line. Acc 3 CHS-5
Occasion: General use.

Blessed are they that consider the poor   Tenor
    Work: FOUNDLING HOSPITAL ANTHEM. Text of excerpt: Psalm 41:1,2.
    Range & Tess: d3-g4   g3-f4

Remarks: Sustained in moderate tempo. Has florid passages. Requires
flexibility. Climactic ending. Generally on MF level. In Anthem No.
16, "Blessed Are They". Acc 3-4 (VS)HI. CHS-5
Occasions: Missions Sunday. Installation for missionary service. Special use with sermon theme: The Beatitudes. General use.

For ever blessed   Tenor
Work: JEPHTHA, oratorio 1752. Text by Thomas Morell.
Range & Tess: g3-g4   bb3-eb4
Remarks: Part of Jephtha. Sustained in slow tempo. Short, generally
on MF level. Slightly climactic ending. Fine as solo introit or res-
ponse to Benediction. Acc 3 CHS-5
Occasion: General use.

R: Sweet flow the strains
A: No unhallowed praise   Tenor
Work: JUDAS MACCABAEUS, oratorio 1747. Text by Thomas Morell.
Range & Tess: f3-g4   g3-f4
Remarks: Subdued secco recitative and an animated, spirited aria in
lively tempo. Has florid passages and climactic passages. Acc 3-4
(VS)GS, NO
Occasions: Memorial services. General use.

R: Thy rebuke ... Behold, and see ... He was cut off
A: But Thou didst not leave His soul   Tenor
Work: MESSIAH, oratorio 1742. Text of excerpt: Psalm 69:20; Lamenta-
tions 1:12; Isaiah 53:8; Psalm 16:10.
Range & Tess: d#3-g#4   e3-e4
Remarks: Three short recitatives and a gently animated air. Air is
graceful, but incisive and vibrant. Agitated accompaniment. Acc 3-
4 (VS)CF-C, NO-S, GS, NO, CP
Occasions: Maundy Thursday. Good Friday.

R: Comfort ye my people
A: Every valley   Tenor
Work: MESSIAH. Text of excerpt: Isaiah 40:1-4
Range & Tess: d#3-g#4   e3-e4
Remarks: Sustained recitative and a very florid air. Requires consider-
able flexibility and agility. Sustained, long lines. Climactic end-
ing. Acc 4 (VS)CF-C, NO-S, GS, NO, CP. ASS-T
Occasion: Advent.

Rejoice greatly   Tenor
Work: MESSIAH. Text of excerpt: Zechariah 9:9-10.
Range & Tess: Version A, d3-ab4   g3-f4
                   Version B, eb3-ab4   g3-g4
Remarks: Animated in lively tempo. Bright, joyous, very florid. Re-
quires considerable flexibility. Version A is in 12/8 time, with
triplet figures in the florid passages. Acc - Version A 3-4; Ver-

sion B 4-5. (VS)CF-C, NO-S. Version B only: (VS)GS, NO, CP
   Occasions: Advent. General use. Christmas. Massed religious gather-
      ings.

Their sound is gone out   Tenor
   Work: MESSIAH. Text of excerpt: Romans 10:18.
   Range & Tess: f3-g4   f3-f4
   Remarks: Version C. Animated in moderate tempo. Short. Version II,
      Shaw edition. Acc 3 (VS)CF-C, NO-S
   Occasions: General use. Missions Sunday.

R: He that dwelleth in heaven
A: Thou shalt break them   Tenor
   Work: MESSIAH. Text of excerpt: Psalm 2:4,9.
   Range & Tess: e3-a4   g3-g4
   Remarks: Version A. Recitative and a sustained air in moderate slow
      tempo. Has florid passages. Quasi-dramatic. Traditionally the aria
      is ended on a4. Acc 4 (VS)CF-C, NO-S, GS, NO, CP. ASS-T
   Occasion: Special use with sermon theme.

He has His mansion fixed on high   Tenor
   Work: OCCASIONAL ORATORIO, 1746. Text by Thomas Morell.
   Range & Tess: e3-g4   f#3-f#4
   Remarks: Sustained in slow tempo. Generally on MF level. Has two flor-
      id passages and slightly climactic passages. Slightly climactic end-
      ing. Acc 3 CHS-5. (VS)EK
   Occasion: General use.

 Jehovah! to my words give ear   Tenor
   Work: OCCASIONAL ORATORIO. Text, see first entry.
   Range & Tess: d#3-f#4   f#3-e4
   Remarks: Sustained in moderate slow tempo. Has some recitative-like
      passages, and slightly climactic passages. Acc 3 ASS-T. (VS)EK
   Occasions: Evening services.

O Lord, how many are my foes!   Tenor
   Work: OCCASIONAL ORATORIO. Text, see first entry.
   Range & Tess: d3-g4   g3-e4
   Remarks: Sustained in slow tempo. Generally on MF level. Syllabic
      treatment of the text. Acc 3 CHS-5. (VS)EK
   Occasions: General use. Evening services. Special use with sermon
      theme.

God is a constant sure defense   Tenor
   Work: SECOND CHANDOS ANTHEM, In The Lord Put I My Trust. Text of ex-
      cerpt: Psalm 9:9,10, paraphrase.
   Range & Tess: d3-a4   g3-f4
   Remarks: Sustained in moderate slow tempo. Has two florid passages and
      some high tessitura. Generally on MF level, with some climactic pas-
      sages. Acc 3 CHS-5. (VS)EK

Occasion: General use.

R: But how? must I then perish in despair?
A: Bow'd with grief   Tenor
   Work: THE PASSION, 1716. Text by Barthold Heinrich Brockes. English
      by J. Troutbeck.
   Range & Tess: d3-g4   g3-f#4
   Remarks: Part of Peter. Short secco recitative and a sustained air
      in slow tempo. Has dramatic passages; intense. Descending ending
      line. Acc 3-4 CHS-5. (VS)EK, OX
   Occasions: Good Friday. Lent.

Though bound and helpless   Tenor
   Work: THE PASSION. Text, see first entry.
   Range & Tess: e3-g4   a3-f4
   Remarks: Sustained in moderate tempo. Generally on MF level. Acc 3
      CHS-5 (VS)EK, OX
   Occasions: Good Friday. Lent.

Baritone and Bass

Vouchsafe, O Lord   Baritone, Bass
   Work: DETTINGEN TE DEUM, 1743. Liturgical texts translated.
   Range & Tess: d2-d#3   e2-c#3
   Remarks: Very sustained in slow tempo. Majestic, serious, intense.
      Requires full-bodied tone. Issued in several transposed editions.
      Acc 3 45A-2(Low), POS-4. (VS)NO, EK. (S)MW
   Occasions: General use.

When Thou tookest upon Thee to deliver man   Baritone, Bass
   Work: DETTINGEN TE DEUM. Text, see first entry.
   Range & Tess: d#2-e3   e2-d3
   Remarks: Sustained in slow tempo. Has florid and climactic passages.
      Requires flexibility. Slightly climactic ending. Acc 3 (VS)NO,EK
   Occasion: General use.

R: I feel the Deity within
A: Arm, arm ye brave!   Baritone, Bass
   Work: JUDAS MACCABAEUS, oratorio 1747. Text by Thomas Morell.
   Range & Tess: b1-e3   c2-d3
   Remarks: Majestic recitative and a spirited, vigorous aria. Requires
      some flexibility. Has some short, florid figures and strong rhythm.
      Available in many editions. Acc 3-4   45A-2(Low), ASS-B, 52S. (VS)
      GS, NO
   Occasions: Special use with sermon theme. Missions Sunday. Massed re-
      ligious gatherings. Festivals.

R: Thus saith the Lord
A: But who may abide   Baritone, Bass
   Work: MESSIAH, oratorio 1742. Text of excerpt: Haggai 2:6,7; Malachi

3:1,2.
Range & Tess: Version A: al-f3   c2-d3
                  Version B: gl(al)-e3   c2-d3
Remarks: Sustained in slow, then fast tempi. Majestic, florid recita-
    tive in moderate tempo. The aria: alternating subdued and slow sec-
    tion with very rapid, animated, very florid, spirited section. Ver-
    sion A is the better known. The Shaw edition gives the version for
    Contralto. Acc 5 (VS)CF-C, NO-S. Version B only: (VS)GS, NO, CP.
    ASS-B
Occasion: Advent.

R: For behold, darkness
A: The people that walked in darkness   Baritone, Bass
    Work: MESSIAH. Text of excerpt: Isaiah 60:2,3; 9:2.
    Range & Tess: f#1(al)-e3   c#2-c#3
    Remarks: Sustained in moderate slow tempo. Has some long and slow-
        moving melismas. The recitative starts very subdued. Often sung too
        slowly. Acc 3-4 (VS)CF-C, NO-S, GS, NO, CP. ASS-B
    Occasion: Advent.

R: Behold, I tell you a mystery
A: The trumpet shall sound   Baritone, Bass
    Work: MESSIAH. Text of excerpt: I Corinthians 15:51-53.
    Range & Tess: al-e3   dl-d3
    Remarks: Subdued recitative and majestic, broad and energetic aria
        with long-sustained notes and florid passages. The second section
        is unfortunately omitted in most performances. Acc 4 (VS)CF-C, NO-
        S, GS, NO, CP. ASS-B
    Occasions: Special use with sermon theme - The Judgement Day. Gener-
        al Use.

Thou art gone up on high   Baritone, Bass
    Work: MESSIAH. Text of excerpt: Psalm 48:18.
    Range & Tess: bb1-e3   d2-d3 (Version A)
    Remarks: Sustained in moderate slow tempo. Long lines with slow-mov-
        ing melismas. See also Version B (range: c3-e4) and Version C
        (range: a2-e4) for Contralto, and Version D (range: d3-a4) for Sop-
        rano in the Appendix of the Coopersmith edition. Acc 3-4 (VS)CF-C,
        NO-S, GS, NO, CP.
    Occasions: Ascension Sunday. Sunday after Easter. Special use with
        sermon theme.

Why do the nations so furiously rage together?   Baritone, Bass
    Work: MESSIAH. Text of excerpt: Psalm 2:1,2.
    Range & Tess: bl-e3   d2-d3
    Remarks: Versions A and B. Animated in rapid tempo. Strong, dramatic,
        very florid. Requires considerable flexibility. Agitated accompani-
        ment. Originally not a Da Capo aria. Version A is best known. Sec-
        tion 2 of Version B is brief and not florid. Acc 5 (VS)CF-C, NO-

S. Version A only: (VS)GS, NO, CP. ASS-B
Occasion: Special use with sermon theme - Conflict among nations.

To God, our strength   Baritone, Bass
  Work: OCCASIONAL ORATORIO, 1746. Text by Thomas Morell.
  Range & Tess: al-e3   d2-d3
  Remarks: Sustained in moderate slow tempo. Slightly faster middle
    section. Generally strong and exultant. Has florid passages, re-
    quires considerable flexibility. Descending ending line. Acc 3-4
    (VS)EK
  Occasions: General use. Massed religious gatherings. New Year's Day.

Now bursting all asunder   Bass-Baritone, Bass
  Work: SAINT JOHN PASSION, 1704. Text of the arias by Christian Hein-
    rich Postel. English texts in MG by R. Snell.
  Range & Tess: fl-f3   b♮l-c3
  Remarks: Animated in fast tempo. Vigorous, very florid, requires con-
    siderable flexibility. Generally strong, energetic, climactic. Dif-
    ficult. Acc 3-4 (VS)MG, EK
  Occasion: Good Friday.

O work of love   Baritone, Bass
  Work: SAINT JOHN PASSION. Text, see first entry.
  Range & Tess: b♮l-f3   d2-e♭3
  Remarks: Sustained in slow tempo. Grave and florid. Has some wide in-
    tervalic skips. Requires flexibility. Ends with quote: It is finish-
    ed. Title in CHS: O work sublime. Acc 3 (VS)MG, EK. CHS-6
  Occasion: Good Friday.

That God is great   Baritone, Bass
  Work: SIXTH CHANDOS ANTHEM, O Praise the Lord. Text of excerpt:
    Psalm 135:5. Handel-Gesellschaft gives this as No. 9.
  Range & Tess: al-f3   d2-d3
  Remarks: Spirited in moderate lively tempo. Vigorous and outpouring.
    Florid, requires considerable flexibility. Climactic. Acc 4 CHS-6
  Occasions: General use. Festivals. National holidays. Massed religious
    gatherings. Evangelistic services. New Year's Day or the Sunday af-
    ter.

Ye to whom God's grace extendeth   All Voices
(Die ihr Gottes Gnad' versäumet)
  Work: THE PASSION, 1716. Text by Barthold Heinrich Brockes.
  Range & Tess: high, f3-g4   g3-f4   low, d2-e3   e2-d3
  Remarks: Best known by its Italian title: Chi sprezzando. Originally
    a Soprano air in the oratorio. Very sustained in moderate slow tem-
    po. Slightly intense. Accompaniment is mainly of full chords. Acc 3
    45A-1. (VS)OX, EK
  Occasions: Lent. Special use with sermon theme.

HANDEL

O praise the Lord   Bass
   Work: TWELFTH CHANDOS ANTHEM, c.1724, O Praise the Lord Ye Angels of
      His. Included as one of the Chandos Anthems by Arnold. Text of ex-
      cerpt: Psalm 103:21.
   Range & Tess: b1-e3   e2-d3
   Remarks: Sustained in moderate tempo. Exultant, has climactic pas-
      sages, one short florid passage, and a low ending. Acc 3 CHS-7
   Occasions: General use. Massed religious gatherings. New Year's Day.

Attributed to Handel

Lord, blessed are we (Dank sei Dir, Herr)   All Voices
   Text: English adaptation by Francis Bernard.
   Range & Tess: high, e3-g4   g3-e4   low, c#3-e4   e3-c#4
   Remarks: Of questionable authenticity. Very sustained in moderate
      slow tempo. Stately, with chordal accompaniment throughout. The
      text is based on the Israelites' journey through the Red Sea. Also
      listed as: Thanks be to Thee. Title in SHS and GAS: Praise be to
      Thee (range: high, e3-g4; medium, c3-eb4). Acc 3 45A-3, SHS
   Occasion: General use. Special use with sermon theme.

HANS LEO HASSLER
1564-1612, Germany

O sacred head now wounded   All Voices
   Text: Latin, 12th century, translation composite of Paul Gerhardt's
      German.
   Range & Tess: f3-eb4   g3-c4
   Remarks: Sustained in moderate tempo. On MF level throughout. Setting
      by George F. Handel, used in the cantata "Ach, Herr, mich armen
      Sunder". See J. S. Bach's harmonization in hymnals. Octavo format.
      Acc 3 (S)CO
   Occasions: Lent. Good Friday.

VERENA HATCH
United States

My soul doth magnify the Lord   High Voice
   Text: Luke 1:46-55.
   Range & Tess: e3-g4   e3-e4
   Remarks: Generally sustained in moderate tempo. Quasi-recitative.
      Starts and ends gently, subdued. Has short middle climactic pas-
      sage. Uses repetitive figures in the accompaniment. Acc 3 SPC
   Occasions: Advent. General use.

RUTH L. HAUSMAN
United States

Suffer the little children   All Voices

Text: Mark 10:13-16.
Range & Tess: c3-f4   f3-d4
Remarks: Starts in recitative style. Sustained in moderate slow tempo; faster, animated middle section. Generally on MF level with two climactic high passages. Subdued, descending ending line. May be transposed. Acc 2-3   52S
Occasions: Children's Day. Special use with sermon theme - faith.

FRANZ JOSEPH HAYDN
1732-1809, Austria

In the beginning   High, Medium Voices
   Work: THE CREATION, 1798. Text of excerpt: Genesis 1:1.
   Range & Tess: high, c3-g4   f3-d4   medium, a2-e4   d3-b3
   Remarks: An arrangement by Mack Harrell. Generally in recitative style. Has some climactic passages and a climactic ending. Incorporates the recitative and the soprano part in the short choral section in the original score. Acc 3   SHS
   Occasions: General use. New Year's Day.

R: And God said, Let the earth
A: With verdure clad   Soprano
   Work: THE CREATION. Texts by Lidley, after Genesis and Milton's "Paradise Lost".
   Range & Tess: e3-bb4   g3-g4
   Remarks: Sustained aria in moderate tempo. Requires flexibility and a fine command of high notes. Has florid passages. Acc 3-4 (VS) GS, CP. ASS-S
   Occasions: General use. Massed religious gatherings. Festivals. New Year's Day.

MICHAEL HEAD
England

The Lord's Prayer   Medium, Low Voices
   Text: Matthew 6:9-13.
   Range & Tess: bb2-eb4   eb3-c4
   Remarks: Sustained in moderate slow tempo. Generally subdued, except climax toward the end. Subdued, descending ending line. Acc 3 (S) B-H
   Occasions: General use. Evening services.

The robin's carol   High Voice
   Text: Patience Strong.
   Range & Tess: c3-ab4   eb3-db4
   Remarks: Animated in moderate lively tempo. Joyous, requires flexibility and precise diction. Verses end with "Alleluyas's". Best for light voices. Acc 3-4 (S)B-H
   Occasions: Christmas Day and the Sunday after.

81

Thus spake Jesus   High, Medium Voices
  Text: John 17:1,5,11,21,23.
  Range & Tess: high, d#3(b2)-g#4   f#3-d#4
                medium, b2(g2)-e4   d3-b3
  Remarks: Sustained in slow tempo. Starts and ends in recitative
    style. Generally on MF level. Climactic and broad ending. Acc 3
    (S)B-H
  Occasions: Lent. Maundy Thursday. General use.

WILBUR HELD
United States

Lord, who at Cana's wedding feast   High, Medium Voices
  Text: Adelaide Thrupp, 19th century.
  Range & Tess: eb3-f4   g3-eb4
  Remarks: Sustained in moderate tempo. Simple vocal lines, generally
    on MF level. Climactic high ending. Organistic accompaniment. Acc
    2-3 TSM
  Occasions: Weddings.

BARTHOLOMAEUS HELDER
16th-17th century, Germany

The Lord my shepherd is   High, Medium Voices
  Text: Psalm 23.
  Range & Tess: e3-f4   a3-e4
  Remarks: Sustained in moderate tempo. Generally on MF level, 3 verses.
    Acc 3 WBB
  Occasions: General use. New Year's Eve. Memorial services.

(ISADORE) GEORGE HENSCHEL
1850-1934, Germany

Morning hymn   All Voices
  Text: Robert Reinick.
  Range & Tess: high, d#3-g#4 g#3-e4   low, a2-d4 d3-bb3
  Remarks: Sustained in slow tempo. Starts gently. Entire song is one
    long crescendo from beginning to end where it becomes dramatic. Ag-
    itated accompaniment. Acc 4 SVR-2
  Occasion: General use.

JOHANNES HERBST
1735-1812, German American
Moravian Composer

TSH Three Sacred Songs of Johannes Herbst. Edited by Karl Kroeger.
    High Voice and organ or piano. An adaptation of the string parts.
    New York: Boosey & Hawkes.

Abide in me (Bleibet in mir)   High Voice
   Text: John 15:4.
   Range & Tess: e3-f4   g3-d4
   Remarks: Sustained in moderate tempo. Gentle, has suggested dynamics
     and a strong ending line. In late Baroque style. Acc 3 TSH
   Occasions: Installation of church officers or Pastor. Evening services.
     Special use in services of personal dedication.

And thou shalt know it (Du solst erfahren)   High Voice
   Text: Isaiah 60:16.
   Range & Tess: d3-g4   a3-f4
   Remarks: Sustained in moderate slow tempo. Has strong high passages,
     some descending scales, and dotted figures requiring flexibility.
     Climactic high ending. Generally dense accompaniment. Acc 4 TSH
   Occasions: Sunday after Easter. General use. Festivals. Massed reli-
     gious gatherings. Trinity Sunday.

I will go in the strength of the Lord   High Voice
(Ich gehe einher in der Kraft des Herrn)
   Text: Psalm 71:16a.
   Range & Tess: c3-g4   a3-d4
   Remarks: Sustained in moderate slow tempo. Majestic, positive-sounding
     with semi-climactic high ending. Extended introduction. Acc 3 TSS.
     (S)B-H
   Occasions: General use. Installation for missionary service. Installa-
     tion of church officers or Pastor. Baptism. Special use in services
     of personal dedication. Missions Sunday.

See Him, He is the Lamb of God   High Voice
(Siehe das ist Gottes Lamm)
   Text: John 1:29.
   Range & Tess: d3-f4   a3-d4
   Remarks: Very sustained in slow tempo. Has suggested dynamics, subdued
     ending section, and subdued, descending ending line. In late Baroque
     style. Acc 3   TSH
   Occasions: Lent. Maundy Thursday. Good Friday. Communion.

IRVIN HINCHLIFFE
United States

Creation   High, Medium Voices
   Text: Edgar Newgass.
   Range & Tess: d3-f4   g3-d4
   Remarks: Sustained vocal part in moderate lively tempo.Calm, tranquil
     middle section. Strong entrance; has climactic passages. Strong de-
     scending ending line. Acc 3-4 (S)CF
   Occasions: Thanksgiving service. General use. New Year's Day or the
     Sunday after. New Year's Eve.

83

ALUN HODDINOTT
England

Medieval carol   All Voices
   Text: Jacqueline Froom.
   Range & Tess: d3-e4   a3-e♭4
   Remarks: Sustained in moderate tempo. Generally gentle; in quasi-
   recitative style. Subdued high ending. First line: The flower is
   fresh and fair of hue. Acc 3-4 (S)OX
   Occasions: Christmas. Christmas Eve programs and services.

GUSTAV HOLST
1874-1934, England

Four Songs for Voice and Violin
Op. 35. Texts from "A Medieval Anthology". London: J. & W. Chester.

(1) Jesu sweet, now will I sing   All Voices
   Range & Tess: d3-e4   e3-c4
   Remarks: Sustained in moderate slow tempo. Gentle, subdued, in
      free, speech-like rhythm.   Violin 3
   Occasions: Christmas Eve programs and services.

(2) My soul has nought but fire and ice   All Voices
   Range & Tess: c3-d4   d3-b3
   Remarks: Sustained in moderate tempo. In gentle recitative style.
      Short, only 8 measures. Violin 2
   Occasions: Special use with sermon theme. Fine as a solo introit.

(3) I sing of a maiden   High Voice
   Range & Tess: e3-g4   a3-e4
   Remarks: Sustained in moderate lively tempo. Generally gentle. Has
      one climactic passage. The first 12 measures are unaccompanied.
      Violin 2
   Occasions: Christmas Eve programs and services. Christmas. New
      Year's Day. Epiphany.

(4) My Leman is so true   High, Medium Voices
   Range & Tess: d3-e4   e3-d4
   Remarks: Sustained in moderate lively tempo. Generally gentle and
      subdued. Requires fine P & PP. Medieval terminology. Violin 3
   Occasions: General use. Good Friday.

Single Song

The heart worships   All Voices
   Text: Alice M. Buckton's "Through Human Eyes".
   Range & Tess: medium, c3-e4   e3-b3   low, b♭2-d4   d3-a3
   Remarks: Sustained in slow tempo. Slightly declamatory. Generally sub-
      dued, has quiet dignity. Acc 3 (S)CF, SB

Occasion: General use.

ALAN HOVHANESS
United States

Three Odes of Solomon

Opus 5. Texts are translations from ancient Syriac. New York: C. F.
Peters.

(1) No way is hard   Medium, Low Voices
    Range & Tess: c3-d4   e3-c4
    Remarks: Sustained in quite slow tempo. Chantlike with slow,
        slightly florid passages. Ends with a short, beautiful "alleluia"
        section which may be used separately as a solo or unison choral
        response. Acc 2-3
    Occasions: General use. Special use with sermon theme.

(2) As the wings of doves   Medium, Low Voices
    Range & Tess: c3-eb4   eb3-d4
    Remarks: Sustained in moderate slow tempo. Chantlike. Gentle first
        section. Strong, dramatic, martial, and accented last section.
        Acc 2-3
    Occasion: General use.

(3) As the work of the husbandman   Medium, Low Voices
    Range & Tess: d3-d4   e3-c4
    Remarks: Sustained in moderate slow tempo. Majestic and strong
        throughout. Dramatic ending. Acc 2-3
    Occasion: General use.

Single Songs

Out of the depths   High Voice
    Text: Psalm 130:1-6.   Range & Tess: e3-a4   f3-f4
    Remarks: Sustained in moderate slow tempo. Simple vocal line with
        chant-like, plaintive quality. Has dissonances. Dramatic ending
        with full-sounding chords in the accompaniment. Acc 3-4 (S)CP
    Occasions: General use. New Year's Eve.

Watchman, tell us of the night   Soprano
    Text: John Bowring.
    Range & Tess: f3-g4   g3-g4
    Remarks: Sustained alternating lively and moderate tempi. Slightly
        florid middle section. Extended instrumental introduction. General-
        ly gentle. Acc 3 (S)CP
    Occasions: Advent. Christmas. New Year's Eve.

HERBERT HOWELLS
England

Come sing and dance   High Voice
  Text: Old carol.
  Range & Tess: d3-ab4   g3-eb4
  Remarks: Joyous, dancelike, requires flexibility and lightness of
    tone. In moderate lively tempo; has some climactic passages. Text
    interpolated with "alleluia" and "eia". Acc 4 (S)OX
  Occasions: Christmas Eve programs and services. Christmas Day or the
    Sunday after.

PELHAM HUMFREY (HUMPHREY)
1647-1674, England

A hymn to God the Father   All Voices
  Text: John Donne.
  Range & Tess: high, c#3-f4 f3-eb4   low, b2-eb4 eb3-db4
  Remarks: Sustained in slow tempo. Declamatory throughout; has some
    quasi-dramatic passages. Impressive setting of a serious and power-
    ful poem. Acc 3 (S)SC
  Occasions: General use. Evening services. Lent.

DON HUMPHREYS
United States

How excellent is Thy loving kindness   All Voices
  Text: Psalm 36:7-10.
  Range & Tess: high, d3-d4 f3-d4   low, c3-eb4 eb3-c4
  Remarks: Sustained in moderate tempo. Animated middle section. Has
    some strong passages, but generally on MF level. Diminishing tone
    on final phrase. Acc 3 (S)WM
  Occasions: Thanksgiving. General use.

I sought the Lord   All Voices
  Text: Psalm 34:1-5,8.
  Range & Tess: high, e3-g4 g3-e4   low, d3-f4 f3-d4
  Remarks: Animated in moderate lively tempo. Slow middle section. Has
    some strong passages, including the ending line. Starts joyfully.
    Acc 3-4 (S)WM
  Occasions: General use. New Year.

Let this mind be in you   High Voice
  Text: Philippians 2:5,1,2.
  Range & Tess: d3-g4(f4)   f3-d4
  Remarks: Sustained in moderate tempo; faster and stronger middle sec-
    tion. Climactic high ending phrase with high tessitura. Acc 3
    (S)WM
  Occasions: General use. World Brotherhood Sunday. Special use with
    sermon theme - like-mindedness in love.

JEREMIAH INGALLS
1764-1828, United States

God we see all around   All Voices
  Text: Anonymous.
  Range & Tess: c3-e4   e3-c4
  Remarks: Sustained in moderate slow tempo. Has climactic passages.
    Bright and joyous. A song of praise and thanksgiving. Acc 3 SEA
  Occasions: Thanksgiving. Massed religious gatherings. General use.

To grace a marriage feast   All Voices
  Text: Anonymous.
  Range & Tess: d#3-e4   e3-d4
  Remarks: Sustained in moderate tempo. Has some climactic passages.
    Generally on MF level. Descending ending line. A prayer. Acc 3
    SEA
  Occasions: Weddings.

JOHN IRELAND
1879-1962, England

The Advent   High Voice
  Text: Alice Maynell.
  Range & Tess: d3-g4   g3-e4
  Remarks: Sustained in slow tempo. Has some declamatory passages. The
    first song in "Songs Sacred And Profane". Acc 3 (SC)SC
  Occasion: Advent.

The Holy Boy   All Voices
  Text: Herbert S. Brown.
  Range & Tess: high, d3-g4(a4) f3-e4   low, c3-f4(g4) eb3-d4
  Remarks: Sustained in slow tempo. Generally subdued, modal, in folk
    style. Acc 2-3 (S)B-H
  Occasions: Christmas. Christmas Eve programs and services.

CHARLES E. IVES
1874-1954, United States

Collections published by Peer International Corp., New York
  10S   Ten Songs   13S   Thirteen Songs   SSI   Sacred Songs
  12S   Twelve Songs   14S   Fourteen Songs   for Voice and
                                                       Piano
114S   114 Songs. Published by Associated Publishers, Theodore
    Presser Co., & Peer International Corp., selling agent.

A Christmas carol   All Voices
  Text: Traditional.
  Range & Tess: d3-c4   f3-a3
  Remarks: Sustained in slow tempo. Subdued with P & PP passages.
    Graceful and gentle. 2 verses. Acc 2 114S

IVES

Occasions: Christmas. Christmas Eve programs and services.

Abide with me   High Voice
   Text: Henry F. Lyte.
   Range & Tess: d3-g4   d3-d4
   Remarks: Sustained in slow tempo. Requires fine command of high PP.
     Same text as the well-known hymn. Acc 3 13S, SSI
   Occasions: Evening services.

Forward into light   High Voice
   Work: THE CELESTIAL COUNTRY, cantata. Text by Alford from Bernard.
   Range & Tess: c3-a4   d3-d4
   Remarks: Sustained in moderate lively tempo. Stately. Requires con-
     siderable dramatic intensity. Has very strong and imposing ending
     section. Acc 4 10S, 114S, SSI
   Occasions: Massed religious gatherings. General use.

His exaltation   Low Voice
   Text: Robert Robinson.
   Range & Tess: a2(g2)-e4   c#3-c#4
   Remarks: Very sustained in slow tempo. Majestic. Extended introduction.
     Starts strongly. Subdued, low ending phrase with a2 sustained for
     9 beats. Adapted from the composer's Second Violin Sonata. Useful
     as a choral unison song. Acc 4-5 114S, SSI
   Occasion: General use.

Hymn   All Voices
   Text: Oliver Wendell Holmes.
   Range & Tess: c#3-e4   g3-d4
   Remarks: Very sustained in slow tempo. Short, chromatic, subdued. Re-
     quires fine P & PP. Generally gentle. Acc 3 114S
   Occasions: General use. Evening services.

Naught that country needeth   Baritone
   Work: THE CELESTIAL COUNTRY. See first entry.
   Range & Tess: al-f3   d2-d3
   Remarks: Sustained in moderate tempo. Requires considerable dramatic
     intensity, some flexibility, and a good command of high PP. Very
     subdued ending. Acc 4 14S, 114S, SSI
   Occasion: General use.

Religion   Medium Voice
   Text: James T. Bixby.
   Range & Tess: db3-ab4   g3-d4
   Remarks: Sustained in moderate slow tempo. Starts strongly. Descend-
     ing ending line after high climax. Partially uses the melody of
     George F. Root. Short, one page. Acc 3 114S, SSI
   Occasion: General use.

The camp meeting   Low Voice
   Text: Charlotte Elliott.
   Range & Tess: ab2-e4   c3-b3
   Remarks: Sustained in slow tempo. Generally on MF level. Has one cli-
      mactic passage. Very subdued ending. Final section uses the melody
      "Just as I am", well-known hymn tune by William B. Bradbury. The
      music is adapted from the composer's "Symphony No. 3". Acc 4 114S,
      SSI
   Occasions: Evening services or prayer meetings. Special use in ser-
      vices of personal dedication. Baptism.

The collection   High, Medium Voices
   Text: from "stanzas of old hymns".
   Range & Tess: e3-f#4   e3-c#4
   Remarks: Sustained in moderate tempo. Generally on MF level. Useful
      also as a solo or unison introit. Acc 3 13S, 114S, SSI
   Occasion: General use.

The waiting soul   Medium, Low Voices
   Text: William Cowper.
   Range & Tess: b2-e4   c#3-c#4
   Remarks: Sustained in moderate slow tempo. Has declamatory passages.
      Requires fine P & PP, some dramatic intensity, flexibility, and
      fluent enunciation. Very subdued low ending. Acc 4 12S, 114S, SSI
   Occasions: Advent. General use.

Watchman!   All Voices
   Text: Lowell Mason and John Bowring.
   Range & Tess: d3-f#4   d3-c#4
   Remarks: Sustained in moderate tempo. Generally on MF level, with
      some accented notes. A setting of texts to a well-known hymn. Acc
      4 14S, 114S, SSI
   Occasions: General use. New Year's Eve. Special use with sermon theme.

               BORGHILD JACOBSON & JOANNA LANGE
                        United States

Now as a rose before the sun unfolds   All Voices
   Text: Borghild Jacobson.
   Range & Tess: d3-eb4   e3-b3
   Remarks: Sustained in moderate tempo. Requires simplicity and an easy
      manner. On MF level, 3 verses. Acc 2 SHC
   Occasion: Communion.

The truest body heaven knows   All Voices
   Text: Borghild Jacobson.
   Range & Tess: c3-d4   d3-bb3
   Remarks: Sustained in slow tempo. Subdued, serious, chantlike, 3 vers-
      es. Acc 2 SHC
   Occasion: Communion.

GEORGE JEFFRIES
dnk-1685, England

Praise the Lord, O my soul   Bass
  Text: Psalm 104: 1,2,24,33,34.
  Range & Tess: e1(d1)-d3   a1-b♭2
  Remarks: Sustained in moderate tempo. Generally on MF level. Has cli-
    mactic high passages, some low tessitura, some wide intervalic
    skips. Closes with melismatic "Alleluia" section ending on f1. Acc
    3 SSM
  Occasions: General use. Festivals.

FREDERICK KOCH

Be not afraid   High Voice
  Text: II Chronicles 20:15b,17; II Timothy 1:7; Isaiah 41:10,13.
  Range & Tess: e♭3-a♭4   g3-d4
  Remarks: Sustained in moderate tempo. Generally on MF & P levels, has
    2 climactic high passages, and a strong high ending. Has mild dis-
    sonances. Requires fine diction. Acc 3 (S)B-H
  Occasions: Evening services. Installation for missionary service.
    Special use with sermon theme: Conquering fear.

A. WALTER KRAMER
United States

Before the paling of the stars   All Voices
  Text: Christina Rossetti.
  Range & Tess: high, a♭3-f4 a♭3-e♭4   low, f3-d4 f3-c4
  Remarks: Sustained in moderate slow tempo. Requires simplicity. Sub-
    dued, with strong ending. Sub-title: A Christmas carol. Acc 3
    (S)JF
  Occasions: Christmas. Christmas Eve programs and services.

GERHARD KRAPF

Morning meditation and hymn of praise   Medium, Low Voices
  Text: Solomon Ben Judah Ibn Gabirol, 11th century.
  Range & Tess: b2-e4   e3-d4
  Remarks: Generally sustained in moderate slow tempo. Has phrases in
    chant style, varied dynamics, a strong ending on "Amen". Translated
    from "Shaharabhaqqesh-kha" by F. P. Bargebuhr. Organ accompaniment.
    Acc 3 (S)CY
  Occasions: General use. Special use with sermon theme.

JOHN LA MONTAINE
United States

Songs of the Nativity
A cycle for Medium Voice and Organ, optional small and large bells (or

tambourine). May be performed singly. New York: H. W. Gray.

(1) Behold, a Virgin shall be with Child   Medium Voice
    Text: Matthew 1:23; Luke 2:14.
    Range & Tess: b♭2-e♭4(f4)   f3-d4
    Remarks: Generally sustained in moderate tempo. Vigorous, rhythmic,
       brisk middle section. Has some florid passages, climactic pas-
       sages, and those requiring fine P & PP. Acc 3
    Occasions: Christmas. Christmas Eve programs and services.

(2) That hallowed season   Medium Voice
    Text: William Shakespeare, from "Hamlet".
    Range & Tess: b2-c#4   c#3-a4
    Remarks: Sustained in slow tempo. Marked "with great sense of mys-
       tery". Subdued throughout; transparent accompaniment. Acc 3-4
    Occasions: Christmas. General use.

(3) Nativity morn   Medium Voice
    Text: John Milton.
    Range & Tess: a#2-e4   e3-c#4
    Remarks: Animated in moderate lively tempo. Starts and ends strong-
       ly, joyfully. Requires fluent enunciation. Low ending. Acc 3-4
    Occasion: Christmas.

(4) Now begin on Christmas Day   Medium Voice
    Text: Gerard Manley Hopkins.
    Range & Tess: a2-d4   e3-c#4
    Remarks: Sustained in slow tempo. Has contrasting strong and gentle
       passages. Climactic high ending. Acc 3
    Occasions: Christmas. Christmas Eve programs and services.

(5) The birds   Medium Voice
    Text: Traditional Czechoslovakian.
    Range & Tess: a2-e4(f#4)   f#3-c#4
    Remarks: Animated in moderate tempo. Requires fluent enunciation
       and flexibility. Narrative, generally on MF level. Subdued end-
       ing after climax. Acc 3
    Occasions: Christmas Eve programs and services.

(6) Rocking   Medium Voice
    Text: Traditional Czechoslovakian.
    Range & Tess: b♭2-e♭4   e♭3-c♭4
    Remarks: First line - Little Jesus, sweetly sleep. Sustained in mod-
       erate tempo. Graceful and buoyant cradle song. Subdued. Gently ag-
       itated accompaniment. Acc 4
    Occasions: Christmas Eve programs and services.

EZRA LADERMAN
United States

From the Psalms

A set of five songs for High Voice and Piano. Texts arranged from the
Psalms.New York: Oxford University Press, 1970. For practical purposes
only numbers 3 and 5 are given here.

(3) From the end of the earth   High Voice
    Text: Psalm 61:2; 69:3.
    Range & Tess: b2-g♭4   e3-e4
    Remarks: Sustained in quite slow tempo. Generally subdued, requires
      fine P & PP. Has one short passage marked FF. Subdued high ending.
     Acc 3-4
    Occasion: Special use with sermon theme.

(5) Thou didst set the earth   High Voice
    Text: Psalm 104:5; 57:6.
    Range & Tess: d♭3-a4   f3-f4
    Remarks: Sustained in moderate tempo. A dramatic song, not for
      light voices. Ending section has many sustained and strong g4's
      and a4's. Vocally demanding. Acc 4
    Occasions: General use. Festivals. Massed religious gatherings.
     New Year's Day.

RICHARD LANE
United States

Rejoice in the Lord   High, Medium Voices
  Text: Philippians 4:4,8.
  Range & Tess: e3-f4(g4)   g3-d4
  Remarks: Sustained in moderate tempo. Majestic, starts and ends
    strongly. High ending. Dissonant. Acc 3 ESS
  Occasions: General use. Festivals. Massed religious gatherings.
    New Year's Day. Installation of church officers or Pastor. Instal-
    lation for missionary service. Missions Sunday. Special use in ser-
    vices of personal dedication.

HENRY LAWES
1596-1662, England

Hymns to the Holy Trinity

A set of three songs which may be performed as a unit or separately.
Texts by John Crofts, c.1613-1670. High Voice and keyboard continuo.
New York: Oxford University Press. Occasions: Trinity Sunday, etc.

(1) To God the Father
    Range & Tess: d3-f4   f3-d4
    Remarks: Sustained in moderate tempo. Has some high tessitura and
      frequent hemiolas. Strong text. Acc 3

(2) To God the Son
   Range & Tess: c#3-f4   f3-d4
   Remarks: Sustained in moderate tempo. Has some quasi-dramatic pas-
      sages. Descending line.

(3) To God the Holy Ghost
   Range & Tess   d3-g4   a3-eb4
   Remarks: Sustained in moderate tempo. Generally on MF level, no
      climactic passages. Requires fine legato throughout. Subdued de-
      scending ending line. Acc 3

LUDWIG LENEL
United States

Lullaby   All Voices
   Text: Isaac Watts.
   Range & Tess: d3-e4   f#3-d4
   Remarks: Sustained in moderate slow tempo. Gentle, somewhat subdued.
      Slightly climactic ending. Best for light voices. First line: Hush,
      my dear, lie still and slumber. Acc 3 SCV
   Occasions: Christmas Eve programs and services. Christmas.

CHARMA DAVIES LEPKE
United States

Great and marvelous are Thy works   High Voice
   Text: Revelation 15:1,3,4.
   Range & Tess: c3-g4(a4)   g3-e4
   Remarks: Animated and joyous in lively tempo. Has strong sections
      with high climaxes. Strong declamatory beginning. Ends with drama-
      tic high notes. Full-sounding accompaniment. Not for light voices.
      Acc 4 ESS
   Occasions: General use. Festivals. Massed religious gatherings.

HENRY GEORGE LEY
1887-1962, England

We praise Thee, O God   All Voices
   Text: Te Deum laudamus, Latin hymn translated.
   Range & Tess: bb2-d4   d3-c4
   Remarks: Quasi-declamatory in moderate lively tempo. Extended, with
      strong passages. Moves in speech fashion. Acc 3 TMB
   Occasion: General use.

SAMUEL LIDDLE
England

How lovely are Thy dwellings   All Voices
   Text: Psalm 84:1-4,8,10.

LIDDLE

Range & Tess in 4 keys:
    (1) eb3-ab4 g3-f4   (3) c3-f4 e3-d4
    (2) db3-gb4 f3-eb4   (4) bb2-eb4 d3-c4
Remarks: Sustained in moderate slow tempo. Has climactic high pas-
 sages, a recitative-style middle section, some broad, sweeping
 lines, and a dramatic high ending. Acc 3-4 (S)B-H
Occasions: General use. Dedication of church building. New Year's
 Day. Massed religious gatherings. Festivals.

The Lord is my shepherd   All Voices
 Text: Psalm 23.
 Range & Tess in 4 keys:
    (1) e3-f4 f3-f4   (3) c#3-d4 d3-d4
    (2) d3-eb4 eb3-eb4   (4) b2-c4 c3-c4

Remarks: Sustained in moderate tempo. Starts strongly. Has some subdued sections and strong, full-sounding passages. Subdued descending ending. Acc 3 (S)B-H
Occasions: General use. Evening services. Funerals. Memorial services. Baptism. New Year's Day.

LUDVIG MATHIAS LINDEMAN
1812-1887, Germany

Built on the rock   Medium, Low Voices
 Text: N. F. S. Gruntvig.
 Range & Tess: c3-eb4 c3-c4
 Remarks: Animated in lively tempo. Energetic, has slightly slower &
  broader sections. Descending ending line. Octavo format. Acc 3
  (S)OX
 Occasions: General use. Dedication of church building or facilities.

AUSTIN C. LOVELACE
United States

Faith is   High Voice
 Text: Hebrews 11:1,2,13,16b; 12:1,2a.
 Range & Tess: d3-a4 f#3-d4
 Remarks: Sustained in moderate lively tempo. Middle section in chant
  style. Has some dramatic high passages. Climactic ending. Organis-
  tic accompaniment. Acc 3 TSL
 Occasions: General use. Evangelistic services. Massed religious gath-
  erings. New Year's Day.

O God of love   All Voices
 Text: William Vaughan Jenkins.
 Range & Tess: c3-eb4 f3-d4
 Remarks: Sustained in moderate tempo. Generally on MF level. Has some
  slightly climactic passages. Requires simplicity. Subdued, descend-

94

ing ending line. Acc 3 (S)AH
Occasions: Weddings.

O God of love, our rest and hope   Medium, Low Voices
   Text: Ernest Fremont Tittle.
   Range & Tess: a2-e♭4   e♭3-c4
   Remarks: Sustained in moderate tempo. Has some slightly faster tem-
      pi, key changes, and a climactic high passage. Subdued, contempla-
      tive ending. Organistic accompaniment. Acc 3 TSM
   Occasions: General use. Special use with sermon theme.

Star in the East   Medium, Low Voices
   Text: Reginald Heber.
   Range & Tess: b♭2-c4   c3-c4
   Remarks: Sustained in moderate tempo. Gentle, in pastoral style. Ge-
      nerally on MF level. First verse is unaccompanied. Tune is from
      "Christian Harmony". Acc 2-3 (S)GA
   Occasion: Epiphany.

                          AUGUSTUS LOWE
                          United States

Creator   Medium, Low Voices
   Text: Edgar Newgass.
   Range & Tess: d3-e4   e3-c4
   Remarks: Sustained in slow tempo. Strong, full-sounding song of
      praise. Not for light, high voices. Descending ending line re-
      quiring Forte strength. Acc 3 (S)CF
   Occasions: General use. Massed religious gatherings.

God is love   High, Medium Voices
   Text: Edgar Newgass.
   Range & Tess: e♭3-f4   g3-e♭4
   Remarks: Sustained in moderate slow tempo. Generally on MF level with
      fuller sounding and majestic final section. Acc 3 (S)CF
   Occasions: General use. Special use with sermon theme - God is love.

                          JAMES LYON
                       1735-1794, United States

Oh Lord, our heav'nly King   All Voices
   Text: Anonymous.
   Range & Tess: c3-e♭4   f3-c4
   Remarks: Sustained in moderate tempo. Has climactic passages. Descend-
      ing ending line. Exultant song of praise. Acc 3 SEA
   Occasions: General use. New Year's Day. Thanksgiving. Massed religious
      gatherings.

                               95

WILLIAM MATHIAS
England

A vision of time and eternity   Contralto
   Text: Henry Vaughan, 1622-1695.
   Range & Tess: bb2-f#4(g#4)   d3-d4
   Remarks: An extended, dramatic piece with various contrasts in dynam-
      ics and tempi. Dissonant. Interpretatively and musically difficult.
      Requires flexibility and fine command of low notes. Very subdued
      ending section. Best for recital. Acc 5 (S)OX
   Occasion: Special use with sermon theme - Eternity.

THOMAS MATTHEWS
United States

The Lord is my shepherd   High Voice
   Text: Psalm 23.
   Range & Tess: d3-g4   f#3-d4
   Remarks: Sustained in moderate tempo. Requires simplicity and free-
      dom. Has very subdued or PP passages as well as full-sounding FF.
      Organ accompaniment. Acc 3   (S)FS
   Occasions: General use. Evening services. Baptism. New Year's Day.

JOHN MAXWELL
United States

When mercy seasons justice   Medium Voice
   Text: William Shakespeare, from "The Merchant of Venice".
   Range & Tess: c3-f#4   f3-d4
   Remarks: Sustained in moderate slow tempo. Slightly faster middle
      section. Generally scale-wise melody. Frequent meter changes. Con-
      stantly moving lines in the accompaniment. Subdued low ending. Acc
      3 SPC
   Occasions: General use. Special use with sermon theme - Mercy and
      power.

KENNETH MEEK
Canada

There is no rose of such virtue   High Voice
   Text: Cambridge manuscript.
   Range & Tess: c3-g4   d3-e4
   Remarks: Sustained in moderate slow tempo. Has slightly faster, ani-
      mated sections, florid passages, "Alleluia" and other Latin phras-
      es. Climactic ending. Best for light, high voices. Acc 3 (S)BL
   Occasion: General use. Christmas.

FELIX MENDELSSOHN (BARTHOLDY)
1809-1847, Germany

Excerpts from Oratorios and Extended Anthems
Arranged according to first lines of the arias.

Soprano

R: My tears have been my meat
A: For I had gone forth   Soprano
  Work: Psalm 42, extended anthem "As the Hart Pants". Text of excerpt:
    Psalm 42:3,4.
  Range & Tess: d3-g4   e3-e4
  Remarks: Recitative and a brilliant, animated air in lively tempo.
    Has dramatic passages, a florid figure, and a climactic ending.
    Solo ends in the measure of the choral entrance, using an A major
    chord. Acc 4 (VS)GS, EK
  Occasion: General use.

For my soul thirsteth for God   Soprano
  Work: Psalm 42. Text of excerpt: Psalm 42:2.
  Range & Tess: e3-a4   a3-f4
  Remarks: Sustained in slow tempo. Has some high tessitura, imposing
    climaxes, climactic ending. Useful as solo introit. Acc 3 (VS)GS,
    EK
  Occasions: Communion. General use.

Hear my prayer, O God   Soprano
  Work: Hear My Prayer, extended anthem. Text of excerpt by W. Bartho-
    lomeo.
  Range & Tess: d3-g4   f#3-d4
  Remarks: Sustained in moderate slow tempo. Generally on MF level. Re-
    quires some fine PP. Has climactic passages and a subdued descend-
    ing ending. Acc 3 (S)GS, EK
  Occasions: Lent. Evening services. General use.

Hear ye, Israel   Soprano
  Work: ELIJAH, oratorio. Texts of excerpt: Isaiah 49:7-10; 53:1;
    51:12,13.
  Range & Tess: d#3-a#4   f#3-f#4
  Remarks: A very sustained adagio and a spirited, vigorous allegro
    maestoso. A short recitative separates the two sections. Has drama-
    tic passages Acc 3-4 (VS)GS, NO, EK. ASS-S. (S)GS
  Occasions: General use. Festivals.

R: So they, being filled
A: I will sing of Thy great mercies, O Lord   Soprano
  Work: SAINT PAUL, oratorio. Text of excerpt: Acts 4:31.
  Range & Tess: e3-f4   g3-f4

97

Remarks: Strong recitative and gently animated air in moderate fast
tempo. Graceful, with dignity. May also be sung by tenor. Acc 3-4
(VS)GS, EK

Occasions: General use. Missions Sunday.

Jerusalem! Thou that killest the prophets   Soprano
Work: SAINT PAUL. Text of excerpt: Matthew 23:37.
Range & Tess: f3-f4   a3-f4
Remarks: Very sustained in slow tempo. Has climactic passages. May al-
so be sung by tenor. Transposed in SCY. Acc 3-4 (VS)GS, EK. ASS-S
Occasions: General use. Special use with sermon theme.

Lord, at all times   Soprano
Work: Praise Jehovah (Lauda Sion). Text adapted from the Psalms.
Range & Tess: d3-g4   f3-d4
Remarks: Sustained in moderate slow tempo. Has climactic passages. May
also be sung by Tenor. Acc 3-4 (VS)EK
Occasions: General use. Evangelistic services.

Praise thou the Lord, O my spirit   Soprano
Work: HYMN OF PRAISE (LOBGESANG). Text of excerpt: Psalm 103:1,2.
Range & Tess: f3-b♭4   a3-g4
Remarks: Sustained in moderate tempo. Has little rhythmic or melodic
variety. High tessitura; effective ending. Has a women's chorus
part, but may be sung as a straight solo. Acc 3 (VS)GS, NO, EK
Occasions: Thanksgiving. New Year's Day. Massed religious gatherings.
Festivals with women's chorus. General use.

Mezzo-Soprano or Contralto

But the Lord is mindful of His own   Contralto, Mezzo-Soprano
Work: SAINT PAUL, oratorio. Text of excerpt: Acts 9:2; Psalm 114:12-
14; II Timothy 2:19; Philippians 4:5.
Range & Tess: a2-d4   d3-b3
Remarks: Sustained air in moderate slow tempo. Subdued ending after
climax. May also be sung by Baritone or Bass. Acc 3 (VS)GS, EK.
ASS-A
Occasions: General use. Funerals.

O rest in the Lord   Contralto, Mezzo-Soprano
Work: ELIJAH, oratorio. Text of excerpt: Psalm 37:7,4,5,1.
Range & Tess: b2-d4   e3-c4
Remarks: Very sustained in moderate slow tempo. Subdued, calm, has
subdued ending. May also be sung by Baritone or Bass. Acc 3 (VS)
GS, NO, EK. ASS-A, 56S. (S)GS, NO
Occasions: General use. Evening services. Funerals.

Tenor

Be thou faithful unto death   Tenor

Work: SAINT PAUL, oratorio. Text of excerpt: Revelation 2:10; Jeremiah 1:8.
 Range & Tess: d3-g4   g3-g4
 Remarks: Sustained in moderate slow tempo. Has some dramatic passages. May also be sung by Soprano. Transposed for medium voice in SHS. Acc 3-4 (VS)GS, EK. ASS-T
 Occasions: General use. Special use with sermon theme.

R: Sing ye praise
A: He counteth all your sorrows   Tenor
 Work: HYMN OF PRAISE, oratorio- Text of excerpt: Psalm 107:2,14,15,19.
 Range & Tess: d3-g4   g3-f4
 Remarks: Animated in moderate lively tempo. Bright, climactic passages. Sustained vocal line. Acc 3-4 (VS)GS, EK, NO. ASS-T
 Occasions: Funerals. General use.

R: Ye people, rend your hearts
A: If with all your hearts   Tenor
 Work: ELIJAH, oratorio. Text of excerpt: Jeremiah 29:13.
 Range & Tess: f#3-ab4   g3-f4
 Remarks: Recitative and a sustained air in moderate slow tempo. Very lyric, with climactic passages and a climactic ending. Acc 3-4 (VS)GS, NO, EK. ASS-T. (S)GS
 Occasions: General use. Evangelistic services. Massed religious gatherings.

Then shall the righteous shine forth   Tenor
 Work: ELIJAH. Text of the excerpt: Matthew 13:43; Isaiah 51:11b.
 Range & Tess: eb3-ab4   ab3-f4
 Remarks: Sustained in moderate tempo. Very lyric, with climactic passages. Transposed for lower voice in SHS. May also be sung by Soprano. Acc 3 (VS)GS, NO, EK. ASS-T
 Occasions: General use. Memorial services. Funerals.

Baritone or Bass

R: God dwelleth not in temples
A: For know ye not that ye are His temple   Baritone, Bass
 Work: SAINT PAUL, oratorio. Text of excerpt: I Corinthians 3:16-17.
 Range & Tess: al-d3   e2-d3
 Remarks: Sustained in moderate tempo. Has dramatic passages. In two sections. End the aria on first note of m.122, then return to the beginning of the aria and end on first note in m.93, using D major chord in the accompaniment. Acc 3-4 (VS)GS, EK
 Occasions: General use. Installation for missionary service. Installation of church officers or Pastor. Massed religious gatherings. Evangelistic services. Special use in services of personal dedication.

MENDELSSOHN

R: I go on my way
A: For the mountains shall depart   Baritone, Bass
   Work: ELIJAH, oratorio. Text of Excerpt: Isaiah 54:10.
   Range & Tess: bl-e3   d2-d3
   Remarks: Sustained in slow tempo. Requires fine P. Has climactic pas-
      sages. Theme: faith. Acc 3 (VS)GS, NO, EK
   Occasions: General use. Special use in services of personal dedica-
      tion. Installation for missionary service. Funerals.

I praise Thee, O Lord, my God   Baritone, Bass
   Work: SAINT PAUL. Text of excerpt: Psalm 86:12,13.
   Range & Tess: c2-c3   e2-c3
   Remarks: Sustained in moderate tempo. The arioso ends on measure 47.
     A short, lyric piece. Acc 3 (VS)GS, EK
   Occasion: General use.

Is not His word like a fire?   Baritone, Bass
   Work: ELIJAH. Text of excerpt: Jeremiah 23:29.
   Range & Tess: bl-f3   e2-d3
   Remarks: Very animated in fast tempo. Vigorous, dramatic, requires
     flexibility and fluent enunciation. Climactic ending. Acc 4 (VS)
     GS, NO, EK. ASS-B
   Occasions: Massed religious gatherings. Festivals. General use.

It is enough   Baritone, Bass
   Work: ELIJAH. Text of excerpt: I Kings 19:4,10.
   Range & Tess: al-e3   f#2-c#3
   Remarks: A dramatic aria in two movements: slow and very fast. Re-
     quires considerable flexibility. Has dramatic high climaxes and ag-
     itated accompaniment. Requires fluent enunciation. Very subdued end-
     ing. Acc 4 (VS)GS, NO, EK. ASS-B, 52S
   Occasion: Special use with sermon theme: The life of Elijah.

R: Draw near, all ye people
A: Lord God of Abraham   Baritone, Bass
   Work: ELIJAH. Text of excerpt: I Kings 18:36,37.
   Range & Tess: bl-eb3   d2-c3
   Remarks: Short recitative and a sustained air in moderate slow tempo.
     A prayer, generally subdued. Subdued ending. Acc 3 (VS)GS, NO, EK.
     ASS-B
   Occasion: General use.

O God, have mercy   Baritone, Bass
   Work: SAINT PAUL. Text of excerpt: Psalm 51:1,11,13,15,17.
   Range & Tess: bl-d3   d2-d3
   Remarks: Very sustained in slow tempo. Has dramatic recitative in the
     middle of the piece. Subdued ending section, a brief restatement of
     the first idea. Acc 3-4 (VS)GS, EK. ASS-B
   Occasions: General use. Missions Sunday. Massed religious gatherings.

Installation for missionary service. Installation of church of officers or Pastor.

The Lord shall bless thee with abundance　　　　　　　　Baritone, Bass
　　Work: Psalm 115, extended anthem. Text of excerpt: Psalm 115:14,15.
　　Range & Tess:　b♭1-e♭3　e♭2-c3
　　Remarks: Sustained in moderate tempo. Has some florid passages.　A
　　　useful song on text rarely set to music.　Acc 3　(VS)GS
　　Occasions: Thanksgiving. General use.

JOHN MERBECKE (MARBECK)
c.1510-c.1585, England

The Lord's Prayer　　　　　　　　　　　　　　　　　　　All Voices
　　Text: Matthew 6:9-13.
　　Range & Tess:　d3-b♭3　f3-a3
　　Remarks: A well-known chant arranged for solo voice by Everett　Jay
　　　Hilty. In free speech rhythm. Piano or organ accompaniment. Octavo
　　　format.　Acc 2　(S)OX
　　Occasions: General use. Evening services.

DAVID MORITZ MICHAEL
1751-1825, United States
Moravian　Composer

I love to dwell in the spirit　　　　　　　　　　　　High　Voice
(Ich bin in meinem Geiste)
　　Text: C. R. von Zinzendorf, translated.
　　Range & Tess:　e3-g4　f3-e4
　　Remarks: Sustained in moderate tempo. Generally on MF level. Descending ending line. Written in Bethlehem, PA, c.1800.　Acc 3-4　3SS
　　Occasions: General use. Whitsunday (Pentecost).

DANIEL MOE
United　States

The greatest of these is love　　　　　　　　　　　　All Voices
　　Text: I Corinthians 13.
　　Range & Tess:　med. high, d♭3-f#4　f3-e♭4　med. low, b♭2-d#4　d3-c4
　　Remarks: Sustained in slow tempo. Slightly faster middle section. Has
　　　climactic high passages. Subdued final section.　Acc 3　(S)AH
　　Occasions: Weddings. General use.

MICHAEL F. MOODY
United　States

The Master's touch　　　　　　　　　　　　　　　　　High Voice
　　Text: Horatius Bonar.
　　Range & Tess:　d3-g4　f3-d4

101

Remarks: Generally sustained in slow tempo. Has passages in gentle
recitative style. Starts very subdued. Has climactic high passages,
changes in meter, very subdued ending. Acc 3 SPC
Occasions: Dedication of church building. Dedication of music facilities. Installation of church officers or Pastor. Installation of
church musician. Special use in services of personal dedication.

WOLFGANG AMADEUS MOZART
1756-1791, Austria

Alleluja   Soprano
Work: Exsultate Jubilate (Motet). Liturgical Latin.
Range & Tess: f3-a4(c5)   a3-g4
Remarks: Animated in lively tempo. Brilliant, florid, joyful. Requires
considerable flexibility. Very florid. Climactic high ending. Widely
used in concert. Issued in many editions. Acc 4-5 (S)GS-3 keys,
CF-3 keys, NO-high only. Motet score: IM, BH.
Occasions: Christmas. Easter. Festivals. Massed religious gatherings.
General use.

Sinners, come! (Kommet her, ihr frechen Sünder. K146)   High Voice
Text: Anonymous. English version by Lorraine Noel.
Range & Tess: e3-g4   g3-f4
Remarks: Sustained in moderate tempo. Has some slightly florid pas-
sages. 3 verses. Acc 3 In "Twenty-one Concert Arias for Soprano",
GS.
Occasion: Lent.

Note: See also Mack Harrell's adaptation of the bass aria "O Isis und
Osiris" from THE MAGIC FLUTE in SHS.

GEORG GOTTFRIED MÜLLER
1762-1821, German-American
Moravian Composer

My Saviour lies in anguish   Soprano
Text: G. G. Müller? English version by Carleton S. Smith.
Range & Tess: d3-a4   a3-f4
Remarks: Sustained in slow tempo. Somber, has high tessitura and a
climactic ending. May also be sung by Tenor. Organ or Piano accom-
paniment and strings ad lib. Acc 3 TSS
Occasion: Lent.

THEA MUSGRAVE
England

A song for Christmas   High Voice
Text: Attributed to William Dunbar, c.1465-c.1530.

Range & Tess: b2-ab4   f3-f4
Remarks: Sustained in moderate tempo. Strong, dramatic, exultant, Has
   recitative passages, florid figures, dramatic high ending on long-
   held ab4. Not for light voices. Text in Scottish dialect, but may
   be edited to sing in modern English. Acc 4-5 (S)CH
Occasions: Christmas or the Sunday after.

GORDON MYERS
United States

Beloved, let us love one another   All Voices
   Text: I John 4:7,8.
   Range & Tess: d#3-eb4   g3-db4
   Remarks: Sustained in moderate slow tempo. Generally on MF level with
      some strong passages. Diminishing final long note. Acc 3 (S)GM
   Occasions: General use. Special use with sermon theme: Love and God.

Except the Lord build the house   All Voices
   Text: Psalm 127:1; 49:16b; 122:7.
   Range & Tess: d3-eb4   g3-d4
   Remarks: Sustained in moderate tempo. Starts strongly in recitative
      style. Has other recitative passages, climactic passages, and those
      marked P. Subdued ending. Acc 3 (S)GM
   Occasions: Dedication of church building or facilities. General use.

Prayer of Saint Francis   All Voices
   Text: St. Francis of Assisi.
   Range & Tess: d3-d#4   e3-d4
   Remarks: Sustained in moderate slow tempo. Has climactic passages,qua-
      si-declamatory phrases, dramatic high ending, contemporary harmo-
      nies. Acc 3-4 (S)GM
   Occasions: General use. Evening services. Special use in services of
      personal dedication. Installation for missionary service. Installa-
      tion of church officers or Pastor. Installation of church musician.
      Missions Sunday. World Brotherhood Sunday.

Thanksgiving   Medium Voice
   Text: Revelation 5:13b; Psalm 95:1,2,7; 96:13.
   Range & Tess: d3-f4   f3-d4
   Remarks: Sustained in moderate tempo. Has slower middle section.
      Starts and ends vigorously in declamatory style. Chant-like second
      section. Acc 3 (S)GM
   Occasions: Thanksgiving. General use. Festivals. Massed religious
      gatherings.

The Lord's Prayer   Medium Voice
   Text: Matthew 6:9-13.
   Range & Tess: eb3-eb4(gb4)   g3-c4
   Remarks: First part in gentle recitative style, using mostly g3 as the
      central tone. Second and final part in lyric style with high climax

before the "Amen". Acc 3 (S)GM
   Occasions: General use. Evening services.

See Myers' setting of "While shepherds watched their flocks by night"
under Traditional Songs.

NEGRO SPIRITUALS

BAN The Books of American Negro Spirituals. Two books in one, combin-
      ing two volumes published separately earlier. Mostly medium keys.
      Edited by James Weldon Johnson and J. Rosamond Johnson. New York:
      Da Capo Press, Inc.
GPS The Green Pastures Spirituals. Edited by Hall Johnson. Medium
      Voice. New York: Carl Fischer, Inc.
NSB Album of Negro Spirituals. Arranged by H. T. Burleigh. High, Low.
      Melville, NY: Belwin-Mills, Inc.
TSJ Thirty Spirituals. Arranged by Hall Johnson. High Voice and Piano.
      New York: G. Schirmer, Inc., 1949.
Note: For other codes, refer to the Bibliography at the beginning of
      the book. Texts of Spirituals are traditional except when indicat-
      ed otherwise.

Balm in Gilead   All Voices
   Text: Jeremiah 8:22.
   Range & Tess: high, b♭3-f4 b♭3-e♭4   low, g3-d4 g3-c4
   Remarks: Sustained in moderate slow tempo. Subdued, tranquil. Acc 2-3
      (S)B-M. TWB, TSJ
   Occasions: General use. Whitsunday (Pentecost). Evening services. New
      Year's Eve.

Deep river   All Voices
   Range & Tess: high, c3-a4 d3-d4 medium, a2-f#4 b2-b3
                           low, g2-e4 a2-a3
   Remarks: Very sustained in slow tempo. Slightly strong middle section.
      Acc 3 (S)B-M-3 keys. BAN, NSB
   Occasions: Evening services. General use.

Every time I feel the spirit   All Voices
   Range & Tess: c3-f4   f3-f4
   Remarks: Slightly animated in moderate tempo. Has passages with high
      tessitura, accented notes, strong passages. Acc 3-4 BAN, NSB, TSJ.
      (S)GA-1 step higher
   Occasions: General use. Evening services. New Year's Eve.

Go down, Moses   All Voices
   Text: Exodus 8:1.
   Range & Tess: high, f#3-f#4 f#3-f#4 low, d3-d4 d3-d4
   Remarks: Sustained in slow tempo. Vigorous, has some dramatic inten-
      sity. Acc 3 (S)GR-2 keys. GPS, BAN, PHP
   Occasion: Special use with sermon theme.

Go tell it on the mountain   All Voices
   Range & Tess: high, e♭3-f4 e♭3-f4 low, c3-d4 c3-d4
   Remarks: Sustained in moderate tempo. Joyous, requires fine diction.
      Slightly climactic ending. Acc 3 (S)GA-2 keys, B-M. TWB, PHP.
   Occasions: Christmas. New Year's Eve.

He's got the whole world in His hands   All Voices
   Range & Tess: f3-d4 a3-c4
   Remarks: Animated, spirited, in lively tempo. Strongly rhythmic, vi-
      brant. 3 verses with refrain. Issued with "When the saints come
      marching in". Acc 3 (S)Walter Kane Publications, NY.
   Occasions: General use. Evangelistic services. National holidays.

In Christ there is no east or west   All Voices
   Text: John Oxenham.
   Range & Tess: c3-e4 g3-c4
   Remarks: Sustained in moderate tempo. Short. After the rise in melo-
      dic line, descends and ends on song's lowest note. Adapted by H. T.
      Burleigh. Acc 2 PHP, TWB
   Occasions: World Brotherhood Sunday. Missions Sunday.

Let us break bread together   All Voices
   Range & Tess: c#3-e4 e3-c#4
   Remarks: Sustained in slow tempo. Serious, has climactic high pas-
      sages. Subdued beginning and ending. Acc 3   PHP
   Occasions: Evangelistic services. Communion. Baptism. Special use in
      services of personal dedication.

Mary had a baby   All Voices
   Range & Tess: c#3-e4 e3-c#4
   Remarks: Sustained in moderate lively tempo. Rhythmic. Requires some
      fluent enunciation. Subdued ending. Acc 2-3 CSV, TSJ, βAN
   Occasions: Christmas. Christmas Eve programs and services.

My Lord, what a morning   All Voices
   Text: Matthew 24:29 paraphrased.
   Range & Tess: high, f3-f4 f3-e♭4 low, d3-d4 d3-c4
   Remarks: Sustained in moderate slow tempo. Generally subdued. Setting
      by William Dawson. Acc 3 (S)FS. TSJ, βAN
   Occasions: Evening services.

Nobody knows the trouble I've seen   All Voices
   Range & Tess: high, e♭3-e♭4 e♭3-e♭4 low, c3-c4 c3-c4
   Remarks: Very sustained in slow tempo. Somber. Has some climactic
      passages. Setting by H. T. Burleigh. Acc 3 (S)GR-2 keys. BAN, NSB
   Occasions: Evening services.

Ride on, King Jesus   All Voices
Range & Tess: high, c3-a4(a♭4) f3-f4 med. b♭2-g4(g♭4) e♭3-e♭4

SPIRITUALS

low,   a♭2-f4(f♭4)   d♭3-d♭4
    Remarks: Animated in moderate tempo. Majestic, starts strongly. Also
      has subdued passages. Climactic, dramatic high ending. Setting   by
      Hall Johnson.   Acc 3 (S)CF
    Occasions: Palm Sunday. Festivals.

Somebody's knocking at your door   All Voices
    Range & Tess: c3-e♭4   e♭3-c4
    Remarks: Sustained in moderate tempo. Has slightly climactic pas-
      sages. Subdued low ending. Acc 4 TWB, BAN
    Occasion: General use.

Steal away   All Voices
    Range & Tess: high, a♭3-f4   a♭3-f4   low, f3-d4   f3-d4
    Remarks: Very sustained in moderate slow tempo. Has some slightly
      climactic passages. Setting by H. T. Burleigh. Acc 3 (S)B-M. BAN
    Occasions: Evening services. General use.

Sweet little Jesus boy   Medium Voice
    Range & Tess: f3-f4   f3-d4
    Remarks: Sustained in slow tempo. In gentle recitative style. Subdued
      throughout, requires simplicity, requires sensitivity to the text.
      Sparse accompaniment consists of chords. Setting by Robert MacGimsey.
      Acc 3 (S)CF
    Occasions: Christmas. Christmas Eve services and programs.

Swing low, sweet chariot   All Voices
    Range & Tess: high, e♭3-f4   a♭3-c♭4   low, c3-d4   f3-c4
    Remarks: Sustained in slow tempo. Slightly animated middle section.
      Has climactic passages and a subdued ending. Setting by H. T. Bur-
      leigh. Acc 3 (S)B-M. BAN, TSJ
    Occasion: Special use with sermon theme.

Talk about a child that do love Jesus   All Voices
    Range & Tess: high, g3-g4   g3-f4   low, e3-e4   e3-d4
    Remarks: Gently animated in moderate lively tempo. Has passages with
      high tessitura. Subdued descending ending. Sustained chords and
      syncopated movement alternate in the accompaniment. Setting by Wil-
      liam Dawson. Acc 3-4 (S)FS
    Occasions: General use. Children's Day.

'Tis me, O Lord (Standing in the need of prayer)   All Voices
    Range & Tess: a♭3-e♭4   a♭3-e♭4
    Remarks: Sustained in moderate tempo. Generally on MF level. Has one
      slightly climactic passage. Setting by H. T. Burleigh. Acc 3 (S)
      GR.
    Occasions: Evening services. General use.

We are climbing Jacob's ladder   All Voices
Range & Tess: d♭3-d♭4   f3-b♭3

Remarks: Sustained in moderate slow tempo. Short. Descending ending
   line. Acc 2 PHP, BAN
Occasions: Installation of church officers or Pastor. Evening services. Special use in services of personal dedication. Special use
   with sermon theme - Challenge for service. Evangelistic services.

Were you there   All Voices
   Range & Tess: high, e♭3-a♭4 a♭3-f4 medium, c3-f4 f3-d4
                        low, b♭2-e♭4 e♭3-c4
   Remarks: Very sustained in slow tempo. Generally subdued and slight-
      ly intense. Setting by H. T. Burleigh. Acc 3 (S)B-M-3 keys. BAN,
      NSB, TSJ, PHP.
   Occasions: Lent. Good Friday. General use.

When the saints come marching in   All Voices
   Range & Tess: e♭3-e♭4 e♭3-b♭3
   Remarks: Animated in moderate tempo. Rhythmic, joyous. Two verses.
      Issued with "He's got the whole world in His hands". Acc 3 (S)
      Walter Kane Publications, NY.
   Occasions: General use. Memorial services.

REID NIBLEY
United States

Let us turn to Bethlehem   High Voice
   Text: Mabel J. Gabbott.
   Range & Tess: d3-f#4 f3-d4
   Remarks: Sustained in moderate slow tempo. Requires smooth and gentle
      movement. Subdued starting and ending. Has some strong passages.
      Simple accompaniment. Acc 2-3 SPC
   Occasions: Christmas. Epiphany.

O thou who bidd'st the torrent flow   High Voice
   Text: John Greenleaf Whittier.
   Range & Tess: d3-g#4 a3-e4
   Remarks: Sustained in moderate tempo. Majestic. Has contrasting dy-
      namics and dramatic high climaxes. Requires very subdued high notes.
      Subdued high ending. Acc 3-4 SPC
   Occasion: General use.

PAUL NORDOFF
United States

Lacrima Christi   All Voices
   Text: Marya Mannes.
   Range & Tess: c3-f4 c3-f4
   Remarks: Sustained in slow tempo. Accompaniment uses ostinato fig-
      ures. English texts. Acc 3 (S)MM
   Occasions: Maundy Thursday. General use.

KNUT NYSTEDT
United States

O perfect love   All Voices
  Text: Dorothy Frances Gurney.
  Range & Tess: c3-d4   e3-c4
  Remarks: Sustained in moderate tempo. In strophic style, generally on
    MF level. Requires simplicity. See the settings by Barnby, Sowerby,
    Wetherill. Acc 3 (S)AH
  Occasions: Weddings.

GEOFFREY O'HARA
United States

Thanks   High Voice
  Text: Raymond Garfield Dandridge.
  Range & Tess: d3-f4(g4)   f3-d4
  Remarks: Sustained in moderate slow tempo. Freedom of delivery need-
    ed, in quasi-recitative style. Generally on MF level with climactic
    ending. Acc 3 52S
  Occasions: Thanksgiving. General use. Evening services.

The waters of Thy love   All Voices
  Text: Daniel S. Twohig.
  Range & Tess: high, c#3-f#4 f#3-d4   low, a2-d4 d3-bb3
  Remarks: Sustained in moderate tempo. After an MF start, volume moves
    into F. Strong high ending. Acc 3-4 (S)RH
  Occasions: Special use in services of personal dedication. Baptism.
    Installation of church officers or Pastor. Trinity Sunday.

There is no death   All Voices
  Text: Gordon Johnstone.
  Range & Tess: high, eb3-ab4 ab3-eb4   medium, c3-f4 f3-c4
                 low, bb2-eb4 eb3-bb3
  Remarks: Generally sustained in moderate tempo. Majestic, generally
    full and strong, with some accented notes. Dramatic and powerful,
    with a dramatic high ending. Acc 3-4 (S)CC
  Occasions: Memorial services. Funerals. General use.

MARY PICKENS OPIE
United States

Communion hymn   All Voices
  Text: Mary Pickens Opie.
  Range & Tess: db3-db4   f3-db4
  Remarks: Sustained in moderate slow tempo. Subdued level, no strong
    passages. Concludes with "Amen". Straightforward reading with em-
    phasis on text is recommended. Acc 3 52S
  Occasion: Communion.

HORATIO PARKER
1863-1919, United States

Excerpts from HORA NOVISSIMA, oratorio
Work for SATB soli, SATB Choir, Orchestra (Piano). Texts by Bernard de
Morlaix. English version by Isabella Parker. Vocal score: H. W. Gray.

Golden Jerusalem (Urbs Syon aurea)   Tenor
  Range & Tess: e♭3-a♭4   a♭3-f4
  Remarks: Very sustained in moderate tempo, with slightly more move-
    ment in the 2nd half. Has dramatic high passages and a dramatic
    high ending. Acc 4
  Occasions: General use. Special use with sermon theme - The new Jeru-
    salem.

O country bright and fair (O bona patria)   Soprano
  Range & Tess: e♭3-a♭4   a♭3-f4
  Remarks: Sustained in moderate tempo. Requires fine high P & PP. Re-
    quires considerable dramatic intensity. Acc 4
  Occasions: General use. Funerals. Special use with sermon theme - The
    country glorious.

People victorious (Gens duce splendida)   Mezzo-Soprano, Contralto
  Range & Tess: c3-e4   c3-c4
  Remarks: Sustained vocal part in moderate tempo. Faster and vigorous
    middle section. Strong and dramatic. Also requires fine P. Subdued
    ending. Acc 4
  Occasions: Memorial services. Funerals. General use. Special use with
    sermon theme - The Holy City.

Zion is captive yet (Spe modo vivitur)   Baritone, Bass
  Range & Tess: a1-e3   e2-d3
  Remarks: Sustained in moderate tempo. Majestic beginning. Has strong
    and dramatic passages as well as those requiring fine P & PP. Has
    several contrasting moods and tempi. Requires flexibility. Subdued
    high ending. An outstanding aria. Acc 4
  Occasions: General use. Special use with sermon theme - The Celestial
    Country.

CHARLES HUBERT HASTINGS PARRY
1848-1918, England

I will sing unto the Lord a new song   Soprano
  Work: JUDITH, oratorio. Text by C. H. H. Parry.
  Range & Tess: c3-a4   a3-f4
  Remarks: Animated in moderate lively tempo. Majestic, vigorous, dra-
    matic, marked. Stately ending. Acc 3-4 ASS-S
  Occasions: General use. Festivals.

The Lord is long-suffering   Contralto, Mezzo-Soprano

PARRY

Work: JUDITH. See first entry.
Range & Tess: d3-e4   f3-d4
Remarks: Sustained and slow beginning and ending sections. Slightly
  animated, vigorous middle section. Has climactic passages and subdued descending ending. Acc 3 ASS-A
Occasions: Special use with sermon theme - Light after darkness, or
  joy after sorrow.

ROB ROY PEERY
United States

God shall wipe away all tears   All Voices
  Text: Revelation 21:3,4.
  Range & Tess: c3-f4   f3-d4
  Remarks: Sustained in generally moderate tempo. Starts with recita-
    tive in majestic, forceful style. The air is generally subdued with
    one climactic, strong passage. Subdued ending.   Acc 3 52S
  Occasions: Funerals. General use. Special use with sermon theme - God
    the Comforter.

FLOR PEETERS
Belgium

Ave Maria   All Voices
  Text: Latin hymn based on Luke 1:28,30,31. English version.
  Range and Tess in 3 keys: high, e♭3-g4 a3-e4
                medium, d♭3-f4 g3-d4   low, b2-e♭4 f3-c4
  Remarks: Sustained in slow tempo. Generally on MF level, with high
    climaxes marked F. Climactic high ending on "Amen". Acc 2-3 (S)CP
  Occasions: General use. Advent.

The Lord's Prayer   All Voices
  Text: Matthew 6:9-13.
  Range & Tess: high, e♭3-g4 g3-d4   medium, d♭3-f4 f3-c4
                low, b♭2-a3 d3-a3
  Remarks: Sustained in slow tempo. In quasi-recitative style. General-
    ly on MF level. Climactic, broad, high ending. Possibly the best
    setting of this text. Acc 3 (S)CP
  Occasions: General use. Evening services.

Wedding song (Wo du hingehst)   All Voices
  Text: Ruth 1:16,17, adaptation by Hugh Ross.
  Range & Tess: high, f3-a4 b♭3-f4   medium, d3-f#4 g3-d4
                low, c3-e4. f3-c4
  Remarks: Sustained in moderate slow tempo. Has meditative and subdued
    passages, and two climactic high passages. See Birch, Cassler, En-
    gel, Gore, Schutz. Acc 2-3 (S)CP
  Occasions: Weddings.

WALTER L. PELZ
United States

Happy are they who dwell in Your house   High, Medium Voices
  Text: Psalm 84:3,4,10-12.
  Range & Tess: e3-f#4   g3-d4
  Remarks: Generally sustained in varied tempi. Starts strongly; end-
    ing section is marked FF. A long-held final note. Not for light,
    high voices. Best for dramatic medium voice. Oboe obbligato. Or-
    gan accompaniment. Acc 3-4 TSL
  Occasions: General use. New Year's Day or the Sunday after. Dedica-
    tion of church building or facilities.

Our soul waits for the Lord   High Voice
  Text: Psalm 33:20-22.
  Range & Tess: e3-a4   a3-e4
  Remarks: Generally sustained and slow first and third sections. Joy-
    ful and animated second section. Has some strong, climactic high
    passages, and a subdued,slow ending. Violoncello obbligato. Organ
    accompaniment. Acc 3 TSL
  Occasions: General use. National holidays.

VINCENT PERSICHETTI
United States

Thou Child so wise   All Voices
  Text: Hilaire Belloc.
  Range & Tess: c3-eb4   f3-b3
  Remarks: Sustained in slow tempo. Requires simplicity. Gentle and
    subdued with a subdued low ending. See Britten's "The birds". Acc
    2-3 (S)EV
  Occasion: Epiphany.

JOHANN FRIEDRICH PETER
1746-1813, United States
Moravian Composer

I will make an everlasting covenant   Soprano
(Ich will mit euch einen ewigen Bund machen)
  Text: Isaiah 55:3.
  Range & Tess: d3-f4   f3-eb4
  Remarks: Sustained in slow tempo. Graceful. Generally subdued. May
    also be sung by Tenor. Acc 3 3SS
  Occasions: General use. Evening services.

Lead me in Thy truth   High Voice
  Text: Psalm 25:5.
  Range & Tess: eb3-g4   g3-eb4
  Remarks: Sustained in moderate slow tempo. Slow second section. Ge-
    nerally on MF level. A short song. Organ (or Piano) and strings ad

111

PETER

lib. Acc 3 TSS
   Occasion: General use.

The days of all thy sorrow (Die Tage Deines Leides)   Soprano
   Text: Isaiah 60:20.
   Range & Tess: d3-a4   a3-e4
   Remarks: Sustained in moderate slow tempo. Generally on MF level.
      Descending ending line. May also be sung by Tenor. Acc 3 3SS
   Occasions: General use. Funerals. Special use with sermon theme.

The Lord is in His holy temple   Soprano
   Text: Habakkuk 2:20-
   Range & Tess: e♭3-f4   g3-e♭4
   Remarks: Sustained in moderate tempo. Stately. Also useful as a solo
      introit. May be sung by Tenor. Organ (or Piano) and strings ad lib.
      Acc 3 TSS. (S)B-H
   Occasion: General use.

                        SIMON PETER
                  1743-1819, Dutch-American
                     Moravian Composer

O, there's a sight that rends my heart   Soprano
(O Anblick, der mir's Herze bright)
   Text: Simon Peter(?). English by Carleton S. Smith.
   Range & Tess: e♭3-g4   a♭3-e♭4
   Remarks: Sustained in slow tempo. Intense. May also be sung by Tenor.
      Acc 3 TSS
   Occasions: Good Friday. Lent.

                        CARL PFLUEGER
                        United States

How long wilt Thou forget me? (O Salutaris)   All Voices
   Text: Psalm 13:1,3,5.
   Range & Tess: high, d3-g4   g3-e4   medium, b♭2-e♭4   e♭3-e4
                        low, a♭2-d♭4   d♭3-b♭3
   Remarks: Sustained air in moderate slow tempo after a short recita-
      tive. Has 2 climactic high passages and a subdued high ending. Best
      for light voices. Acc 3 (S)RH
   Occasion: General use.

                       DANIEL PINKHAM
                       United States

              Eight Poems of Gerard Manley Hopkins
A set of songs for Baritone or Tenor-Baritone and Viola. Boston: Ione
Press, c/o ES. Note: Only the movements with definite Christian themes
are given here.

                            112

(1) Jesus to cast one thought upon
    Range & Tess: c3-f#4   e3-c#4
    Remarks: Sustained in moderate slow tempo. Slightly faster middle
       section. Starts subdued; generally on MF level. Subdued low end-
       ing. Viola 3
    Occasions: Evening services. General use. Special use in services
       of personal dedication.

(4) Pied beauty
    Range & Tess: c3-f4   f#3-c#4
    Remarks: Animated in moderate tempo. Requires flexibility for some
       wide intervalic skips. Generally on MF level. Subdued low ending.
       Viola 3
    Occasion: Thanksgiving.

(7) Christmas Day
    Range & Tess: b♭2-f4   g3-d4
    Remarks: Sustained in slow tempo. Strong passages in the first
       part; second part is subdued. Short song. Subdued low ending.
       Viola 2
    Occasions: Christmas or the Sunday after.

(8) Jesu that dost in Mary dwell
    Range & Tess: g♭2-c4   e♭3-c4
    Remarks: Sustained in moderate tempo with forward movement. Gene-
       rally subdued, with some inner intensity. Requires flexibility
       for the wide intervalic skips and low tessitura. Viola 3
    Occasions: Trinity Sunday or the Sundays after.

Letters From Saint Paul

Six songs for High Voice and Organ or Piano. Boston: E. C. Schirmer Music Co.

(1) Wherefore seeing
    Text: Hebrews 12:1,2.
    Range & Tess: f#3-a♭4   a3-e4
    Remarks: Sustained in moderate slow tempo. Starts strongly. Has
       climactic high passages and a strong ending. Acc 3
    Occasions: General use. Evangelistic services. Trinity Sunday. Spe-
       cial use with sermon theme - Author and finisher of our faith.

(2) Who shall separate us from the love of Christ
    Text: Romans 8:35,37-39.
    Range & Tess: c#3-a♭4   g3-e4
    Remarks: Starts with declamatory passage in slow tempo. In moderate
       slow tempo, with variations. Has climactic passages and subdued
       ending. Acc 3
    Occasions: Massed religious gatherings. Evangelistic services. Mis-
       sions Sunday. Reformation Sunday. Special use with sermon theme-

love of Christ. General use.

(3) Let the word of Christ dwell in you
   Text: Colossians 3:16.
   Range & Tess: c3-g4   g3-d4
   Remarks: Sustained in slow tempo. On MF level, no strong contrasts.
      Subdued high ending. Short: one page. Useful as a Benediction
      solo.   Acc 3
   Occasions: General use. Installation of church officers or Pastor.
      Special use with sermon theme - The word of Christ.

(4) But of the times and the seasons
   Text: I Thessalonians 5:1-6.
   Range & Tess: c#3-a4   f3-e4
   Remarks: Animated in varied tempi and moods. Declamatory, with dra-
      matic passages. Requires flexibility. Subdued, "falling" ending.
      Acc 3
   Occasions: New Year's Eve. Evening services. Special use with ser-
      mon theme: Watching for the Lord's coming. General use.

(5) Rejoice in the Lord alway
   Text: Philippians 4:4-7.
   Range & Tess: d3-g4   g3-g4
   Remarks: Animated in rapid tempo. Joyous. Has frequent meter chang-
      es, high sustained climactic notes, and a dramatic high ending.
      Requires fluent enunciation and flexibility. Acc 4
   Occasions: Massed religious gatherings. Festivals. New Year's Day.
      General use.

(6) Now it is high time to awake
   Text: Romans 13:11,12.
   Range & Tess: cb3-a4   g3-d4
   Remarks: Generally sustained in moderate slow tempo. Starts on MF
      level, then becomes strong with frequent F & FF indications. Dra-
      matic high ending. Acc 3-4
   Occasions: Advent. New Year's Eve. New Year's Day. Evangelistic
      services. National holidays. Reformation Sunday. General use.

Man That is Born of a Woman

Three songs for Mezzo-Soprano and Guitar. Text from "Book of Common
Prayer". Boston: E. C. Schirmer Music Co. Note: These songs fit the
Contralto voice better. The songs may be performed separately.

(1) Man, that is born of a woman
   Range & Tess: g2-e4   c3-d4
   Remarks: Sustained in moderate lively tempo. Has contrasting strong
      and subdued passages, phrases with sustained low notes, frequent
      meter changes, wide intervalic skips. Subdued ending phrase.
      Guitar 3-4

Occasion: Special use with sermon theme.

(2) In the midst of life
   Range & Tess: f#2-c4   c3-g3
   Remarks: Sustained in moderate slow tempo. Requires fine P & PP.
      Has one short climactic passage, many low notes, and low tessi-
      tura. Very subdued "falling" ending.   Guitar 3
   Occasions: Lent. Special use with sermon theme.

(3) Thou knowest, Lord, the secrets of our hearts
   Range & Tess: a2-f4   d3-c4
   Remarks: Sustained in moderate slow tempo. Has contrasting soft and
      strong passages, climactic high phrases, and a subdued, "falling"
      ending.   Guitar 3-4
   Occasions: General use. Special use with sermon theme.

See also Two Motets for Soprano (Tenor), Flute and Guitar. Boston: E.C.
   Schirmer Music Co. Total range: c3-b 4. Titles:
   (1) I will not leave you comfortless (Non vos relinquam orphanos)
       For: General use. Funerals. Ascension Sunday.
   (2) Before the ending of the day (Te lucis ante terminum)
       For: Evening services. New Year's Eve.

The Lamb   High Voice
   Text: William Blake.
   Range & Tess: d3-g4   g3-e4
   Remarks: Sustained in moderate tempo. Moves syllabically, generally
      subdued. Very subdued low ending. Sparse accompaniment. Best for
      light voices. Octavo format.   Acc 2-3 (S)ES
   Occasions: Children's Day. Special use with sermon theme - The Lamb.
      Special use in services of personal dedication.

                        CHARLES PROCTOR
                            England

King David   High Voice
   Text: Walter de la Mare.
   Range & Tess: d3-g4   g3-eb4
   Remarks: Sustained in slow tempo. Sorrowful, mostly subdued, no forte
      passage. Very subdued ending line. Extended introduction and harp-
      like accompaniment in middle section.   Acc 3 (S)LK
   Occasion: Special use with sermon theme - King David's sorrow.

                        Five Mystic Songs
Songs for High Voice and Piano (or Organ). London: Alfred Lengnick Co.

(1) Christ my beloved
   Text: Baldwin, 1594.
   Range & Tess: g#3-f4   a3-e4
   Remarks: Sustained in slow tempo. Subdued, gentle. Unmetered,

                              115

slightly free rhythm. Acc 3
Occasion: General use.

(2) Our Lady's lullaby
Text: Richard Verstegen (Rowlands).
Range & Tess: e3-g4   g3-e4
Remarks: Gently animated in moderate tempo. Delicate, graceful,
    gentle, in folk style. Best for light soprano. Acc 2-3
Occasions: Christmas Eve programs and services.

(3) Love bade me welcome
Text: George Herbert, 1593-1633.
Range & Tess: c#3-g4   f3-d4
Remarks: Sustained in moderate tempo. Generally subdued, requires
    fine P & PP. In free speech rhythm. Very subdued ending. Inter-
    pretatively not easy. Acc 3
Occasion: Special use with sermon theme.

(4) That He whom the sun serves
Text: Richard Crashaw, 1613-1648.
Range & Tess: b2-a4   f3-e4
Remarks: Sustained in moderate slow tempo. Graceful, generally
    subdued. Requires fine high PP. Ends with extended, descending
    cadenza. Acc 3
Occasions: Epiphany. Special use with sermon theme.

(5) Lord, Thou art mine, and I am Thine
Text: George Herbert, 1593-1633.
Range & Tess: d#3-f#4   e3-e4
Remarks: Sustained in moderate tempo. Generally on MF level,
    slightly majestic, has climactic passages and chordal accompani-
    ment. Acc 3
Occasions: Evening services. Palm Sunday.

RICHARD PROULX
United States

Nuptial blessings   All Voices
  Text: John Newton, 1779.
  Range & Tess: d3-e4   e3-b3
  Remarks: Sustained in moderate tempo. Starts in recitative style. Ge-
    nerally gentle, with a climactic passage. Subdued ending with "A-
    men". Acc 2-3 (S)AH
Occasions: Weddings.

HENRY PURCELL
c.1659-1695, England

HPS Henry Purcell. High, Low. Edited by John Edmunds. New York: R. D.

Row Music Co.

HSP   Harmonia Sacra. Three Divine Hymns. Henry Purcell. Realised by Benjamin Britten. Medium Voice. New York: Boosey & Hawkes.

TDH   Two Divine Hymns and Alleluia. Henry Purcell. London: Boosey & Hawkes.

16S   16 Songs. Henry Purcell. Edited by Maureen Lehane and Peter Wishart. Books 1, 3. - medium keys. London: Stainer & Bell.

40S   40 Songs. Henry Purcell. High, Low. Edited by Sergius Kagen. New York: International Music Co.

A morning hymn thou wakeful shepherd   High Voice
   Text: Anonymous.
   Range & Tess: d3-g4   eb3-eb4
   Remarks: Generally sustained in moderate tempo. In recitative style.
      Has climactic passages, florid passages, subdued ending. Requires
      fine P. Acc 3 TDH
   Occasion: General use.

Alleluia   High Voice
   Text: Alleluia.
   Range & Tess: f3-g4   a3-eb4
   Remarks: Animated in lively tempo. Brilliant, has florid passages, re-
      quires flexibility. Starts gently. Dramatic, slow, and broad
      high ending. A charming "Alleluia". Acc 3-4   TDH
   Occasions: Christmas. New Year's Day. Easter. General use.

An evening hymn   All Voices
   Text: Dr. William Fuller.
   Range & Tess: high, d3-g4 f#3-e4   low, bb2-eb4 d3-c4
   Remarks: Very sustained in slow tempo. Has long, sustained phrases.
      Requires some flexibility.Ends with extended "Hallelujah" section.
      Uses ostinato bass in accompaniment. Acc 3 40S-4, HSP, 16S-3.
      (S)SC-2 keys
   Occasions: Evening services.

Lord, what is man   All Voices
   Text: Hebrews 2:6; Purcell(?).
   Range & Tess: high, d3-a4 f#3-g4   low, bb2-f4 d3-eb4
   Remarks: A florid recitative-style song in 3 movements. A short solo
      cantata. Requires considerable flexibility. Forceful and dramatic,
      interpretatively not easy. The last section is perhaps the most im-
      pressive and dynamic setting of "Hallelujah". A remarkable song.
      Acc 4 40S-3, HSP-½ tone lower for low voice, 16S-1.
   Occasions: Easter. General use.

O Lord, rebuke me not   All Voices
   Text: Psalm 6:1-4.
   Range & Tess: high, c3-g4 f#3-eb4   low, a2-e4 d#3-c4
   Remarks: Generally sustained song of supplication with an impressive,

extended, florid "Alleluia" section. Requires flexibility. Acc 4
HPS
Occasion: General use.

The blessed Virgin's expostulation   Women's Voices
   Text: Nahum Tate, a paraphrase of Luke 2:42.
   Range & Tess: high, d♭3-g♭4 f3-f4   low, b♭2-e♭4   d3-d4
   Remarks: An extended solo or cantata with recitatives and airs. Has
      florid passages. Declamatory, requires flexibility. Interpretative-
      ly difficult. Acc 4 40S-2. (S)SC and B-H soprano key only
   Occasions: Christmas Eve programs and services. Special use with ser-
      mon theme.

We sing to Him   All Voices
   Text: Jean Ingelow.
   Range & Tess: high, c#3-g4 f#3-f#4   low, a2-e♭4 d3-d4
   Remarks: Broad, majestic first section; graceful, lighter second sec-
      tion with rhythmic complexity. Climactic ending. Acc 3 40S-1;
      HPS, HSP
   Occasions: Dedication of music facilities. Installation of church
      musician. General use.

ROGER QUILTER
1877-1953, England

Non nobis, Domine (Not unto us, Lord)   Medium, Low Voices
   Text: Rudyard Kipling.
   Range & Tess: c3-e♭4(f4)   e3-d4
   Remarks. Text is in English. Sustained in moderate tempo. Subdued be-
      ginning. Has some strong passages and a dramatic high ending. Acc 3
      (S)B-H
   Occasions: Communion. New Year's Day. General use.

NATALIA RAIGORODSKY
United States

I will lift up mine eyes   High, Medium Voices
   Text: Psalm 121.
   Range & Tess: c3-f4(f#4)   f3-d4
   Remarks: Generally in recitative style, in moderate slow tempo. Starts
      gently; has two climactic high passages. Majestic, declamatory end-
      ing. Dissonant. Organistic accompaniment. Acc 3-4 ESS
   Occasion: General use.

SERGEI RAKHMANINOF
1873-1943, Russia

RAS Rachmaninoff Songs. Complete in 2 volumes. Original Russian texts
      and English versions by Edward Agate. New York: Boosey & Hawkes.

A prayer   High Voice
   Text: Aleksei N. Plescheyef, after Goethe.
   Range & Tess: c3-a4   f3-eb4 (original key)
   Remarks: Intended for soprano. Sustained in moderate tempo. Various
      dynamics, strong high climaxes, subdued descending ending line.
      Full-sounding accompaniment of chords. Not for light voices. Acc 3
      RAS-1
   Occasion: Lent.

Christ is risen!   Mezzo-Soprano, Baritone
   Text: Dmitrij S. Merejkovsky. English by Rosa Newmarch.
   Range & Tess: medium, d3-f4   f3-eb4   low, b2-d4   d3-c4
   Remarks: Sustained in moderate tempo. Majestic, dramatic, intense,
      with forceful climax. Not for light voices. Medium key is original.
      Acc 3-4 (S)GA. RAS-2
   Occasions: Easter. Massed religious gatherings. Evangelistic servic-
      es. General use.

Glorious forever   All Voices
   Text: Nikolai Nekrasof. English by Nathan H. Dole.
   Range & Tess: high, d#3-g4   g3-e4   low, b2-eb4   eb3-c4
   Remarks: Sustained in moderate tempo. Majestic, with effective cli-
      max. Acc 2-3 (S)BM
   Occasions: National holidays. General use.

ALAN RAWSTHORNE
England

Carol   High, Medium Voices
   Text: W. R. Rodgers.
   Range & Tess: db3-f4   f3-d4
   Remarks: Sustained in slow tempo. Gentle, requires simplicity. Has
      mild dissonances. Atmospheric, descriptive text. Generally sub-
      dued, with one short high climax near the end. Acc 3 (S)OX
   Occasions: Christmas. General use.

DOROTHY DASCH REESE
United States

Let not your heart be troubled   High Voice
   Text: John 14:1,2,27.
   Range & Tess: d3-g4   f#3-d4
   Remarks: Sustained in moderate slow tempo. Has some high tessitura.
      Generally on MF level. In lyric style, with subdued, "floating"
      ending line: Peace I leave with you. Acc 3 (S)FS
   Occasions: Maundy Thursday. Funerals. Special use with sermon theme-
      Jesus' final charge to His disciples.

MAX REGER
1873-1916, Germany

12S 12 Sacred Songs. Op. 137. Max Reger. English text edition by Jean
      Lunn. Frankfurt: C. F. Peters Corp. Mostly medium keys, but may
      be transposed for other voices.

Evening   All Voices
    Text: Anonymous.
    Range & Tess: e3-e4   g#3-c#4
    Remarks: Sustained in moderate slow tempo. Descending ending line. 3
      verses. Acc 3 12S
    Occasions: Evening services.

Lamentation on Christ's passion   All Voices
    Text: Anonymous.
    Range & Tess: d3-f4   e3-c#4
    Remarks: Sustained in quite slow tempo. Requires some flexibility.
      Somber, sad texts. Acc 3 12S
    Occasions: Good Friday. Lent.

Let evil not deceive thee   All Voices
    Text: Paul Fleming.
    Range & Tess: e3-e4   g3-d4
    Remarks: Sustained in slow tempo. Generally gentle. 3 verses. Acc 3
      12S
    Occasions: Special use with sermon theme. General use.

Lo, a Child is born to us   All Voices
    Text: Anonymous.
    Range & Tess: f3-e4   f3-c4
    Remarks: Sustained in moderate slow tempo. Graceful in quiet jubila-
      tion. Simple and charming melody. 2 verses. Acc 2 12S
    Occasions: Christmas. Christmas Eve programs and services. Advent.

Lord Jesus Christ, we wait for Thee   All Voices
    Text: Erasmus Alberus.
    Range & Tess: f3-e4   g3-d4
    Remarks: Sustained in slow tempo. Generally on MF level. 3 verses.
      Acc 3 12S
    Occasion: General use.

Morning song   All Voices
    Text: Erasmus Alberus.
    Range & Tess: e3-f#4   g3-e4
    Remarks: Animated in moderate lively tempo. Bright and joyous. 3 vers-
      es. Acc 3 12S
    Occasions: Christmas. Advent.

O Christ, with Thine own graciousness   All Voices
    Text: Anonymous.
    Range & Tess: d3-e4   f#3-c#4
    Remarks: Sustained in slow tempo. Subdued ending.3 verses. Acc 3 12S
    Occasion: General use.

O Lord my God, take Thou from me   All Voices
    Text: Anonymous.
    Range & Tess: eb3-eb4   g3-c4
    Remarks: Very sustained in moderate slow tempo. Generally gentle. Sub-
      dued ending. 3 verses. Acc 2 12S
    Occasions: Special use in services of personal dedication. Installation
      of church officers or Pastor. Installation for missionary service.
      General use.

Prayer for a blessed death   All Voices
    Text: Nicolaus Herman.
    Range & Tess: c3-ab4   eb3-c4
    Remarks: Sustained in slow tempo. Gentle and tranquil. 2 verses. Acc
      3 12S
    Occasions: Evening services. Lent.

The Christ Child's lullaby   All Voices
    Text: Anonymous.
    Range & Tess: e3-e4   f#3-c#4
    Remarks: Slightly animated in moderate lively tempo. Graceful, slight-
      ly subdued with quiet jubilation. Acc 3 12S
    Occasions: Christmas Eve programs and services. Christmas Day.

The Virgin's slumber song (Mariä Wiegenlied)   Women's Voices
    Text: Martin Boelitz. English by Ed. Teschemacher.
    Range & Tess: highest key, ab3-ab4   ab3-f4 (Key of Ab). Also pub-
      lished in four other keys: G, F, E, D.
    Remarks: Not suitable for very dark, heavy voices. Sustained in mod-
      erate slow tempo. Graceful, gentle, rather subdued, requires very
      fine P & PP. Acc 3 (S)AM
    Occasions: Christmas Eve programs and services. Christmas.

Thy will, O Lord, befall me!   All Voices
    Text: Joseph Freiherr von Eichendorff.
    Range & Tess: e3-e4   f3-d4
    Remarks: Sustained in slow tempo. Short, simple, generally subdued.
      Acc 3 12S
    Occasions: Evening services. Special use in services of personal dedi-
      cation.

JOSEPH (GABRIEL) RHEINBERGER
1839-1901, Germany

Bethlehem   Baritone, Bass
   Work: DER STERN VON BETHLEHEM (The Star of Bethlehem). Text by the
     composer(?). English by Mrs. John P. Morgan.
   Range & Tess: c#2-eb3 f2-d3
   Remarks: Sustained in moderate slow tempo. Has passages with high
     tessitura and some strong high climaxes. Climactic ending. Acc 3-
     4 (VS)EK
   Occasions: Advent. Christmas.

Maria   Soprano
   Work: DER STERN VON BETHLEHEM. See first entry.
   Range & Tess: eb3-g4 a3-e4
   Remarks: Sustained in moderate tempo. Starts gently in quasi-recita-
     tive style, then moves into a majestic second section with con-
     trasts of strong and soft phrases. Descending ending line. Acc 3-4
     (VS)EK
   Occasion: Sunday after Christmas.

THOMAS RICHNER
United States

Rise up and walk!   High Voice
   Text: Acts 3:1,2.
   Range & Tess: c3-g4 e3-eb4
   Remarks: In recitative, narrative style in moderate tempo. Requires
     precise diction. Dissonant, with bold unprepared key shifts. Very
     strong high ending on g4 held 17 beats. Acc 3-4 SPC
   Occasions: Special use with sermon theme - Faith and healing. Gener-
     al use.

DALE G. RIDER
United States

Every good and perfect gift is from above   High Voice
   Text: James 1:17; Joseph Smith, Jr.
   Range & Tess: d3-g4 g3-eb4
   Remarks: Sustained in moderate, freely moving tempo. Has passages in
     recitative style, climactic phrases, subdued ending section. Organ-
     istic accompaniment. Fine as Offertory Solo. Acc 3 (S)CY
   Occasion: General use.

Establish a house   High Voice
   Text: Joseph Smith, Jr.
   Range & Tess: eb3-g4 g3-eb4
   Remarks: In gentle recitative style. Has climactic high passages.
     Broad, soft ending. May be transposed for lower voices. Organistic

accompaniment. Acc 2-3 (S)CY
Occasion: Dedication of church building or facilities.

GODFREY RIDOUT
England

What star is this?   High Voice
  Text: Charles Coffin, 1676-1749.
  Range & Tess: g3-f4   g3-d4
  Remarks: Sustained in moderate tempo. Gentle, with descending ending.
    No bold contrasts. First verse is unaccompanied. Text is a transla-
    tion of Coffin's Latin hymn: Qua stella sole pulchrior. Octavo for-
    mat. Acc 2 (S)OX
  Occasions: Christmas Eve programs and services. Sunday after Christ-
    mas.

McNEIL ROBINSON
United States

In the beginning was the word   High, Medium Voices
  Text: John 1:1-14.
  Range & Tess: c3-g4   g3-d4
  Remarks: In broad recitative style, in slow tempo. Has many triplet
    figures. Melody hinges around the dominant. Generally dissonant,
    has chromaticisms, requires excellent diction. Subdued ending. Acc
    3-4 ESS
  Occasions: New Year's Day. Special use with sermon theme - The Word
    made flesh. General use. Evangelistic services.

ROBERT A. ROESCH
United States

Christ, the living way   High Voice
  Text: Simon Browne, 1720.
  Range & Tess: e♭3-a♭4   f3-c4
  Remarks: Sustained in moderate tempo. Has slight element of declama-
    tion. Strong and climactic middle section with high passages. De-
    scending, subdued ending passage. Organistic accompaniment. Acc 2-
    3 (S)HF
  Occasions: Whitsunday (Pentecost). Trinity Sunday. General use.

BERNARD ROGERS
United States

Psalm 68   Baritone
  Range & Tess: al-g3   c2-d3
  Remarks: First line - Let God arise, let His enemies be scattered.
    Extended song in varied tempi and moods. Has dramatic high passages.
    Joyous, exultant, majestic. Dramatic high ending on g3. Acc 4-5

ROREM

(S)SM
Occasions: Massed religious gatherings. New Year's Day. General use.

NED ROREM
United States

FSR Four Songs for Medium-High Voice and Piano. Ned Rorem. Boston: E.
    C. Schirmer Music Co.

Cycle of Holy Songs
Four songs for High Voice and Piano. Ned Rorem. New York: Southern Music Publishing Co. Note: Best for dramatic high voice.

(1) Psalm 134 (Behold, bless ye the Lord)
    Range & Tess: d3-g#4   e3-e4
    Remarks: Animated in moderate lively tempo. Stately, vigorous, and
       strong. Requires flexibility. Subdued ending. Acc 4
    Occasions: New Year's Eve. General use.

(2) Psalm 142 (I cried unto the Lord)
    Range & Tess: b2-g4   d3-d4
    Remarks: Sustained in moderate slow tempo. Requires fine high P and
       flexibility. Has climactic high passages. Subdued high ending.
       Acc 3-4
    Occasions: Evening services. General use.

(3) Psalm 148 (Praise ye the Lord)
    Range & Tess: c3-g4   d3-e4
    Remarks: Animated in rapid tempo. Spirited, vigorous. Requires some
       flexibility and fluent enunciation. Has passages with considerable
       dramatic intensity. Vocally demanding. Dramatic ending. Acc 4
    Occasions: Festivals. Massed religious gatherings. General use.

(4) Psalm 150 (Praise ye the Lord)
    Range & Tess: d3-a4   f#3-g4
    Remarks: Sustained in moderate tempo. Stately, quite vigorous in
       parts. Starts strongly. Requires considerable dramatic intensity.
       Has impressive quasi-chant ending. Acc 3-4
    Occasions: Massed religious gatherings. Festivals. New Year's Day or
       the Sunday after. General use.

Single Songs

A Christmas carol   All Voices
   Text: Anonymous, c.1500.
   Range & Tess: c3-f4   e3-d4
   Remarks: Sustained in moderate lively tempo. Plaintive, generally subdued. Has unaccompanied passages. Acc 2-3 (S)EV
   Occasions: Christmas. Christmas Eve programs and services.

A psalm of praise   High, Medium Voices
  Text: Psalm 100.
  Range & Tess: c3-g4   g3-d4
  Remarks: Animated in fast tempo, with variations. Rhythmically vigor-
    ous. Requires fluent enunciation. Has 5/8 and 7/8 meters, declama-
    tory passages, frequent meter changes. Vigorous climax. In contem-
    porary vein. Acc 3-4 (S)AM
  Occasions: General use. Thanksgiving. New Year's Day. Festivals.

A song of David   High Voice
  Text: Psalm 120.
  Range & Tess: d3-g4   d3-c4
  Remarks: Sustained in moderate slow tempo. Generally subdued, with one
    short, climactic passage. Subdued ending section. Acc 3 (S)AM
  Occasions: Evening services. Special use with sermon theme. General
    use.

Alleluia   Soprano
  Text: Alleluia.
  Range & Tess: b2-g#4   f#3-f#4
  Remarks: Best for dramatic soprano voice. Animated in fast tempo. Vig-
    orous, dramatic, brilliant, in uneasy mood. Has florid passages.
    Effective ending. In 7/8 meter. Acc 4-5 (S)HM
  Occasions: Christmas. Easter.

An angel speaks to the shepherds   High Voice
  Text: Luke 2:9-15.
  Range & Tess: d3-ab4   e3-e4
  Remarks: Very sustained in slow tempo. Has some soaring lines. Inter-
    pretatively not easy. Narrative, requires considerable dramatic in-
    tensity. Subdued ending. Acc 4 (S)SM
  Occasion: Christmas.

The resurrection   High Voice
  Text: Matthew 27:62-66,28.
  Range & Tess: bb2-ab4   eb3-eb4
  Remarks: An extended dramatic narrative. In varied tempi and moods.
    Mostly declamatory. Requires dramatic intensity. Slow ending sec-
    tion. Acc 4 (S)SM
  Occasions: Easter. Special use with sermon theme.

Note: Other sacred songs by Ned Rorem, reviewed in the second edition
  of this book - 1. Cradle song (S)CP; 2. The Lord's Prayer (S)HR; 3.
  The mild mother, FSR.

GIOACCHINO ROSSINI
1792-1868, Italy

Through the darkness   Baritone, Bass
  Work: STABAT MATER. Liturgical Latin, with English version.
  Range & Tess: al-e3   c#2-c3
  Remarks: Generally sustained vocal part in moderate tempo. Has animat-
    ed sections, dramatic passages, florid figures. Requires some flex-
    ibility. Acc 3-4 (VS)GS
  Occasions: General use. Evening services. Massed religious gatherings.

ALEC ROWLEY
1892-1958, England

A Cycle of Three Mystical Songs
A cycle for High Voice and Piano (or Organ). Texts from traditional
sources. Accompaniment level, 3. London: Boosey & Co.

(1) Three jolly shepherds
    Range & Tess: d3-g4   f#3-f#4
    Remarks: Animated in lively tempo. Rhythmic, requires fluent enun-
      ciation, and a light tone. Subdued ending.
    Occasions: Christmas Eve programs and services.

(2) The prophecy
    Range & Tess: e3-g4   f#3-f4
    Remarks: Sustained in moderate tempo. Has climactic passages. Cli-
      mactic high ending.
    Occasions: Christmas. Epiphany.

(3) The birthday
    Range & Tess: e3-a4   e3-g4
    Remarks: Sustained in moderate lively tempo. The 2nd half is a
      strong, vigorous, and climactic "Allelujah" section, with F and
      FF indications. Dramatic high ending.
    Occasion: Christmas.

EDMUND RUBBRA
England

FSR Four Short Songs for Medium Voice. Edmund Rubbra. London: Alfred
    Lengnick & Co., 1976.
TSR Two Songs for Voice and Harp (or Piano). Edmund Rubbra. London:
    Alfred Lengnick & Co., 1953.

Three Psalms for Low Voice
Songs for Contralto or Bass. Op. 61. London: Alfred Lengnick & Co.

(1) Psalm 6 (O Lord, rebuke me not)
    Range & Tess: f#2-e♭4   c3-c4

Remarks: Sustained in slow tempo. Rhythmically intricate, follows speech flow. Has some quasi-recitative passages and dramatic phrases. Requires fluent enunciation and fine P & PP. Acc 3-4
Occasions: Special use with sermon theme - Supplication. General use.

(2) Psalm 23 (The Lord is my shepherd)
Range & Tess: a2-d4   d3-c4
Remarks: Sustained in moderate slow tempo. Rhythmically intricate, follows speech flow. Requires fluent enunciation and flexibility. Has climactic passages. Acc 4
Occasions: Evening services. New Year's Day. Memorial services. General use.

(3) Psalm 150 (Praise ye the Lord)
Range & Tess: b♭2-f4   e3-d4
Remarks: Animated in lively tempo. Vigorous, has dramatic passages. Requires considerable flexibility. Imposing and strong ending. Acc 3-4
Occasions: Festivals. Trinity Sunday. General use.

Two Sonnets by William Alabaster
A diptych for Medium Voice, Viola and Piano. Op. 87. London: Alfred Lengnick & Co. Text is in Old English.

(1) Upon the crucifix
Range & Tess: c#3-e4   f#3-c4
Remarks: Sustained in slow tempo. Generally on MF level. Has some climactic passages and a very subdued, descending ending line which moves without interruption into the next song or second part.
(2) On the reed of our Lord's passion
Range & Tess: a2-f♭4   f3-c4
Remarks: Starts gently, then moves into varied dynamics. Has climactic passages on the peaks of vocal lines. In parlando style. Has frequent changes in meter without affecting note values (istesso tempo). Acc for both songs Piano 3 Viola 3
Occasions for both songs: Lent. Good Friday.

Single Songs

A Duan of Barra   High Voice
   Text: Murdoch Maclean.
   Range & Tess: d3-g4   e3-e4
   Remarks: Sustained in moderate tempo. Delicate and subdued. Requires fine P. Quasi-sacred text. Acc 3 (S)LK
   Occasion: Special use with sermon theme.

RUBBRA

A hymn to the Virgin   High Voice
    Text: Anonymous Medieval.
    Range & Tess: d3-g4   e3-e4
    Remarks: Sustained in slow tempo. Generally subdued, has frequent me-
        ter changes, requires some free movement of lines, has some brief
        florid figures. Subdued descending ending. Acc 3 TSR
    Occasions: Advent. Christmas.

Jesukin   High Voice
    Text: St. Ita, 480-570 A.D.
    Range & Tess: e3-f#4   f#3-e4
    Remarks: Slightly animated, has one strong passage, generally subdued.
        Irregular meter; subdued low ending. Acc harp or piano 3 TSR
    Occasions: Epiphany. General use.

Rosa Mundi   Medium Voice
    Text: Rachel Annand Taylor.
    Range & Tess: d3-e♭4   a3-d4
    Remarks: Sustained in moderate slow tempo. Generally on MF level. Re-
        quires simplicity. Has one climactic high passage. Accompaniment
        for keyboard or violins playing in two parts. Symbolic texts. Acc 3
        FSR
    Occasion: Lent.

The mystery   All Voices
    Text: Ralph Hodgson.
    Range & Tess: f3-e4   f3-c4
    Remarks: A short, unaccompanied song in slow tempo. Generally on MF
        level; descending ending after strong, high climax. FSR
    Occasion: General use.

                                JOHN RUTTER
                                  England

Shepherd's pipe carol   High Voice
    Text: John Rutter.
    Range & Tess: c3-g4   f3-e4
    Remarks: Joyous, light, in lively tempo. Requires fine diction and
        flexibility. Has some quick meter changes. Subdued high ending. Acc
        3 (S)OX
    Occasions: Christmas Eve programs and services. Christmas or the
    Sunday after.

                            CAMILLE SAINT-SAËNS
                             1835-1921, France

In my heart I believe, O Lord   Tenor (Soprano)
    Work: CHRISTMAS ORATORIO, 1863.
    Range & Tess: f3-a4   a3-f4

Remarks: Sustained in moderate tempo. Very lyric, has high tessitura.
   Has climactic high passages. There are brief choral passages for
   treble voices.Very fine as solo introit, especially before and after The Creed. Acc 3 (VS)GS
Occasion: General use.

Patiently have I waited for the Lord   Mezzo-Soprano, Contralto
   Work: CHRISTMAS ORATORIO. Text of the excerpt: Psalm 40:1.
   Range & Tess: b2-f#4   e3-c#4
   Remarks: Sustained in moderate slow tempo. Graceful. Generally on MF
      level. Acc 3 (VS)GS
Occasions: General use. Evening services.

ALESSANDRO SCARLATTI
1660-1725, Italy

O humble city of Bethlehem (O di Betlemme altera)   Soprano
   Text: Cardinal Antonio Ottoboni. English by Edward Dent.
   Range & Tess: c3-a4   a3-e4
   Remarks: A Christmas solo cantata in 3 movements, each with a recita-
      tive and arioso. Has some florid figures and a climactic ending.
      Fine English version. Accompaniment: string quartet and continuo.
      Acc 3-4 (SC)OX
Occasions: Christmas or the Sunday before.

JOHANN HERMANN SCHEIN
1586-1630, Germany

Holy Redeemer   High Voice
   Text: Anonymous.
   Range & Tess: d3-g4   e3-d4
   Remarks: Sustained in moderate tempo. Has some rhythmic complexities.
      In quasi-recitative style. Organ accompaniment, with violin obbliga-
      to. English version by Georgia Otto and Richard Gore. English and
      German texts. Acc 3 (S)CY
Occasions: Lent. Maundy Thursday. Good Friday. General use.

FRANZ SCHUBERT
1797-1828, Austria

Ave Maria   Women's Voices
   Text: Sir Walter Scott, from "The Lady of the Lake". English adapta-
      tion by Theodore Baker.
   Range & Tess: high, f#3-f#4 a#3-d#4   medium, e♭3-e♭4 g3-c4
                           low, d♭3-d♭4 f3-b♭3
   Remarks: Sustained in very slow tempo. Requires some flexibility. Ge-
      nerally on MF level, no strong climaxes. Acc 3-4 52S. (S)GS-3
      keys, CF-3 keys
Occasion: General use.

SCHUBERT

Christmas song of the shepherds (Weihnachtslied der Hirten) All Voices
  Text: Christof F. D. Schubert.
  Range & Tess: b♭2-c4 e♭3-c4
  Remarks: Gently animated in moderate slow tempo. Subdued, graceful,
    gentle. Very subdued refrain. Original key. 3 verses. Acc 3 CPS
  Occasions: Christmas. Christmas Eve programs and services.

Every sorrow (Sohn des Vaters)   Baritone, Bass
  Work: STABAT MATER. Text, translated from the Latin hymn.
  Range & Tess: g1-e3 e2-c3
  Remarks: Sustained in moderate slow tempo. Requires flexibility. Has
    some wide intervalic skips. High climaxes and a subdued, descending
    ending line. Acc 3-4 (VS)BH
  Occasions: Lent. Good Friday. General use.

Gazing on the crucifixion (Bei des Mittlers Kreuze)   Soprano
  Work: STABAT MATER. See first entry.
  Range & Tess: f3-a♭4 b♭3-f4
  Remarks: Sustained in moderate slow tempo. Has climactic high passages
    and a climactic ending. Acc 3-4 (VS)BH
  Occasions: Good Friday. Lent.

Litany (Litanei)   All Voices
  Text: J. C. Jacobi. English version by Lloyd Pfautsch.
  Range & Tess: high, c3-e♭4 e♭3-c4 low, b♭2-d♭4 d♭3-b♭3
  Remarks: Very sustained in slow tempo. Generally subdued. Not for
    light, high voices. Acc 3 SCY
  Occasions: Funerals.

May the fervent contemplation (Ach, was hätten wir empfunden)   Tenor
  Work: STABAT MATER. See first entry.
  Range & Tess: g3-a♭4 c3-g4
  Remarks: Sustained in slow tempo. High tessitura in some passages. Re-
    quires good command of high notes. Short. Acc 3-4 (VS)BH
  Occasions: Good Friday. Lent.

O how lovely is Thy world (Im Abendrot)   All Voices
  Text: Carl Lappe. English by Mack Harrell.
  Range & Tess: high, e3-f#4 a3-e4 medium, c3-d4 f3-c4
  Remarks: Very sustained in slow tempo. Subdued, requires fine PP and
    simplicity. Acc 3 SHS, POS-1, FSS
  Occasions: General use. Evening services.

Omnipotence (Die Allmacht)   All Voices
  Text: Johann L. Pyrker. English by Willis Wager.
  Range & Tess: high, c3-a4(b♭4) a♭3-f4 low, g2-e4(f4) e♭3-c4
  Remarks: Very sustained in slow tempo. Majestic, vigorous, dramatic.
    Has some low tessitura. Not vocally easy. Not for light, high voic-
    es. Dramatic ending. Acc 3-4 FSS. (S)GS-high only

Occasions: General use. Massed religious gatherings. Evangelistic
services. New Year's Day. Easter.

To the infinite God (Dem Unendlichen)   All Voices
  Text: Friedrich G. Klopstock. English by Mack Harrell.
  Range & Tess: high, bb2-ab4 eb3-eb4 low, ab2-gb4 db3-db4
  Remarks: Dramatic recitative and a sustained, majestic, vigorous sec-
    tion in moderate tempo. Imposing, climactic ending. Difficult. Not
    for light, high voices. Acc 4-5 SHS
  Occasions: General use. New Year's Day.

HEINRICH SCHÜTZ
1585-1672, Germany

FSS Five Sacred Songs. Heinrich Schütz. High Voice and Piano or Organ.
     German texts with fine English versions. Edited by Richard Gore.
     St. Louis: Concordia Publishing House. Note: The songs are not
     too high for Medium and some Low Voices. May also be transposed.
3SC 3 Short Sacred Concertos. Heinrich Schütz. In two editions: German
     text, and English text. Edited by Arnold Mendelssohn. Frankfurt &
     New York: C. F. Peters.
5SC 5 Short Sacred Concertos. Heinrich Schütz. In two editions: German
     text, and English text. Edited by Heinrich Spitta. Frankfurt & New
     York: C. F. Peters.

Be not afraid   Soprano
  Work: THE CHRISTMAS STORY, oratorio. Text of excerpt: Luke 2:10-12.
  Range & Tess: d3-e4 g3-e4
  Remarks: Sustained in moderate lively tempo. Graceful. Has florid pas-
    sages, climactic passages, and ends on a long-held note with 21
    beats plus fermata. An admirable setting of the angel's song to the
    shepherds. Acc 3 (VS)GS
  Occasion: Christmas.

Bring to Jehovah (Bringt her dem Herren)   All Voices
  Text: Psalm 29:1,2; 66:4.
  Range & Tess: d3-f4 eb3-eb4
  Remarks: Has sustained as well as animated sections. Bright, has flor-
    id passages, impressive "alleluia" passages, and a climactic ending.
    Acc 3 FSS, 5SC
  Occasions: New Year's Day or the Sunday after. Reformation Sunday.
    Missions Sunday. General use.

Haste Thee, Lord God, haste to save me   All Voices
(Eile, mich, Gott, zu erretten)
  Text: Psalm 40:13-17 or Psalm 70:1-5.
  Range & Tess: c3-g4 e3-d4
  Remarks: Sustained in varied tempi. Has declamatory passages, drama-
    tic phrases, and a slow, subdued ending. One step higher in 5SC.

    Acc 3 FSS, 5SC
  Occasion: General use.

How hast Thou offended (Was hast du verwirket)   All Voices
  Text: St. Augustine's Meditations.
  Range & Tess: db3-f4   f3-eb4
  Remarks: Mostly declamatory in moderate slow tempo. Has dramatic pas-
    sages. Not easy. An impressive setting. One step higher in 3SC.
    Acc 3 FSS, 3SC
  Occasions: Good Friday. Lent. Evening services.

Now will I praise the Lord with all my heart   All Voices
(Ich danke dem Herren loben allezeit)
  Text: Psalm 34:1-7.
  Range & Tess: c3-g4   g3-d4
  Remarks: Animated in moderate tempo. Bright, joyful, in recitative
    style. Has florid passages and an impressive "alleluia" section.
    Acc 3 FSS, 5SC
  Occasions: New Year's Day. Massed religious gatherings. Missions Sun-
    day. Installation for missionary service. Easter. Evangelistic ser-
    vices. General use.

O God, I will praise Thee (Ich danke dem Herrn)   All Voices
  Text: Psalm 111.
  Range & Tess: c3-f4   g3-e4
  Remarks: Sustained in generally slow tempo. Has rhythmic complexi-
    ties, climactic and florid passages, and an imposing and stately
    climax. Title in 5SC: I sing to the Lord. Acc 3 FSS,5SC
  Occasions: Massed religious gatherings. Thanksgiving. Installation
    for missionary service. National holidays. Reformation Sunday.
    Ascension Sunday. Memorial services.

O God, my heart is ready (Paratum cor meum)   Medium Voice
  Text: Latin hymn. English version by W. K. Stanton.
  Range & Tess: d3-f4   f3-e4
  Remarks: Sustained in generally moderate tempo. Graceful, rhythmic,
    bright, exultant. Has florid passages and an impressive ending.
    From "Symphoniae Sacrae", 1629. Acc 3 (SC)HI
  Occasions: New Year's Day. National holidays. Reformation Sunday.
    Ascension Sunday. Dedication of music facilities. Installation of
    church officers or Pastor. Installation for missionary service.

O Jesu, name most lovely (Vom Namen Jesu)   All Voices
  Text: Anonymous. English version by Jean Lunn.
  Range & Tess: d3-f4   g3-d4
  Remarks: Sustained in moderate tempo. Bright, in recitative style.
    Has climactic passages and florid phrases. Requires some flexibili-
    ty. May be transposed for lower voices. Acc 3 3SC
  Occasions: Evening services. Special use in services of personal de-

dication. General use.

O most kind and most merciful Jesu   All Voices
(O du allerbarmherzigster Jesu)
   Text: Anonymous. English version by Jean Lunn.
   Range & Tess: c3-g4   f3-d4
   Remarks: Sustained in moderate tempo. In recitative style. Has cli-
      mactic passages, phrases with some emotional intensity, and a sub-
      dued ending. May be transposed. Acc 3 3SC
   Occasions: Evening services. General use.

O tender, O bountiful, O kind and gracious Lord Jesus Christ
(O süsser Herr Jesu Christe)   All Voices
   Text: St. Augustine's Meditations.
   Range & Tess: c3-g4   f3-eb4
   Remarks: Sustained in slow tempo. In gentle recitative style. Has cli-
      mactic passages and florid figures. Requires fine P. May be trans-
      posed. Acc 3 5SC
   Occasions: Easter. New Year's Day. Special use in services of person-
      al dedication. Ascension Sunday. General use.

Wedding song   All Voices
   Text: Ruth 1:16,17.
   Range & Tess: high, f3-f4 g3-d4   low, d3-d4 e3-b3
   Remarks: Sustained in moderate slow tempo. Requires simplicity. Two
      verses, each preceded and ended with ritornelli. Gentle, generally
      on MF level. See Birch, Cassler, Engel, Gore, Peeters. Acc 2-3
      (S)CY
   Occasions: Weddings.

                          ROGER SESSIONS
                          United States

Psalm 140   High Voice
   Range & Tess: db3-b4   g3-g4
   Remarks: Sustained in varied tempi and moods. Has dramatic high pas-
      sages, quasi-recitatives, climactic ending on a4. Requires fine P &
      PP. Extended festive solo with organ accompaniment. Not for light
      voices. Orchestra version available. Acc 4-5 (S)EM
   Occasions: Massed religious gatherings. Festivals. New Year's Day. Ge-
      neral use.

                          ALLEN SHAWN
                          United States

Thou wilt keep him in perfect peace   Medium Voice
   Text: Isaiah 26:3,4,12.
   Range & Tess: bb2-f4   e3-c#4
   Remarks: Sustained in moderate slow tempo. Generally on MF level. Has
      some slight climaxes, dissonances, subdued high ending. Requires

                               133

flexibility for the wide intervalic skips. See Thiman. Acc 3-4 ESS
Occasions: General use. World Brotherhood Sunday.

JEAN SIBELIUS
1865-1957, Finland

There comes another morrow   All Voices
   Text: Geoffrey O'Hara.
   Range & Tess: high, ab3-f4   ab3-eb4 low, f3-d4 f3-c4
   Remarks: An arrangement from "Finlandia". Sustained in moderate slow
     tempo. The text of the hymn arrangement "Be still, my soul" may be
     used instead of O'Hara's sometimes careless prosody. Acc 3 (S)RH
Occasions: General use. Funerals.

MAX SINZHEIMER
United States

Blessed are those who fear the Lord   Contralto, Baritone
   Text: Psalm 128.
   Range & Tess: d3-f4   f3-d4
   Remarks: Uses motives from the chorale "Erhalt' uns, Herr". Declama-
     tory, unmeasured. First section in moderate lively tempo on MF lev-
     el. Second section very subdued in moderate tempo. Acc 3 (S)CO
Occasion: General use.

TIM SMITH
United States

Jesus! the name high over all   Medium Voice
   Text: Charles Wesley, 1707-1788.
   Range & Tess: c3-e4   e3-c4
   Remarks: Sustained in moderate tempo. Broader second half with key
     change. Starts and ends subdued. Full-sounding start in the second
     half. Acc 3 (S)CO
Occasion: General use.

LEO SOWERBY
1895-1968, United States

I will lift up mine eyes   Medium Voice
   Text: Psalm 121.
   Range & Tess: b2-e4   d3-d4
  Remarks: Sustained in slow tempo. Has some long phrases, and a fairly
     subdued ending section. Generally contemplative. See Dvorak, Gober,
     and "Watchful's song" by Vaughan Williams. Organ accompaniment.
     Acc 3 (S)HG
  Occasions: Installation for missionary service. Installation of
    church officers or Pastor. General use.

Little Jesus, sweetly sleep　　　　　　　　　　　　　　　　All Voices
　　Text: Czech carol. English by Percy Dearmer.
　　Range & Tess:　d3-f4　f3-d4
　　Remarks: Sustained in slow tempo. Requires simplicity. Gentle, gener-
　　　ally subdued lullaby.　Acc 3　(S)FS
　　Occasions: Christmas Eve programs and services.

O be joyful in the Lord　　　　　　　　　　　　　　　　Medium Voice
　　Text: Psalm 100.
　　Range & Tess:　c3-eb4　f3-d4
　　Remarks: Animated in fast tempo. Vigorous, has climactic passages.
　　　Bright and outgoing.　Acc 4　(S)HG
　　Occasion: General use.

O perfect love　　　　　　　　　　　　　　　　　　　　All Voices
　　Text: Dorothy Frances Gurney.
　　Range & Tess:　high,　eb3-ab4　eb3-eb4　low,　c3-f4　c3-c4
　　Remarks: Sustained in slow tempo. Has some effective climaxes. Climac-
　　　tic ending. In lush, romantic style. See Barnby, Nystedt, Wetherill.
　　　Acc 3　(S)HG
　　Occasions: Weddings. General use.

The Lord is my shepherd　　　　　　　　　　　　　　　　　　Bass
　　Text: Psalm 23.
　　Range & Tess:　f1-db3　c2-bb3
　　Remarks: Sustained in slow tempo, with slightly more animated section.
　　　Generally subdued. Has some low tessitura and a high, dramatic cli-
　　　max.　Acc 3-4　(S)HG
　　Occasions: Evening services. New Year's Eve. Memorial services. Gen-
　　　eral use.

Whoso dwelleth　　　　　　　　　　　　　　　　　　　Medium Voice
　　Text: Psalm 91.
　　Range & Tess:　a2-f#4　e3-d#4
　　Remarks: Sustained in moderate slow tempo. Quasi-recitative. Requires
　　　flexibility, fluent and rapid enunciation, and fine command of high
　　　PP. Has climactic passages, some low tessitura, and a very subdued
　　　ending.　Acc 3　(S)HG
　　Occasions: New Year's Day or the Sunday after. General use.

JOHN STAINER
1840-1901, England

My hope is in the everlasting　　　　　　　　　　　　　High Voice
　　Work: THE DAUGHTER OF JAIRUS, cantata 1878.
　　Range & Tess:　d#3-ab4　ab3-f4
　　Remarks: Generally sustained in moderate slow tempo; faster middle
　　　section. Varied and contrasty dynamics from PP to FF. High climactic
　　　passages. Subdued beginning and ending. Theme: Joy and hope in the

STARER

Saviour. Acc 3-4 52S
Occasions: Memorial services. Festivals. Massed religious gatherings.
General use.

ROBERT STARER
United States

TSS Two Sacred Songs. Robert Starer. High Voice and Piano. New York:
Southern Music Publishing Co.

Give thanks unto the Lord   High Voice
Text: Psalm 136:1-9.
Range & Tess: c3-a4   g3-f4
Remarks: Animated in fast tempo. Light, generally on MF level. Re-
quires fine P. Has some strong phrases and a majestic climax. Acc
3-4 TSS
Occasions: Thanksgiving. New Year's Day or the Sunday after. Massed
religious gatherings. General use.

Have mercy upon me, O Lord   High Voice
Text: Psalm 31:1,9,10,15,16.
Range & Tess: d3-g4   f#3-d4
Remarks: Sustained in moderate tempo. Generally gentle; also has some
climactic passages. Requires fine PP. Has some quasi-recitative
passages. Subdued final phrase. Acc 3 TSS
Occasions: Evening services. General use.

THEODORE STEARNS
1875-1935, United States

I lift up mine eyes   Medium, High Voices
Text: Psalm 121:1-4, paraphrase.
Range & Tess: c3-f4   f3-d♭4
Remarks: Sustained in slow tempo. Generally on MF level. Subdued
high ending. Lyric in style, no strong or climactic passages. Not
for light, high voices. Organistic accompaniment. Acc 3 (S)CM
Occasions: Installation for missionary service. Installation of
church officers or Pastor. General use.

WILLIAM STICKLES
United States

Grant me, dear Lord, deep peace of mind   All Voices
Text: Helen Boardman Knox.
Range & Tess: high, e♭3-g4 g3-e♭4   low, c3-e4 e3-c4
Remarks: Sustained in moderate tempo. Slightly faster middle section.
Has some climactic high passages and a subdued low ending. Also in
the publisher's "Sacred Songs Especially Suited for Christian
Science Services"; High, Low. Acc 3 (S)RH

136

Occasions: Evening services. Funerals. Special use in services of personal dedication.

ALESSANDRO STRADELLA
c.1645-1682, Italy

O Lord, have mercy (Pieta, Signore!)   All Voices
  Text: Anonymous. English by H. Millard.
  Range & Tess: high, c3-f4 g3-eb4   low, a2-d4 e3-c4
  Remarks: Sustained in moderate slow tempo. Has some climactic passages.
    Requires flexibility. Ends on lowest note in descending vocal line.
    A prayer of penitence. Acc 3 24I, ARB
  Occasions: Lent. Evening services.

ARTHUR SULLIVAN
1842-1900, England

And God shall wipe away all tears   Mezzo-Soprano
  Work: THE LIGHT OF THE WORLD, oratorio. Texts by the composer.
  Range & Tess: b2-e4   d#3-b3
  Remarks: Sustained in moderate slow tempo. Starts strongly with "The
    Lord is risen". Has some very gentle as well as climactic passages.
    Subdued low ending. Chordal accompaniment. Acc 3 52S
  Occasion: Easter or the Sunday after.

The Lord is risen   Mezzo-Soprano, Contralto
  Work: THE LIGHT OF THE WORLD. See first entry.
  Range & Tess: b2-e4   d#3-b3
  Remarks: Sustained in moderate slow tempo. Has climactic passages. Majestic, with strong starting phrase. Acc 3 ASS-A
  Occasions: Easter or the Sunday after.

CONRAD SUSA
United States

Hymns for the Amusement of Children
A set of six songs in contemporary vein with semi-popular rhythms thrown
in. Text by Christopher Smart, 1722-1771. For Medium Voice and Harpsichord or Piano. Boston: E. C. Schirmer Music Co. All are musically
difficult, not intended to be sung by young people. Only the first, second and sixth are given here.

(1) For Sunday   Medium Voice
  Range & Tess: c3-g4 f3-d4
  Remarks: In gentle calypso rhythm, moderately slow. Requires considerable flexibility and rhythmic sensitivity. Generally on MF level
    with some climactic passages. Acc 4-5
  Occasion: Easter for children.

(2) At dressing in the morning   Medium Voice
    Range & Tess: b2-f#4   e3-c#4
    Remarks: Animated in blues style, with strong beat and prominent
      bass figures in the accompaniment. Vocal part is generally strong
      and outgoing. Climactic ending section. Acc 4-5
    Occasion: Children's Day.

(6) The conclusion of the matter   Medium Voice
    Range & Tess: c3-f4   eb3-d4
    Remarks: Animated in slow tempo. Gently rhythmic, subdued through-
      out, requires flexibility. Slower ending on descending line with
      soft melisma on "Hosanah!" Acc 4-5
    Occasion: General use.

ROBERT F. SWIFT
United States

Hast thou not known?   Medium Voice
  Text: Isaiah 40:28-31.
  Range & Tess: c3-f4   f3-d4
  Remarks: Sustained in moderate slow tempo. Faster middle section. Has
    some climactic high passages. Subdued ending. In gentle recitative
    style. Has dissonances. Organistic accompaniment. Acc 3 ESS
  Occasions: Special use with sermon theme - Trust in God. Evangelistic
    services. General use.

RAYNOR TAYLOR
1747-1825, United States

The Lord my shepherd is   All Voices
  Text: Psalm 23, paraphrase.
  Range & Tess: b2-e4   e3-c4
  Remarks: Sustained in moderate tempo. Generally on MF level. May be
    transposed for higher voices. Acc 3 SEA
  Occasions: Evening services. Funerals. Memorial services. General use.

PIOTR ILYICH TCHAIKOVSKY
1840-1893, Russia

Prayer (Lord, Almighty God)   High Voice
  Work: MOSCOW CANTATA. Text by Apollon N. Maikof, English by Stewart
    Wille.
  Range & Tess: ab2(cb3)-ab4(fb4)   eb3-eb4
  Remarks: Starts sustained in slow tempo; slightly animated middle sec-
    tion. Imposing climaxes. Requires some dramatic intensity. Arpeg-
    giated accompaniment. Acc 3-4 (S)GA
  Occasion: General use.

GEORG PHILIPP TELEMANN
1681-1767, Germany

Alleluia   All Voices
   Text: Alleluia.
   Range & Tess: c#3-e4   e3-d4
   Remarks: Animated in quite fast tempo. Florid, joyous. Requires flexi-
      bility and lightness of tone. Climactic ending. Acc 3 TMB
   Occasions: Easter. Christmas. General use.

ERIC H. THIMAN
England

TCS   The Church Soloist by Eric H. Thiman. High or Medium Voice. Lon-
      don: Novello & Co., 1981.
TSS   Two Sacred Songs for Low Voice. Eric H. Thiman. London: Novello &
      Co., 1954.

In the bleak midwinter   High Voice
   Text: Christina G. Rossetti.
   Range & Tess: c3-g4   f3-d4
   Remarks: Sustained in moderate tempo. Generally subdued, requires fine
      P & PP, has "floating" lines. Subdued, slower ending. Best for light,
      lyric voices. Acc 3-4 TCS
   Occasions: Christmas. Christmas Eve programs and services.

Jesus, the very thought of Thee   Medium, Low Voices
   Text: Bernard of Clairvaux.
   Range & Tess: medium high, d3-f#4 d3-e4 low, bb2-d4 bb2-c4
   Remarks: Sustained in moderate tempo. Generally on MF level. Has cli-
      mactic passages, frequent meter changes, and a descending ending
      line. Acc 3 TCS-medium, TSS & (S)NO-low
   Occasions: Palm Sunday. General use.

The God of love my shepherd is   All Voices
   Text: George Herbert.
   Range & Tess: high/medium, c3-f4 f3-eb4 low, a2-d4 d3-c4
   Remarks: Slightly animated in moderate lively tempo. Contrasting dy-
      namics from PP to FF. Soaring lines and climactic high ending. Acc
      3-4 TCS & (S)NO-medium high; TSS-low
   Occasion: General use.

The wilderness   Medium, Low Voices
   Text: Isaiah 35:1,2,6-8,10.
   Range & Tess: bb2-e4   eb3-c4
   Remarks: Sustained in moderate tempo. Has a faster and stronger mid-
      dle section. Requires some considerable dramatic intensity. Subdued
      ending. Acc 3-4 TCS
   Occasion: General use.

139

THIMAN

Thou wilt keep him in perfect peace   High Voice
   Text: Isaiah 26:3,4.
   Range & Tess: d3-g4   e3-c#4
   Remarks: Sustained in moderate slow tempo. Subdued except for one
      high climactic passage. Requires calm, assured delivery, and sim-
      plicity. Generally chordal accompaniment, organistic. Issued also
      in low key. See Shawn. Acc 3-4 (S)HG
   Occasions: Evening services. Special use in services of personal ded-
      ication. Funerals. General use.

RANDALL THOMPSON
United States

Lullaby   Soprano
   Work: THE NATIVITY ACCORDING TO SAINT LUKE, musical drama. Text a-
      dapted by Richard Rowlands.
   Range & Tess: c3(bb2)-g4   f3-f4
   Remarks: First line - Upon my lap my Sov'reign sits. Sustained in mod-
      erate slow tempo. Gentle, subdued, has hummed passages. Gently-
      moving accompaniment. Extended prelude. Acc 3 (S)ES. (VS)ES
   Occasions: Christmas Eve programs and services. Christmas.

My Master hath a garden   All Voices
   Text: Anonymous.
   Range & Tess: eb3-eb4   f3-c4
   Remarks: Sustained in moderate tempo. Requires simplicity and fluent
      enunciation. Generally on MF level. See Virgil Thomson. Acc 3 (S)
      ES
   Occasions: Special use with sermon theme. General use.

My soul doth magnify the Lord   Soprano
   Work: THE NATIVITY ACCORDING TO SAINT LUKE. See first entry.
   Range & Tess: b2-g4   e3-e4
   Remarks: Other title - Magnificat. Sustained in varied slow to moder-
      ate tempi. Requires simplicity. Generally gentle, subdued, has flor-
      id passages. Acc 3-4 (S)ES. (VS)ES
   Occasions: Christmas Eve programs and services. Christmas.

VIRGIL THOMSON
United States

PAP Praises and Prayers for Medium Voice and Piano. Virgil Thomson. A
      set of five songs issued separately. New York: G. Schirmer, Inc.

Before sleeping   Medium Voice
   Text: Anonymous.
   Range & Tess: d3-d4   f3-c4
   Remarks: Sustained in moderate slow tempo. Requires simplicity. Sub-
      dued. The text is based on the child's prayer: Matthew, Mark, Luke

and John, bless the bed that I lie on. Acc 2-3 PAP
  Occasions: Evening services and prayer meetings. Children' Day.

Consider, Lord   Medium, Low Voices
  Text: John Donne.
  Range & Tess: bb2-d4   d3-c4
  Remarks: Sustained in slow tempo. Majestic. Useful as solo introit or
    before extended prayer. Acc 2-3 (S)SM
  Occasions: Baptism. Installation for missionary service. General use.

From The Canticle of the Sun   High, Medium Voices
  Text: Saint Francis of Assisi.
  Range & Tess: c#3-e4(f#4) g#3-d#4
  Remarks: First line - Most high, Omnipotent Lord. Sustained in moder-
    ate tempo. Generally strong, majestic. Subdued, descending and con-
    templative ending phrase after high climax. Acc 3-4 PAP
  Occasions: Thanksgiving. New Year's Day or the Sunday after. Massed
    religious gatherings. General use.

Jerusalem, my happy home   High, Medium Voices
  Text: from "The Meditations of Saint Augustine".
  Range & Tess: d3-f#4   f#3-e4
  Remarks: Animated in moderate tempo. Rhythmic, straightforward. Has
    climactic passages and a strong, climactic ending. Acc 3 PAP
  Occasion: Special use with sermon theme - The Holy City.

My Master hath a garden   High, Medium Voices
  Text: Anonymous.
  Range & Tess: f3-eb4   g3-eb4
  Remarks: Sustained in moderate tempo. Generally light, with some flor-
    id figures. Subdued ending. Gently agitated single line accompani-
    ment on each hand. See Randall Thompson. Acc 3 PAP. (S)GS
  Occasions: Special use with sermon theme. General use.

Sung by the shepherds   High, Medium Voices
  Text: Richard Crashaw.
  Range & Tess: d3-g4   e3-c4
  Remarks: Sustained in moderate tempo. Starts gently. Requires fine P
    & PP. Has climactic passages, dramatic ending section, and full
    chords in the accompaniment. Not for light voices. The tune is
    based on the Pange Lingua. Acc 3-4 PAP
  Occasions: Christmas Eve programs and services. Christmas.

See Thomson's setting of "My shepherd will supply my need" in Traditional Songs.

141

LOUISE C. TITCOMB
United States

Christ's healing power   High Voice
   Text: John Greenleaf Whittier.
   Range & Tess: f3-ab4   ab3-f4
   Remarks: Sustained, generally in moderate tempo with variations. Has
      quasi-recitative passages, varied dynamics, and a high dramatic end-
      ing. Acc 3-4 (S)CF
   Occasions: Installation of church officers or Pastor. Installation
      for missionary service. General use.

TRADITIONAL SACRED SONGS

TFC   Three French Carols. Arranged for unison voices by Gerald Cock-
         shott. Texts in French and English. Octavo edition, suitable as
         solos. London: Novello & Co.

A carol of Bethlehem   All Voices
   Source: France - Il est beau ce fils de Dieu le pere.
   Range & Tess: d3-c4   d3-b3
   Remarks: Sustained in moderate slow tempo. Graceful, generally sub-
      dued, 3 verses. Acc 1-2 TFC
   Occasions: Christmas Eve programs and services. Christmas.

A star in the sky   High, Medium Voices
   Source: Poland. English text by John H. Payne.
   Range & Tess: eb3-eb4   g3-c4
   Remarks: Slightly animated in moderate tempo. Graceful in 6/8 meter,
      dancelike. Generally on MF level, ends with "Amen" section. Setting
      by David N. Johnson. Acc 3 (S)AH
   Occasions: Christmas. Epiphany.

Amazing grace   All Voices
   Text: John Newton.
   Range & Tess: d3-d4   d3-b3
   Remarks: Sustained in moderate slow tempo. Generally on MF level.
      Gently rhythmic. Setting by John Coates, Jr. Acc 3 (S)SP, CF-½
      higher in last verse.
   Occasions: Special use with sermon theme: God's grace, finding the
      lost. Evangelistic services. General use.

At the river   All Voices
   Source: United States, text by Robert Lowry.
   Range & Tess: eb3-eb4   g3-c4
   Remarks: Sustained in moderate tempo. Hymn-like. Slightly majestic,
      marked "with dignity". Acc 3 OAS-2
   Occasions: Evangelistic services. Special use with sermon theme.

142

Carol of the birds   All Voices
   Source: Spain.
   Range & Tess: b2-e4   g3-d4
   Remarks: Gently animated in moderate tempo. Generally on MF level. Re-
      quires fine P. Acc 3 CSV
   Occasions: Christmas. Christmas Eve programs and services.

Carol of the crib   All Voices
   Source: France.
   Range & Tess: e3-e4   g3-e4
   Remarks: Sustained in moderate tempo. Gentle, subdued, except the
      strong ending. Three verses. Acc 1-2 TFC
   Occasions: Christmas. Christmas Eve programs and services.

His voice, as the sound of the dulcimer sweet   High, Medium Voices
   Source: Southern United States.
   Range & Tess: e3-f#4   a3-e4
   Remarks: Sustained in moderate tempo. Simple, quasi-modal. Setting by
      Robert Fairfax Birch. Acc 3 (S)TP
   Occasion: General use.

I wonder as I wander   All Voices
   Source: United States.
   Range & Tess: high, e♭3-g4   g3-e♭4   low, b♭2-d4   d3-b♭3
   Remarks: Sustained in moderate slow tempo. Requires fine P. Graceful,
      gentle. Setting by John Jacob Niles. Acc 3 (S)GS
   Occasions: Christmas Eve programs and services.

In Bethlehem, that fair city   All Voices
   Source: France - C'etait a l'heure de minuit.
   Range & Tess: d3-d4   d3-d4
   Remarks: Slightly animated and dancelike. Joyous, each verse ending
      with Alleluias. Acc 3 TFC
   Occasions: Christmas. Christmas Eve programs and services. Epiphany.

In heaven above, in heaven above (I himmelen, i himmelen)   All Voices
   Source: Norway. Text by Laurentius Laurinius (d.1655), Norwegian
      hymn writer.
   Range & Tess: e3-d4   e3-c#4
   Remarks: Folk-hymn from Heddal, site of Norway's largest stave-church.
      Sustained in moderate tempo, 4 verses. Acc 2-3 In: Norway Sings,
      Norsk Musikforlag, Oslo.
   Occasions: Special use with sermon theme - The Book of Revelation.
      General use.

Infant Jesus   All Voices
   Source: Poland.
   Range & Tess: c3-e♭4   g3-e♭4
   Remarks: Sustained in moderate slow tempo. Requires simplicity. Gen-

erally on MF level. Acc 2-3 CSV
Occasions: Christmas. Christmas Eve programs and services.

Jesu! Thou dear Babe divine   High, Medium Voices
   Source: Haiti. English text by Helen A. Dickinson.
   Range & Tess: eb3-f4   eb3-eb4
   Remarks: Sustained in moderate slow tempo. A gentle cradle song, gen-
      erally on MF level. Subdued final section. Low ending phrase. May
      be transposed. Setting by Dr. Clarence Dickinson. Acc 3 (S)HG
   Occasions: Christmas. Christmas Eve programs and services.

Jesus, Jesus rest your head   All Voices
   Source: North Carolina.
   Range & Tess: high, d3-g4 g3-e4   medium, bb2-eb4 eb3-c4
                                  low, g2-c4 c3-a3
   Remarks: Sustained in moderate tempo. Subdued, gentle, generally on
      MF level. Acc 2-3 (S)RR-arr., Edmunds; GS-arr.,John Jacob Niles,
      high and low. AEI-2
   Occasions: Christmas Eve programs and services. Christmas.

My shepherd will supply my need   All Voices
   Source: United States. Text, Psalm 23, metrical version by Isaac
      Watts.
   Range & Tess: d3-f#4   d3-d4
   Remarks: Sustained vocal part in moderate lively tempo. Strong final
      section with subdued, descending ending. Tune: Resignation, from
      William Walker's "Southern Harmony", 1854. Setting by Virgil Thom-
      son. Acc 3 (S)HG. TWB-one step lower
   Occasions: Evening services. Weddings. Memorial services. General use.

O leave your sheep (Quittez pasteurs)   All Voices
   Source: France. English version by "A. R."
   Range & Tess: high, d3-g4 g3-d4   medium, c3-f4 f3-c4
                                  low, bb2-eb4 eb3-bb3
   Remarks: Agitated in lively tempo. Requires lightness of tone and
      simplicity. Has some climactic high passages. Very subdued low end-
      ing with a long-sustained final note. Setting by Cecil Hazlehurst.
      Acc 3 (S)B-H
   Occasion: Epiphany.

Praise we the Lord   All Voices
   Source: England. Text by Sir Steuart Wilson.
   Range & Tess: high, f3-f4 f3-f4   low, d3-d4 d3-d4
   Remarks: Animated in lively tempo. Strong, outgoing, exultant. Adapt-
      ed by John Edmunds from Oxford Book of Carols. Acc 3 (S)RR. AEI-2
   Occasions: Thanksgiving. New Year's Day. Massed religious gatherings.

Simple gifts   All Voices
   Source: United States. Traditional Shaker song.

Range & Tess: eb3-eb4   ab3-eb4
Remarks: Sustained in moderate slow tempo. Generally on MF level. Re-
   quires simplicity and straightforward treatment. Setting by Aaron
   Copland. Now included in some hymnals. See this melody in a lively
   setting "Lord of the dance", words by Sydney Carter, No. 426, TWB.
   Acc 3 AEI-1. (S)B-H
Occasions: General use. Children's Day.

Sweet was the song the Virgin sang   High Voice
   Source: Southern United States. Text by William Ballet(?), 17th cent.
   Range & Tess: c3-f4   f3-eb4
   Remarks: Sustained in moderate slow tempo. Tranquil, gentle, requires
      fine P & PP. Very subdued, descending ending line. Setting by David
      H. Johnson.   Acc 3 (S)AH
   Occasions: Christmas Eve programs and services. Christmas.

Wexford carol   All Voices
   Source: England.
   Range & Tess: d3-d4(f#4)   g3-d4
   Remarks: Animated in moderate lively tempo. Vigorous, bright, has a
      climactic ending. Setting by John Edmunds in RR and Philip Maue in
      HF. Acc 3 (S)RR, HF
   Occasions: Christmas. Christmas Eve programs and services.

What Child is this   All Voices
   Source: England. "Greensleeves" melody, text by William C. Dix.
   Range & Tess: b2-d4   e3-d4
   Remarks: Sustained in moderate tempo. Has some slightly strong pas-
      sages. Graceful. Acc 3 PHP, TWB. (S)Pembroke Music Co., New York
   Occasions: Christmas. Christmas Eve programs and services.

When Jesus left His Father's throne   All Voices
   Source: Southern United States. Folktune: Fairfield. Text by James
      Montgomery, 1816, subst.
   Range & Tess: d3-d4(f4)   f3-d4
   Remarks: Sustained in moderate slow tempo. Generally on MF level. Sub-
      dued descending ending line. Setting by David N. Johnson. Acc 3
      (S)AH
   Occasions: General use. Children's Day or Youth Sunday.

While shepherds watched their flocks by night   All Voices
   Source: United States. Text by Nahum Tate.
   Range & Tess: a2-e4   e3-c#4
   Remarks: Gently animated in moderate slow tempo. Graceful, generally
      on MF level. Descending ending line. May be transposed. Setting by
      Gordon Myers. Acc 3 SEA
   Occasions: Christmas. Christmas Eve programs and services.

FRANZ TUNDER
1614-1667, England

Wake, awake   High, Medium Voices
   Text: Philip Nicolai.
   Range & Tess: high, f3-bb4 f3-g4 medium, d3-g4 d3-e4
   Remarks: Sustained in moderate tempo. Majestic, with strong beginning.
      Has some high tessitura, climactic passages, climactic high ending.
      Requires fine P. Acc 3 (S)HG
   Occasions: Advent. Special use with sermon theme - The coming of the
      Bridegroom. General use.

RALPH VAUGHAN WILLIAMS
1872-1958, England

Five Mystical Songs
A cycle of five songs for Baritone and Orchestra (or Piano or Organ).
Texts by George Herbert. Has choral parts as background material. Lon-
don: Stainer & Bell. Note: Mezzo-Sopranos have also sung this cycle.
The songs may also be performed separately.

(1) Easter
    Range & Tess: eb3-f4   g3-eb4 (Read one octave lower)
    Remarks: Sustained in moderate tempo. Majestic, exultant, elevating.
       Has climactic passages and optional choral background. Possibly
       the finest setting on the subject of Easter. Acc 4
    Occasions: Easter. Massed religious gatherings. Festivals. General
       use.

(2) I got me flowers
    Range & Tess: db3-eb4   eb3-eb4
    Remarks: Sustained in moderate tempo. Short, slightly declamatory.
       Has frequent meter changes. Climactic ending. Acc 3
    Occasion: Special use with sermon theme.

(3) Love bade me welcome
    Range & Tess: d3-f4   e3-d4
    Remarks: Sustained in moderate tempo. Requires some fine PP. Inter-
       pretatively not easy. Narrative text. Acc 3
    Occasion: Special use with sermon theme.

(4) The call
    Range & Tess: eb3-f4   eb3-e4
    Remarks: Very sustained in slow tempo. Generally subdued, tranquil.
       Mostly sustained chords in the accompaniment. Acc 3 (S)SB
    Occasions: Weddings. Special use with sermon theme.

(5) Antiphon
    Range & Tess: eb3-f4(g4)   f3-d4
    Remarks: Sustained vocal part in lively tempo. Vigorous, spirited.

Imposing climax. Accompaniment uses ostinato figures. Acc 3
Occasions: Massed religious gatherings. Special use with sermon
theme - One world, one God. General use.

Four Hymns for Tenor Voice
Songs for Tenor with Piano accompaniment and Viola obbligato. London:
Boosey & Hawkes. Viola difficulty 3.

(1) Lord! Come away!
Text: Bishop Jeremy Taylor.
Range & Tess: d3-bb4   g3-f4
Remarks: Generally sustained, with some quasi-recitative passages.
  Has animated passages, vigorous phrases, and some dramatic sec-
  tions. Dramatic ending. Acc 3-4
Occasions: Palm Sunday.

(2) Come love, come Lord
Range & Tess: g3-g4   g3-e4
Remarks: Sustained. The text is interspersed with viola passages.
  Acc 3
Occasion: General use.

(3) Who is this fair one?
Text: Isaac Watts.
Range & Tess: eb3-a4   g3-f4
Remarks: Sustained. Has contrasts in mood and tempi. Acc 3-4
Occasion: Special use with sermon theme - Christ the bridegroom and
  the church the bride.

(4) Evening hymn
Text: Robert Bridges, from the Greek.
Range & Tess: e3-a4   a3-f#4
Remarks: Sustained. Has contrasts in mood and tempi. Imposing end-
  ing. Acc 3-4
Occasions: Evening services.

Ten Blake Songs
Songs for Tenor (or Soprano) and Oboe. Text by William Blake, 1757-
1827. London: Oxford University Press. For practical reasons, only numbers 5, 6 and 9 are given here.

(5) The Lamb
Range & Tess: eb3-f4   f3-eb4
Remarks: Sustained in moderate tempo, generally on MF level. Re-
  quires precise diction and simplicity. Mystical verse. Oboe 3
Occasions:Special use with sermon theme - The Lamb. General use.

(6) The shepherd
Range & Tess: d3-g4   f3-d4

VAUGHAN WILLIAMS

> Remarks: Sustained in moderate lively tempo. Generally on MF level. Short, with descending ending line. Note on the score: "This song may be transposed down a semitone, a tone, or a minor third", therefore may be sung also by medium or low voices. Oboe tacet.
> Occasions: Children's Day. New Year's Day or the Sunday after. General use.

(9) The Divine Image
Range & Tess: d3-f4   f3-eb4
> Remarks: Sustained in moderate tempo. On MF level, requires simplicity and fine diction. Text extols mercy, pity and love. Descending ending line. Oboe tacet.
> Occasions: Special use with sermon theme on the three qualities. General use.

THE PILGRIM'S PROGRESS
Excerpts from the Opera-Morality

The songs listed here are published singly by Oxford University Press. They differ slightly or considerably from the opera score. Alphabetical listing.

The bird's song   Medium Voice
> Text: John Bunyan, adapted from Psalm 23.
> Range & Tess: db3-f4   e3-c4
> Remarks: Sustained in moderate slow tempo. Generally subdued and tranquil. Rhythmically varied and complex. Acc 3
> Occasions: Evening services. Memorial services. General use.

The pilgrim's psalm   Medium Voice
> Text: Psalm 18:32,37; 144:1,2; 91:5; Ephesians 6:11; Rev. 21:7.
> Range & Tess: d3-f4   f3-e4
> Remarks: Animated in moderate march tempo. Vigorous, spirited, accented. Climactic ending. Has declamatory passages. Acc 3-4
> Occasions: New Year's Day. General use.

The song of the leaves of life and the water of life   Medium Voice
> Text: Revelation 22:1,2.
> Range & Tess: d3-e4   g3-e4
> Remarks: Sustained in moderate slow tempo. Plaintive, generally subdued, gentle. Acc 3
> Occasions: Evening services. New Year's Eve. General use.

The song of the pilgrims   Tenor, Baritone
> Text: John Bunyan.
> Range & Tess: d3-e4   f#3-d4
> Remarks: Sustained vocal part in moderate lively tempo. Vigorous, spirited. Climactic high ending. Acc 3
> Occasions: Massed religious gatherings. General use.

The woodcutter's song   Medium Voice
   Text: John Bunyan.
   Range & Tess: d3-e4   e3-d4
   Remarks: Sustained in moderate slow tempo. Subdued, plaintive, pastor-
      al. See "The shepherd boy sings in The Valley of Humiliation" by
      David Diamond. Acc 2-3
   Occasion: General use.

Watchful's song   Medium, Low Voices
   Text: Psalm 31:5; 127:1,121; Isaiah 14:7.
   Range & Tess: c#3-e4   e3-e4
   Remarks: Very sustained in moderate slow tempo. Subdued. Has some un-
      accompanied, quasi-recitative passages. Interpretatively not easy.
      See "I will lift up mine eyes" by Dvorak, Gober, Sowerby. Acc 3-4
   Occasions: Evening services. Installation for missionary service.
      General use. New Year's Eve.

LUDOVICO VIADANA
c.1560-1627, Italy

Lord Jesus Christ   All Voices
   Text: Traditional sacred Latin, translated.
   Range & Tess: d#3-d4   f#3-c4
   Remarks: Sustained in moderate tempo. Generally on MF level. Acc 3
      TMB
   Occasion: General use.

ANTONIO VIVALDI
c.1685-1741, Italy

Deliver Thy people from evil   Contralto, Mezzo-Soprano
(Qui sedes ad dexteram Patris)
   Work: GLORIA. Liturgical Latin text, translated.
   Range & Tess: c#3-d4   e3-c4
   Remarks: Animated in lively tempo. Generally strong; has florid pas-
      sages. Climactic ending. GR edition, edited by Joseph Machlis. Acc
      3 (VS)GR, GS, IM, EK, B-M
   Occasions: Evening services. Good Friday.

O Lord most holy (Domine Deus)   Soprano
   Work: GLORIA. See first entry.
   Range & Tess: f3-f4   g3-e4
   Remarks: Sustained in quite slow tempo. Generally gentle, lyric. Has
      a slightly climactic ending. Extended prelude and postlude. Has flor-
      id passages. Acc 3 (VS)GR, GS, IM, EK, B-M
   Occasions: Christmas Eve programs and services. Trinity Sunday.

VULPIUS

MELCHIOR VULPIUS
Real name: FUCHS, c.1560-1615, Germany

Abide with them, dear Savior   All Voices
    Text: Josua Stegmann.
    Range & Tess: high, e3-f4 f3-e4 medium, c3-d4 d3-c#4
    Remarks: Sustained in slow tempo. Requires simplicity; generally on
      MF level. Climactic high ending. Acc 3 TWS
    Occasions: Weddings.

PETER WARLOCK
Real name: PHILIP HESELTINE, 1894-1930, England

PWS Warlock Songs. Mixed collection. London: Boosey & Hawkes.

Balulalow   Soprano
    Text: Anonymous English, 16th-17th centuries.
    Range & Tess: eb3-f4 ab3-eb4
    Remarks: A cradle song. Sustained in slow tempo. Very subdued & gen-
      tle throughout. Fine for light, high voices. Acc 3 (S)OX
    Occasions: Christmas Eve programs and services. Christmas.

Bethlehem down   All Voices
    Text: Bruce Blunt.
    Range & Tess: c#3-eb4 d3-d4
    Remarks: Sustained in very slow tempo. Requires fine high PP & PPP.
      Acc 3 (S)B-H
    Occasion: Christmas.

The first mercy   Medium Voice
    Text: Bruce Blunt.
    Range & Tess: f3-f4 g3-d4
    Remarks: Animated in moderate tempo. Gentle, requires flexibility. Acc
      3-4 (S)B-H. PWS
    Occasions: Christmas Eve programs and services.

The frostbound wood   All Voices
    Text: Bruce Blunt.
    Range & Tess: d3-e4 e3-g3
    Remarks: Sustained, very slow, soft throughout. Requires simplicity.
      In quiet recitative style, atmospheric, mystical. The melody is
      built around the repetition of four notes: d3, e3, g3, a3. Acc 2-3
      (S)OX
    Occasions: Lent. General use.

SAMUEL SEBASTIAN WESLEY
1810-1876, England

Praise the Lord, O my soul   All Voices
    Text: Psalm 103:1; 5:8.

Range & Tess: high, c3-g4 g3-f4 medium, a2-e4 d3-d4
Remarks: Sustained in moderate slow tempo. The choral setting of this
tune is familiar to most choirs. Acc 2-3 SHS
Occasion: General use.

EDWARD H. WETHERILL
United States

A marriage prayer   High Voice
Text: Dorothy F. Gurney.
Range & Tess: c3-f4 g3-d4
Remarks: Sustained in moderate tempo. Generally on MF level, with
some slight climaxes. Descending, subdued ending. The same text as
"O perfect love". See Barnby, Nystedt, Sowerby. Organ accompani-
ment. Acc 2-3 (S)HF
Occasions: Weddings.

ROBERT WETZLER
United States

Psalm 128   Medium Voice
Range & Tess: c3-e4 d3-c4
Remarks: First line - Blessed is everyone who fears the Lord. Sus-
tained in moderate tempo. Has passages in chant style. Very subdued
ending. Acc 3 (S)AH
Occasion: General use.

LEWIS E. WHIKEHART
United States

O sing unto the Lord   All Voices
Text: Psalm 96. Revised Standard Version.
Range & Tess: d3-a♭4 f3-e♭4
Remarks: Vigorous and spirited. Requires flexibility. In contemporary
vein.Organ accompaniment. Acc 4 (S)HG
Occasions: Festivals. Massed religious gatherings. General use.

PAUL WHITE
United States

God walks with me   High, Medium Voices
Text: George Graff.
Range & Tess: d3-f4 f3-d4
Remarks: Sustained in moderate tempo. Generally on MF level with a
few climactic passages. Subdued, descending ending line. Acc 3
(S)EV
Occasions: Evening services. Installation for missionary service.
Special use in services of personal dedication. General use. Fu-
nerals. Whitsunday (Pentecost).

RICHARD WIENHORST
United States

I will sing the story of Thy love   All Voices
   Text: Psalm 89:1; 100:5; Jeremiah 33:11.
   Range & Tess: c#3-e4 e3-c4
   Remarks: Sustained in moderate tempo. Except in one short section,
     the active flute part plays separately, alternating with the vocal
     sections. Starts unaccompanied in chant style. Organ accompaniment
     and flute solo. Acc 3 Flute 3 (S)CY
   Occasions: Weddings.

HEALEY WILLAN
1880-1968, England

Come unto me, all ye that labor   All Voices
   Text: Matthew 11:28-30.
   Range & Tess: e3-e4 g3-d4
   Remarks: Sustained in moderate tempo. Generally on MF level. Requires
     both gentleness and firmness of tone. Acc 3 TMB. (S)CO
   Occasions: Communion. General use.

Create in me a clean heart, O God   All Voices
   Text: Psalm 51:10-12.
   Range & Tess: e♭3-e♭4 f3-b♭3
   Remarks: Sustained in moderate tempo. Requires simplicity and straight-
     forward treatment. Generally on MF level. Octavo format. Acc 2 (S)
     CO
   Occasions: Evening services. General use.

The Lord's Prayer   All Voices
   Text: Matthew 6:9-13.
   Range & Tess: d3-b♭3 f3-a3
   Remarks: A setting of a Gregorian chant, and must be performed in a
     style similar to it. Generally on MF level. Acc 3 TMB
   Occasion: General use.

HUGO WOLF
1860-1903, Austria

SPL Spanisches Liederbuch. Hugo Wolf. Original keys. German texts by
     Paul Heyse and Emanuel Geibel; English versions by John Bernhoff.
     10 songs. Frankfurt: C. F. Peters.
65S 65 Songs. Hugo Wolf. High, Low. Edited by Sergius Kagen. German
     texts, with English versions. New York: International Music Co.
Note: There are many more collections of songs by Wolf. The above were
     chosen for the English versions by John Bernhoff and Marie Boileau.
     The few awkward spots in prosody may be adjusted by the singer
     without changing any of the original notes.

Bowed with grief, Oh Lord, behold me   High Voice
(Mühvoll komm' ich und beladen)
  Text: Spanish songbook, translated by Geibel and Heyse.
  Range & Tess: d3-g4   a3-e4
  Remarks: Sustained in very slow tempo. Starts gently. Intense, peni-
    tential texts. Has dramatic passages. Subdued, descending ending
    line. May be transposed. Acc 3 SPL
  Occasions: Lent. Evening services.

Lead me, Child, to Bethlehem!   High Voice
(Führ' mich, Kind, nach Bethlehem!)
  Text: Spanish songbook.
  Range & Tess: e3-f#4   g3-e4
  Remarks: Sustained in slow tempo. Starts gently. Has some climactic
    passages and descending ending line. May be transposed. Acc 3-4
    SPL
  Occasion: Christmas.

Lord, what doth the soil here bear   Medium, Low Voices
(Herr, was trägt der Boden hier)
  Text: Spanish songbook.
  Range & Tess: b2-e4   f#3-d4
  Remarks: Sustained in very slow tempo. Requires dramatic intensity.
    Interpretatively not easy. Acc 3-4 65S, SPL
  Occasion: Special use with sermon theme.

Now wander, Mary (Nun wandre, Maria)   All Voices
  Text: Spanish songbook.
  Range & Tess: high, g3-f#4 b3-f4   low, eb3-d4 g3-db4
  Remarks: Very sustained in slow tempo. Interpretatively difficult.
    Subdued, narrative. Illustrative setting of Joseph comforting Mary
    during their journey to Bethlehem. Acc 3-4 65S, SPL, FSS
  Occasion: Advent.

On the cross, love, Thou art bleeding   High Voice
(Wunden trägst du, mein Geliebter)
  Text: Spanish songbook.
  Range & Tess: f#3-f#4   a3-d4
  Remarks: Sustained in slow tempo. Intense and serious. Requires fine
    P & PP. Has some climactic passages and a subdued high ending. May
    be transposed. Acc 3 SPL
  Occasions: Lent. Good Friday.

Prayer (Gebet)   All Voices
  Text: Eduard Mörike. English by Marie Boileau.
  Range & Tess: high, d#3-e4 g#3-e4   low, c#3-d4 f#3-d4
  Remarks: Very sustained in slow tempo. Generally subdued, solemn,
    prayerful. Requires simplicity and quiet dignity. Acc 3 65S, SCS-6
  Occasions: Evening services. Special use with sermon theme - Content-
    ment.

153

DARWIN WOLFORD
United States

Christis arisen   High, Medium Voices
   Text: Johann Wolfgang von Goethe, translated.
   Range & Tess: d3-f4   f3-c4
   Remarks: Animated in lively tempo. Joyful, rhythmic, outgoing, bright.
      Has some strong passages and a sustained, high ending. The simple
      accompaniment is organistic. Acc 3 SPC
   Occasion: Easter.

Now, let us give thanks!   High Voice
   Text: Ruth H. Barrus.
   Range & Tess: d3-f4   g3-eb4
   Remarks: Generally sustained in lively tempo. Exultant, outgoing,
      forceful. Has high, sustained climaxes. Very strong, sustained high
      ending. Has frequent meter changes. Organistic accompaniment. Acc
      3 SPC
   Occasions: Thanksgiving. Massed religious gatherings. Festivals.

Oh Father, as the steadfast sea   High, Medium Voices
   Text: Marylou Cunningham Shaver.
   Range & Tess: c3-eb4   eb3-c4
   Remarks: Sustained in moderate slow tempo. Simple, gently flowing mel-
      ody, generally subdued. 2 verses. Low ending line. Acc 3   SPC
   Occasions: Evening services. Evangelistic services. Special use with
      sermon theme - Faith. General use.

JULIE LOFGREN WOLFORD
United States

The shepherd   Medium Voice
   Text: William Blake and Scottish metrical paraphrase of Psalm 23.
   Range & Tess: c3-f4   eb3-d4
   Remarks: Sustained first section in moderate tempo; slightly animated
      second section with repetitive and arpeggiated figures in the ac-
      companiment.   Acc 3 SPC
   Occasions: Evening services. Funerals. General use.

ABRAHAM WOOD
1752-1804, United States

Angels tell the Lord is ris'n   All Voices
   Text: J. Hart.
   Range & Tess: d3-e4   e3-d4
   Remarks: Animated in moderate tempo. Majestic, joyous. Climactic end-
      ing. Acc 3 SEA
   Occasion: Easter or the Sunday after.

Settings Of

PSALM 23 and THE LORD'S PRAYER

Used in this Book

PSALM 23

V. Archer
"Brother James"
P. Creston
A. Dvorak
J. Edmunds
N. Espina
G. Flowers
B. Helder

S. Liddle
T. Matthews
E. Rubbra
L. Sowerby
R. Taylor
Traditional Songs
R. Vaughan Williams
J. Wolford

THE LORD'S PRAYER
(Matthew 6:9-13)

P. Earls
P. Genchi
M. Head
J. Merbecke

G. Myers
F. Peeters
H. Willan

S U P P L E M E N T

A SELECTED LIST OF CHORAL MUSIC

Vocal Scores of Oratorios, Masses, Passions, Cantatas, and Extended
Anthems. Solo Voices are indicated by the SATB designation; more than
four simply by "Soli".

ARNOLD, MALCOLM
   Song of Simeon. SATB soli, mixed choir, orchestra. English. OX

BACH, CARL PHILIPP EMANUEL, 1714-1788
* Holy is God (Heilig). SATB soli and Choir. English, German. CO;
    OX(rental)
* Magnificat. SATB soli & Choir. Latin, English. GS
   The Resurrection and Ascension of Jesus. TB soli & Choir. German,
    English. SP

BACH, JOHANN CHRISTIAN, 1735-1782
* Kyrie in D. SATB soli, Mixed Choir, instruments. Keyboard reduction
    by Wesley Vos. CO

BACH, JOHANN CHRISTOPH, 1732-1795
* The Childhood of Christ. SATB soli, Choir, keyboard. English by
    Lowell P. Beveridge, and the original German. JF

BACH, JOHANN SEBASTIAN, 1685-1750
* A Stronghold Sure (Ein feste Burg ist unser Gott). Cantata 80, SATB
    soli & Choir. GS-English; BH-German, English
* Beautify Thyself, my Spirit!(Schmücke dich, o liebe Seele). Cantata
    180, SATB soli, Choir, keyboard. GS-English; BH-German, English
* Christ Lay in Death's Dark Prison (Christ lag in Todesbanden). Can-
    tata 4, SATB soli, Choir, keyboard. GS & HG-English; BH-German;
    NO-English
* Christmas Oratorio. BWV248, SATB soli & Choir, keyboard. GS-Eng-
    lish; CP-German; NO-English; BH-German, English
* For Us a Child is Born (Uns ist ein Kind geboren). Cantata 142, ATB
    soli, Choir, keyboard. GA-German, English; GS-English
* God, the Lord, is Sun and Shield. Cantata 79, AB soli, Choir, key-
    board. GS-English; BH-German
* God's Time is Best (Gottes Zeit ist die allerbeste Zeit). Cantata
    106, SATB soli, Choir, keyboard. GS & NO-English; BH-German,
    English
* Heart and Mouth and Deed and Life (Herz und Mund und Tat und Leben).
    Cantata 147, SATB soli, Choir, keyboard. Has the well-known
    "Jesu, joy of man's desiring" chorale. BH-German
* Jesus, Thou my Wearied Spirit (Jesu, der du meine Seele). Cantata
    78, SATB soli, Choir, keyboard. GS-English; BH-German,English

CHORAL MUSIC

* Magnificat. BWV243, SATB soli, Choir, keyboard. GS, CP & BH - Latin; NO-English, Latin
* Mass in B Minor. BWV232, SATB soli, Choir, keyboard. Latin. GS, CP, NO, BH
* Now Thank We All Our God (Nun danket Alle Gott). Cantata 192, SB soli, Choir, keyboard. GS-English, German; BH-German
* Praise Him, the Lord, the Almighty, the King and Adore Him (Lobe den Herren, den mächtigen König). Cantata 137, soli, Choir, keyboard. BH-German, English
* Singet dem Herrn ein neues Lied. Cantata 190, ATB soli, Choir, keyboard. BH-German
* Sleepers, Wake! (Wachet auf ruft uns die Stimmel). Cantata 140, STB soli, Choir, keyboard. GS & NO-English; BH-German, English, French
  The Heavens Declare the Glory of God (Die Himmel erzählen). Cantata 76, SATB soli, Choir, keyboard. BH-German, English
* The Passion According to Saint John. BWV245, SATB soli, Choir, keyboard. GS-English; NO-English; CP & BH-German
  The Passion According to Saint Luke. Selections only, with TB soli, Choir, keyboard. PP-English
* The Passion According to Saint Matthew. BWV244, SATB soli, Choir, keyboard. GS & NO-English; CP & BH-German
* Motets: I.   Sing Ye to the Lord a New Song
          II.   The Spirit Also Helpeth Us
          III. Jesu, My Great Pleasure
          IV.   Be Not Afraid
          V.   Come, Jesus, Come
          VI.   Praise the Lord, All Ye Nations
  CP-German, English; NO-German & English, Nos. 1,2,3,6

BARBER, SAMUEL, 1910-1981
  Prayers of Kierkegaard. Soprano solo, Choir, keyboard. English. GS

BEETHOVEN, LUDWIG VAN, 1770-1828
* Mass in C Major. SATB soli, Choir, keyboard. Latin. NO, CP
* Missa Solemnis (Mass in D Major). SATB soli, Choir, keyboard. Latin. CP, NO, GS
* The Mount of Olives. STB soli, Choir, keyboard. NO-English; EK-German

BERLIOZ, HECTOR, 1803-1869
* L'Enfance du Christ (The Childhood of Christ). Soli, Choir, keyboard. GS-English; NO-English; EK-English, French, German
* Requiem. Tenor solo, Choir, keyboard. Latin. GS
* Te Deum. Tenor solo, Triple Choir, keyboard. Latin. GS, NO.

BOYCE, WILLIAM, 1710-1779
* Lord, Thou Hast Been Our Refuge. AT soli, SATB Choir, orchestra. OX

BRAHMS, JOHANNES, 1833-1897
* Requiem. SBr soli, Choir, keyboard. GS & NO-English; CP-German
* Triumphal Hymn. Br solo, Choir, keyboard. English. GS

BRITTEN, BENJAMIN, 1913-1976
* A Boy Was Born. Men's, Women's, Boys' Voices, optional organ accompaniment. OX
* A Ceremony of Carols. Soprano solo, Choir, Keyboard. English. B-H
* Rejoice in the Lamb. SATBr soli, Choir, keyboard. English. B-H
* Te Deum in C. Soprano solo, SATB Choir, organ or orchestra. English only. OX
* War Requiem. STBr soli, Boys' Choir, Mixed chorus, orchestra or keyboard. English, with interpolations in Latin. B-H

BRUCKNER, ANTON, 1824-1896
* Te Deum Laudamus. SATB soli, Choir, keyboard. Latin. CP

BUXTEHUDE, DIDERIK (DIETRICH), 1637-1707
* Command Thine Angel That He Come (Befiehl dem Engel, dass er komm'). SATB Choir. AB-German, English
* Jesu, Joy and Treasure (Jesu, meine Freude). STB soli and Choir. German & English. HI
* Open to Me, Gates of Justice (Aperite Mihi Portas Justitiae), Psalm 118. ATB Choir. Latin, English. CP, CO
* Rejoice, Beloved Christians. Twilight Music. SAB soli & Choir. English HG
* Rejoice, Earth and Heaven. SATB soli & Choir. CP
* The Infant Jesus (Das neugeborne Kindelein). SATB Choir, strings & continuo. CO

CHARPENTIER, MARC-ANTOINE, 1633-1704
* Magnificat in G. Soli, Choir, strings, flute, organ. CO
* Mass. Soli, Mixed Double Choir, orchestra. Latin. OX

COPLAND, AARON
* In the Beginning. Soprano solo & Choir. English. B-H

DARKE, HAROLD EDWIN, 1888-1976
The Sower. STB soli & Choir. English. OX

DUBOIS, THÉODORE, 1837-1924
* The Seven Last Words of Christ. STB soli, Choir, keyboard. English. Piano or Organ score. GS

DVOŘÁK, ANTONÍN, 1841-1904
* Requiem Mass. SATB soli & Choir. Laton. NO
* Stabat Mater. SATB soli & Choir. Latin. GS, NO, EK

CHORAL MUSIC

ELGAR, EDWARD, 1857-1934
  • The Apostles. SATBB soli, Choir, keyboard. English. NO
  • The Dream of Gerontius. MzS,T,B soli, Choir, keyboard. English. NO
  The Light of Life. SATB soli, Choir, keyboard. English. NO

FAURÉ, GABRIEL, 1845-1924
  • Requiem. SB soli, Choir, orchestra or piano. Latin, English. FS,GS,
    NO

FRANCK, CÉSAR, 1822-1890
  • The Beatitudes. Soli, Choir, keyboard. English. GS

GOUNOD, CHARLES, 1818-1893
  • St. Cecilia Mass (Messe Solennelle). SATB soli, SATB Choir, keyboard.
    NO-Latin; GS-Latin, English

GRAUN, KARL HEINRICH, 1704-1759
  • The Passion of Our Lord (Der Tod Jesu). STBr soli, Choir, orchestra
    piano. English, German. NK

HANDEL, GEORGE FRIDERIC, 1685-1759
  • Dettingen Te Deum. ATB soli, Choir, orchestra or keyboard. NO-Eng-
    lish; CP-German
  • Funeral Anthem on the Death of Queen Caroline. SATB soli, Choir,
    keyboard. English. AB
  • Israel in Egypt. Soli, Choir, keyboard. GS & NO-English; CP-German
  • Judas Maccabaeus. Soli, Choir, keyboard. GS & NO-English;CP-German
  • Messiah. SATB soli, Choir, orchestra or keyboard. English. CF-Coo-
    persmith; NO-Shaw & Prout eds.; GS; CP-German
  • Psalm 112 (Laudate Pueri Dominum). Soprano solo, Choir, keyboard.
    Latin. CP
  • Samson. Soli, Choir, keyboard. English. GS & NO-English; CP-English
    & German
  • The Passion According to Saint John. Soli, Choir, keyboard. MG-Eng-
    ligh & German; AB-English
  • The Passion of Christ. 1716, abridged. STB soli, SATB Choir, key-
    board. OX, ed. by Denys Darlow, English; EK
  • Utrecht Te Deum. AB soli, SATB Choir, keyboard. English, German. MG;
    NO; B-M

HAYDN, FRANZ JOSEPH, 1732-1809
  • Mass in C (Paukenmesse in Tempore Belli), Mass No. 2 - Mass in Time
    of War. SATB soli, Choir, keyboard. Latin. GS; NO
  Te Deum Laudamus. SATB soli, Choir, keyboard. Latin. NO
  • The Creation. SATB soli, Choir, keyboard. LG & NO-English; CP-Eng-
    lish & German
  • The Seasons. STB soli, Choir, keyboard. GS & NO-English; CP-German
    & English
  • The Seven Last Words of Christ. SATB soli, Choir, keyboard. NO &

GS-English; CP-German
* <u>Third Mass</u> (The Imperial or Lord Nelson Mass). SATB soli, Choir,
    keyboard. GS-Latin, English; NO-English; CP-Latin

HONEGGER, ARTHUR, 1892-1955
* <u>King David</u>. Soli, Narrator, Choir, keyboard. English. ES

HOVHANESS, ALAN
    <u>Glory to God</u>. SA soli, Choir. English. CP
    <u>I Will Lift Up Mine Eyes</u>. SATB Choir (Bass solo & Boys' Choir ad
        lib.) English. CP
* <u>Magnificat</u>. SATB soli, Choir, keyboard. English, Latin. CP
    <u>Make a Joyful Noise</u>. Br(T) solo, Choir. English. CP

JACOB, GORDON
* <u>The New-Born King</u>. Br solo, SATB Choir, orchestra or piano. English.
    OX

KUHNAU, JOHANN, 1660-1722
* <u>How Brightly Shines the Morning Star</u>. T solo, SATB Choir, organ.
    English by H. Fishback III. HG

LEO, LEONARDO, 1694-1744
    <u>Mass in F Major</u>. TB soli, Choir, keyboard. Latin. LG

MENDELSSOHN, FELIX, 1809-1847
* <u>Elijah</u>. Soli, Choir, keyboard. GS & NO-English; CP-German
* <u>Hymn of Praise</u>. SST soli, Choir, keyboard. GS & NO-English; CP-Ger-
    man
* <u>St. Paul</u>. SATB soli, Choir, keyboard. GS-English; CP-English,Ger-
    man

MONTEVERDI, CLAUDIO, 1567-1643
* <u>Magnificat</u>. Soli, Double SATB Choir. Latin. NO; CP

MOZART, LEOPOLD, 1719-1787
    <u>Mass in C</u>. SATB soli, Choir, keyboard. Latin. Sam Fox Publishers.

MOZART, WOLFGANG AMADEUS, 1756-1791
* <u>Coronation Mass</u> (Kronungs-Messe). C Major, K.317. SATB soli, Choir,
    keyboard. Latin. BH; BA; GS; NO; CP; EK
* <u>Grand Mass</u>. C Minor, K.427. SATB soli, Choir, keyboard. Latin. GS;
    CP; EK
* <u>Missa Brevis</u>. F Major, K.192. SATB soli, Choir, keyboard. Latin. GS
* <u>Requiem</u>. D Minor Mass, K.626. SATB soli, Choir, keyboard. Latin. GS;
    CP; NO

PALESTRINA, GIOVANNI PERLUIGI DA, 1525-1594
    <u>Missa Brevis</u>. A cappella Choir. Latin. GS

CHORAL MUSIC

* Missa Papae Marcelli. SATTBB soli & a cappella Choir. Latin. GS-
    Latin, English; CP-Latin

PARKER, HORATIO, 1863-1919
 · Hora Novissima. SATB soli, Choir, keyboard. Latin, English. HG

PERGOLESI, GIOVANNI BATTISTA, 1710-1736
 · Stabat Mater. SA Choir & Strings. Latin, English. OX

PINKHAM, DANIEL
    St. Mark Passion. STBrB soli & SATB Choir, piano or organ. English.
    CP

POULENC, FRANCIS, 1899-1963
 · Gloria. Soprano solo, Choir, keyboard. Latin. SA

PUCCINI, GIACOMO, 1858-1924
 · Messa di Gloria. TBrB soli, SATB Choir, orchestra. Latin. Piano-Vo-
    cal score: B-M

RHEINBERGER, JOSEF (GABRIEL), 1839-1901
 · The Star of Bethlehem (Der Stern von Bethlehem). Op. 164. SB soli,
    mixed Choir, orchestra or piano. English, German. EK

ROSSINI, GIOACCHINO A., 1792-1868
 · Stabat Mater. SSTB soli, Choir, keyboard. GS & NO-Latin, English.

SAINT-SAËNS, CAMILLE, 1835-1921
 · Christmas Oratorio. SMzTBr soli, Choir, keyboard. English, Latin.GS

SCARLATTI, ALESSANDRO, 1660-1725
    St. Cecilia Mass. Soli, Choir, keyboard. Latin. NO

SCHEIDT, SAMUEL, 1587-1654
    In Dulci Jubilo. Motet for 2-part Choir and 2 clarinets ad lib. Lat-
    in. BA

SCHUBERT, FRANZ, 1797-1828
 · Mass in A Flat. SATB soli, Choir, keyboard. Latin. CP
 · Mass in G. STB soli, Choir, keyboard. Latin. GS; AB; NO; CP

SCHÜTZ, HEINRICH, 1585-1672
 · A German Requiem. Soli, Choir, keyboard. German, English. GS
 · Psalm 84 (How Lovely is Thy Dwelling Place). Double Choir. German,
    English. GS
 · The Christmas Story (Historia von der Geburt Jesu Christi). STB soli,
    Choir, keyboard. English, German. GS
 · The Passion According to Saint John. Narrator & a cappella Choir.
    English. B-H; OX

* The Passion According to Saint Luke. A cappella Choir. English. OX;
    CP-German
* The Passion According to Saint Matthew. Soli & a cappella Choir.
    English. CO; OX
* The Seven Words of Christ on the Cross. Soli, Choir, keyboard. Eng-
    lish. CO; OX
  Symphonia Sacra. SAB soli, SATB Choir, instruments. OX

SPITTA, HEINRICH
* From Heaven Above, Ye Angels All. Choir. English. CO

STAINER, JOHN, 1840-1901
* The Crucifixion. TB soli, Choir, keyboard. English. NO; GS

STRAVINSKY, IGOR, 1882-1971
* Mass. SATB soli, Choir, orchestra or piano. Latin. B-H
* Symphony of Psalms. Choir, orchestra or piano. Latin. B-H

TALLIS, THOMAS, 1505-1585
  Lamentations of Jeremiah. SATTB a cappella; also ATTB a cappella.
    2 eds.: English & Latin. OX
  Spem in Alium Nunquam Habui. 40-part mixed chorus, optional organ.
    Latin. OX

THOMPSON, RANDALL
* The Nativity According to Saint Luke. Musical drama for soloists,
    chorus, church bells, organ, and chamber orchestra. English. ES
* The Peacable Kingdom. A cappella Choir. English. ES

THOMSON, VIRGIL
  Missa Pro Defunctis (Requiem Mass). Men's and Women's Choirs. Latin.
    HG

VAUGHAN WILLIAMS, RALPH, 1872-1958
* Dona Nobis Pacem. SBr soli, SATB Choir. English, with Latin in the
    first movement only. OX
* Hodie (This Day). STB soli, SATB Choir, Children's Choir, orchestra.
    English. OX
* Magnificat. Alto solo & SSA Choir. English. OX
* The First Nowell. Soli, SATB Choir, orchestra (small). Vocal score
    available. English. OX

VERDI, GIUSEPPE, 1813-1901
* Requiem. SATB soli, Choir, keyboard. GS-Latin, English; CP-Latin
  Stabat Mater. Choir. Latin. CP
  Te Deum. Soprano solo & two Choirs. Latin. CP

VIVALDI, ANTONIO, c.1680-1743
* Gloria. SSA soli, Choir, keyboard. GR-Latin; IM & GS-Latin, English

163

CHORAL MUSIC

· <u>Dixit</u>. SATB soli, double SATB Choirs, 2 orchestras. Piano and organ
    editions available. Latin. GS

WALTON, WILLIAM
    <u>Coronation Te Deum</u>. Double chorus, orchestra. Vocal score on hire.
      OX
    <u>Gloria</u>. ATB soli, mixed chorus, orchestra. Latin. OX

I N D I C E S

BY

OCCASIONS

(See page 166 for Detailed Listing)

VOICES

TITLES

COMPOSERS

OCCASIONS TABLE OF CONTENTS

OCCASIONS INDEX

General Use

General use

169

General Use

General Use

General Use

Advent

Christmas
(Christmas Day, Christmas season, the Sunday after Christmas)

177

Christmas

Christmas Eve Programs and Services

179

Christmas Eve Programs and Services

New Year's Eve

New Year's Day and the Sunday After

181

Lent

Song of penitence (Beethoven) 33
The crucifixion (Barber) 29
The frostbound wood (Warlock) 150
The Holy Passiontide now brings to mind again (Bach) 11
Though bound and helpless (Handel) 77
Thus spake Jesus (Head) 82
Upon the crucifix / On the reed (Rubbra) 127
Were you there (Spiritual) 107
What if this present (Britten) 40
When Jesus wept (Billings) 35
Where sin sore wounding (Dowland) 50
Wherefore, Jesus, didst Thou thirst (Handel) 71
Ye to whom God's grace extendeth (Alt. Handel) 79
Ye to whom God's grace extendeth (Soprano. Handel) 72

Palm Sunday
Any exultant song of praise may also be used.

Bridegroom of my soul (Bach) 6
Jesus, the very thought of Thee (Thiman) 139
Lord! Come away! (Vaughan Williams) 147
Lord, Thou art mine, and I am Thine (Proctor) 116
Ride on, King Jesus (Spiritual) 105
The palms (J. Faure) 58
Thou only hast the words of life (Elgar) 56
Within my heart of hearts (Bach) 16

Communion
Many of the songs under Lent may also be used.

Come unto me, all ye that labor (Willan) 152
Communion hymn (Opie) 108
Dearest Immanuel (Bach) 6
For my soul thirsteth for God (Mendelssohn) 97
How precious are the gifts (Bach) 14
I love my Jesus every hour (Bach) 7
Jesus, Thy humiliation (Bach) 9
Let not your heart be troubled (Haeussler) 66
Let us break bread together (Spiritual) 105
Non nobis, Domine (Quilter) 118
Now as a rose before the sun unfolds (Jacobson/Lange) 89
O Lord most holy (Franck) 61
Our God, the heavenly circle filling (Handel) 72
Out of my soul's depth to Thee (Campian) 42
See Him, He is the Lamb of God (Herbst) 83
The truest body heaven knows (Jacobson/Lange) 89

Maundy Thursday

Good Friday

186

Trinity Sunday

Thanksgiving

Baptism

Children's Day or Youth Sunday

Dedication of Music Facilities

Installation of Church Musician

Installation of Church Musician

O Lord, Thy faithfulness (Bartlet) 30
Prayer of Saint Francis (Myers) 103
So shall the lute and harp awake (Handel) 68
The Master's touch (Moody) 101
To music bent (Campian) 43
We sing to Him (Purcell) 118

Dedication of Church Building or Facilities
Songs under Dedication of Music Facilities may also be used.

Blessed are they that dwell in Thy house (Greene) 64
Built on the rock (Lindeman) 94
Establish a house (Rider) 122
Except the Lord build the house (Myers) 103
Happy are they who dwell in Your house (Pelz) 111
How lovely are Thy dwellings (Liddle) 93
Lord, I have loved the habitation of Thy house (Baumgartner) . . 31
The Lord's name is praised (Greene) 65
The Master's touch (Moody) 101
Thou, whose unmeasured temple stands (Cunwick) 46

Installation of Church Officers or Pastor

Abide in me (Herbst) 83
Ah, happy are ye, steadfast spirits (Bach) 5
Behold, how good (Edmunds) 53
Blessed are they that dwell in Thy house (Greene) 64
Christ's healing power (Titcomb) 142
Create in me a clean heart, O God (Bernhard) 35
For know ye not. R: God dwelleth (Mendelssohn) 99
God my shepherd walks beside me (Bach) 13
How beautiful are the feet (Contralto. Handel) 73
How beautiful are the feet (Soprano. Handel) 70
I lift up mine eyes (Stearns) 136
I will go in the strength of the Lord (Herbst) 83
I will lift up mine eyes (Sowerby) 134
Let the word of Christ dwell in you (Pinkham) 114
O God, have mercy (Mendelssohn) 100
O God, my heart is ready (Schütz) 132
O Lord, my God, take Thou from me (Reger) 121
Peace be unto you (Elgar) 54
Prayer of Saint Francis (Myers) 103
Proficiscere, anima Christiana (Elgar) 55
Rejoice in the Lord (Lane) 92
Take me, Saviour, for Thine own (Bach) 20
The Master's touch (Moody) 101
The sun shall be no more thy light (Greene) 65
The voice of thy watchman (Elgar) 54
The waters of Thy love (O'Hara) 108
We are climbing Jacob's ladder (Spiritual) 106

190

Installation (or Dedication) for Missionary Service

Missions Sunday

Evening Services or Prayer Meetings

Memorial Services

Massed Religious Gatherings

Massed Religious Gatherings

Festivals

Festivals

Reformation Sunday

World Brotherhood Sunday

Special Use in Services of Personal Dedication

Evangelistic Services

Evangelistic Services

Special Use With Sermon Theme

Special Use With Sermon Theme

VOICES INDEX

For All Voices

For High Voices

High Voices

For Medium Voices
Mezzo-Soprano, High Alto, Low Tenor, Baritone.

216

Soprano

For Mezzo-Soprano or Contralto
See also For Medium Voices and For Low Voices.

For Tenor
See also For High Voices.

221

Baritone or Bass

TITLES INDEX

232

236

C O M P O S E R S   I N D E X

240